How to Mi

How to Misunderstand Tolkien

The Critics and the Fantasy Master

BRUNO BACELLI

McFarland & Company, Inc., Publishers

Jefferson, North Carolina

LIBRARY OF CONGRESS CATALOGUING-IN-PUBLICATION DATA

Names: Bacelli, Bruno, author.
Title: How to misunderstand Tolkien :
the critics and the fantasy master / Bruno Bacelli.
Description: Jefferson, North Carolina : McFarland & Company,
Inc., Publishers, 2022 | Includes bibliographical references and index.
Identifiers: LCCN 2022031497 |
ISBN 9781476686943 (paperback : acid free paper) ∞
Subjects: LCSH: Tolkien, J. R. R. (John Ronald Reuel), 1892–1973.
Lord of the rings. | Tolkien, J. R. R. (John Ronald Reuel),
1892–1973—Appreciation. | BISAC: LITERARY CRITICISM /
Science Fiction & Fantasy | LCGFT: Literary criticism.
Classification: LCC PR6039.O32 L63236 2022 |
DDC 823/.912—dc23/eng/20220705
LC record available at https://lccn.loc.gov/2022031497

BRITISH LIBRARY CATALOGUING DATA ARE AVAILABLE

ISBN (print) 978-1-4766-8694-3

Front cover: J.R.R. Tolkien in his sixties. Artist Silvia Bacelli

Printed in the United States of America

*McFarland & Company, Inc., Publishers
Box 611, Jefferson, North Carolina 28640
www.mcfarlandpub.com*

Table of Contents

Acknowledgments

For the help my work received, I am grateful
to Thomas Honegger; Guido Schwarz;
Davide Mana; Katherine Williams,
who helped me with the first editing;
and my family, in particular my sister Silvia,
who provided the illustrations for this book.

Preface

My interest in the beautiful world of Middle-earth began with reading The Lord of the Rings trilogy. I was young and enjoyed the books without thinking that they were communicating a "message" to me, although it's very clear that the author was committed to bringing out traditional and religious values (Christian in all but name) under the fairytale form of his works. Later I discovered that Michael Moorcock, another fantasy author, had written somewhat disparaging comments about Tolkien and his work. Reading about it, I discovered it was a strong negative criticism. I didn't know what to think about it, because although they are different from each other, I liked both authors. I started to be more interested in the world of Middle-earth and its meaning. It was not just the beautiful setting of a great adventure story, but something that had stirred the cultural world of the twentieth century and continues to be a riddle to anyone looking for its significance today. Due to Tolkien's popularity, I think it's necessary that readers know about the debate surrounding him as an author and as a man.

In this book I'll try to cover all the aspects the critics touched, but positive criticism will not be the main focus. I'll talk about negative criticism and misinterpretations, about the political battles to decide whose side Tolkien is on, about unusual viewpoints. Tolkien was not only attacked but also interpreted in misleading ways. His thought was distorted, his political affiliation inferred, sometimes in bad faith. This author is difficult to pigeonhole; during his life he was loyal to no party and had no political affiliation. Therefore, any precise definition you can find needs to be examined with more than a grain of wariness. For this reason, this work will not be limited to negative criticism or slander, although Tolkien received plenty of both. Attempts to "enlist" Tolkien in ecological crusades or political parties also need to be examined.

The book is divided into chapters that cover many topics: Tolkien's style and themes, political and social ideas, alleged sexism and racism, religion. We will meet some critics in more than one of these chapters,

1

when necessary. Some notable names will be mentioned, as will those of some lesser-known critics. Also, since some analyses don't precisely fit into just one part, I had to decide what the more relevant topic was.

I encourage the reader to cultivate his or her own opinion about Tolkien's work and the criticism about him.

Introduction

J.R.R. Tolkien: A Short Biography

I do not wish to dwell on boring repetition of data and facts already written everywhere, so I will limit myself to essential data only, which is needed in order to understand the author. Tolkien was born into a middle-class family in 1892, in what is now known as independent South Africa, a British colony at the time. While his father's death left the family in a very precarious situation, Tolkien knew a happy and carefree childhood with his mother and brother in the English countryside, near Birmingham. He grew up as a Catholic, as his mother had converted, a fact that caused a permanent rift among the family and the loss of any financial assistance. When his mother died, the future author was entrusted to Father Morgan, a Catholic priest; thanks to him, he was given a good education and was able to secure a scholarship at Oxford. However, when Tolkien met Edith, an orphan girl who would go on to become his wife, Father Morgan forbade him from seeing her, as he did not want him to be distracted from his studies, and because Edith was a Protestant. Tolkien eventually regained contact with Edith, who converted to Catholicism in order to marry him. At the outbreak of the First World War, the young Tolkien, evidently little influenced by the patriotism of the time, postponed his conscription for educational reasons, until after his graduation. In 1916, shortly after his marriage, he left for France, fully aware of the massacre that was taking place on the battlefields. He fell ill with trench fever during the Battle of the Somme (July–November 1916), and soon returned to England; he remained in poor health until the near end of the conflict.

After the war, Tolkien began his academic career; during the Second World War he did not take up active service. Always interested in languages and mythology, he started to produce his own non-fiction and literary works, comparing his writings to those of his circle of friends (notable among them C.S. Lewis, the author of The Chronicles of Narnia). He published *The Hobbit* in 1937 and the books that composed The Lord of the Rings trilogy between 1954 and 1955. These are his fundamental works, as well as the essay on the fairy tale of 1947 and *The Silmarillion*, published posthumously in 1977. Tolkien had four children. Widowed in 1971, he died in 1973.

A Strange Myth Penetrates the Twentieth Century

Who was Tolkien? Why is he important? It is likely that enthusiasts rarely wonder about the cultural world's opinion regarding J.R.R. Tolkien and his work. Apart from the success that has lasted for decades, and the affection of readers, what value is given to Tolkien by the literary world?

Tolkien is considered by some to be the father of the fantasy genre; on the one hand, this may be considered a false attribution, given that other renowned authors had written fantasy before him. On the other hand, however, his extraordinary success redefined the genre, making a mark that conditioned it for decades, and which is still felt today. Still, the popularity achieved by Tolkien, especially with The Lord of the Rings, was such that the author could not remain in the mistreated limbo of the fantasy genre. The cultural environment had to come to terms with him, but often did so with little affection.

The author disconcerts many of those who assess his work. On the one hand, his immense popularity may be seen as a deterrent when attempting to critique his work. On the other hand, his success may be considered an anomaly in the cultural landscape; Tolkien's work stands apart from existing literary trends to the point of rendering literary criticism almost unthinkable, aside from those who feel entitled to attack it because they have identified something alien to their own value system.

In such cases, there is the risk of adverse evaluation, branding Tolkien's work as pure entertainment (and maybe foolish at that) as well as bestowing scorn and sarcasm onto his readers, as it is they who take away the power to judge what may or may not be considered valid from the critics.

As stated above, we should bear in mind that Tolkien, if considered a mere fantasy author, is not the progenitor of this literary genre; in his time, it was already fertile territory. If, however, we find it restrictive to simply consider his work as pure entertainment, then it becomes difficult to define it and even more difficult to place it, not only in his time's cultural panorama, but in current ones as well. Modernism, structuralism, and a predominantly progressive cultural environment: these are the trends in the period in which Tolkien's work was published. For some of the intellectuals who confronted him, excluding those limiting themselves to some quick mockery, Tolkien was an enemy, despised for the alleged cultural nullity and hated for public success. Such was this success that, in a survey by Britain's Waterstones bookshop chain, the public acclaimed him as the "author of the century," which provoked further reviews, full of dismay. Of them all, I cite that of the feminist and Marxist writer Germaine Greer: "It has been my nightmare that Tolkien would turn out to be the most influential writer of the 20th century. The bad dream has been realised."[1]

Other critics have simply spared themselves the trouble of talking about him, even going so far as to refuse to take him into consideration. The fact that Tolkien succeeded in the "unthinkable" task of resurrecting mythology and the epic in modern times contributed to him digging himself into an even greater hole, excluding himself from the intellectuals who predominated the cultural landscape of the time, more interested in a future of revolution and progress, or in the challenges of the social sphere, rather than in a mythical past. For themes and authors, we will look at some examples of negative criticism regarding both the content and the form of Tolkien's work, finding food for thought where possible.

1

Criticism of Tolkien's Style and Themes

The Contempt of Edmund Wilson (and Others)

In Edmund Wilson's April 14, 1956, review, titled "Oo, Those awful Orcs!,"[1] we have an excellent example of an "intellectually superior" attitude from a critic who unleashes all weapons of mockery onto Tolkien's work, not sparing ammunition against the enthusiastic readers.

Edmund Wilson (1895–1972), an influential critic with an interest in the works of Marx and Freud, appreciated many of those authors whose works are today considered classics, including F. Scott Fitzgerald and Ernest Hemingway. He was the classical intellectual of his time: progressive, a supporter of civil liberties, a strong proponent of realism in literature. He took a stance against Cold War politics in the United States after the Second World War, and later he opposed involvement in the Vietnam War.

Wilson initially cites a number of reviews and positive opinions on Tolkien's work. He then goes on to question if The Lord of the Rings really is, contrary to The Hobbit, a work intended for adults. According to Wilson, it is a children's book unexpectedly grown, fantasy developed by the author for its own sake, so that it was to be aimed to the adult readership instead of the juvenile market.

With this statement, Wilson suspected that Tolkien himself did not take his own work seriously and believed it was created as a philological exercise, just for the sake of it, considering the great pleasure that creating languages gave him (we should remember that he was always extremely modest about his "dilettantism," and about any pretense of giving his work a particular meaning). Wilson took this as an opportunity to feel entitled to consider the book a linguistic toy, created by an expert in the field, without literary value.

We get a feel of what Tolkien was writing about in his letter 165

7

(pages 219–222), in which the author reports some notes about his work and himself for the benefit of his U.S. publisher. Tolkien states that the backbone of the stories is the languages' creation. The worldbuilding is there to make use of these languages, not the other way around. In Tolkien's creative process a name came first, then a story developed. He loved the linguistic aesthetic, the sound of his invented languages and names.

Letter 180 is also interesting, as Tolkien observes that legends depend on the language to which they belong. Greek mythology benefits the most from the marvelous aesthetics of language and the nomenclature of places and people, unbeknownst to the reader, while the content is less important. In addition to this, he observes that artificial languages, such as Esperanto, would be even deader than the now extinct ancient languages, as there are no such legends or myths in said language.

If Wilson is wrong in minimizing the significance of The Lord of the Rings, it is therefore clear that Tolkien's interest in language was an essential, but not the sole, motive, as we shall see.

The aforementioned letter was intended to provide the editor with effective, easy-to-quote phrases to promote the book: therefore, we should not take from this that, for Tolkien, the motivations were only those explained.

Be that as it may, Wilson saves Tolkien the accusation of taking himself seriously, even though his generosity is venomous. Instead he discharges his weapons against the admirers of the English professor, attributing to them the pretentiousness that, at the end of the day, the author himself did not have regarding his writing, the limits of which he knew. Frodo's search is a simple comparison, a confrontation between good and evil, direct and

Edmund Wilson.

uncomplicated: "The hero has no serious temptations; is lured by no insidious enchantments" (one has to wonder in how much detail Wilson read the book). For the reviewer, Tolkien does not show any ability in developing his plot, instead bundling "more and more of the same stuff" and demonstrating a lack of talent for narrative or literary form. In addition to this, Wilson also criticized the characters' vocabulary and their dull personalities.

Gandalf is an eminent figure in the book, but Wilson states that he could not visualize him. Frodo is a dull little Englishman, Sam a dog-like servant, with a poor language and respectful attitude, so that he never leaves his master. Characters are not real, their interminable adventures display scarce ability on the part of the writer, the overall effect is almost pathetic.

Wilson admits, however, that despite Tolkien's words, the modesty displayed towards his own work, the fight against Sauron and the contention for the Ring seems to take on some greater significance than the fact itself. The Ring, bestowing power but exerting a sinister influence on the bearer, is recognized by the critic as an interesting element: the situation could be used by a creative writer to get a satisfactory outcome. Wilson anticipates a dilemma for Frodo, seduced by the enemy's power and tempted to go over to the enemy. He could become a monster himself, looking at the horrible enemy realm as at a pleasant place. However, even the monsters and evil entities have limits, no less than the protagonists. To Wilson they appear stereotyped: the Black Riders seem to terrify everyone, but the reader just sees specters that the good guys easily fend off. There's no real threat, the enemy has no real power, the monsters lack substance and presence. The horrors evoked by Tolkien are immaterial: they have no real contact with their victims, who are able to drive them away like a bad dream. Even Sauron, after appearing convincing (as a flaming eye that scrutinizes everything from his remote tower), lacks any subsequent development. The reader is not given a chance to get close enough to really taste his power, which fades into an anticlimactic collapse when the Ring is destroyed. This is convenient for the author, Wilson argues, because then he doesn't need to tell the reader what was so terrible.

We must note here, if need be, that grievous bodily harm does occur in the book: many characters die, and the "ghost" commander, the Witch-king of Angmar, hits Frodo with a weapon during the beginning of his journey, inflicting a wound that will never completely disappear.

The same specter, during the battle of the Pelennor Fields, destroys Éowyn's shield and breaks her arm with a violent blow. Not so harmless it seems.

We have another comment on the effectiveness of the Black Riders (Nazgûl) by Tom Shippey.[2] He thinks that, in the first chapter of *The Fellowship of the Ring*, we have several instances in which this menace seems pretty impotent. The Riders are scary, but they don't seem able to do much. Tolkien was writing this first part of his work without a definite plot; the Hobbits traveled out of the Shire having some bad encounters but also receiving help (for example, from Tom Bombadil); the Riders are trying to find them and ask for information about them. Several Hobbits are quite frightened, but, apart from this, the Riders "seem to have no special power." Later, during the attack on Weathertop, they don't press their attacks home, and probably lose a good opportunity to conclude victoriously their search. Shippey explains this lack of development of the Nazgûl with Tolkien having not yet made up his mind about what story to tell.

Tolkien is charged, by Wilson, with having not only a poor imagination, but also an inability to involve readers or to make them really feel the horror, fear, and evil, whether it be the wars, the torments and pains of the characters, or monsters. Even in the ladies we meet along the way, Wilson finds no quality capable of making the reader's heart beat.

Therefore, we have to ask ourselves a question: If this is the case, why did Tolkien succeed? Wilson's answer is that people love juvenile trash; he thinks this is even truer in Britain than elsewhere. He could think this way because Tolkien's success in the United States was yet to come. When fans talk about Tolkien, "they bubble, they squeal, they coo," Wilson writes. In short, for Wilson, Tolkien is a third-rate writer, and his opinion regarding the readers who have established Tolkien's success is even more drastic. A fierce and certainly simplistic criticism guided more by bewilderment about Tolkien's work, which was not so appropriate for the era, than by a real analysis.

Another observation about the style: like others after him, Edmund Wilson was surprised by Tolkien's opinion about the importance of words and their sound. Tolkien, a philologist, was serious about it. His work was not just about the thankless interpretation of ancient texts. As noticed by Tom Shippey in *The Road to Middle-earth*, philology worked with the evolution of language, the understanding of older, now dead, forms. Through philology, you can understand the relationship between different peoples whose languages may derive from a common ancestor. Language can tell you about a civilization. The names of cities or places of interest can tell you about their history. Even if not in use anymore, a language tells a story of changing meaning and sound. For the philologist, a word is not considered just for its immediate use, but for its role in the context: the word is not like a brick to build a sentence, but like a stalactite, an element with a meaning in the immediate interpretation, but evolving and growing in time.

So, Tolkien perceived a strong relationship between philology and literature, the writing of stories. To work with languages, real or imagined, was a stimulus to use words to tell tales. Languages are the foundation, and stories are needed to give languages a world in which to live.[3]

In Wilson's critique there is little space for in-depth analysis: he limits himself to bestowing his scorn on Tolkien's work and relying on an all-too-modest declaration by the author. He takes this opportunity to wipe him out as a literary entity, claiming that even Tolkien did not take himself seriously. As for the judgment on readers, it is pure contempt with no hint of explanation. Probably Wilson's stance against Tolkien should not be a surprise. It shouldn't even surprise us that, in 1945, he gave a disparaging review about the work of famous horror writer H.P. Lovecraft. We can't have Lovecraft's reaction because he died in 1937; other critics defended his style from Wilson's onslaught. Whether Wilson's criticism of Lovecraft's style was on target of not, the latter was to become the father of the modern horror story. So treating him like a "hack" was maybe a bit of over-criticism. Do we need to put the critics "in context," too, as we do authors? Edmund Wilson was in tune with the mainstream trends of his times, with a bit of added sarcasm. Writers like Tolkien or Lovecraft were probably on the wrong side for him. What is useful, or at least interesting, about his commentary about Tolkien? Certainly, the reference to an assumed, though scarce, expressiveness, to the bogeymen that don't really scare, to empty threats. Valid or not, these themes are at least based on a textual critique and have been taken up and re-evaluated by others.

On the other hand, mockery and sharp jibes against Tolkien have never been lacking.

The author himself (letter 163[4]) mentioned one from the journalist and writer Maurice Richardson: "Adults of all ages! Unite against the infantilist invasion."[5]

Another who wished for Tolkien's rapid fall into oblivion was Philip Toynbee, English writer and journalist of communist ideals who also tried his hand at epic writing (title: *Pantaloon*). Toynbee is baffled by the enthusiastic reception Tolkien received from critics (W.H. Auden, Edwin Muir, and others). He thinks the books are dull and childish, so Tolkien enthusiasts must be mad. But he's pleased because this enthusiasm is finally fading[6]: "Most of his more ardent supporters were soon beginning to sell out their shares in Professor Tolkien, and today those books have passed into a merciful oblivion."[7]

Here too, the same misunderstanding—exchanging fairy tale for infantilism—can be seen. The truth of the matter is that the fortunes of Tolkien's work grew slowly with time as opposed to declining, and would go on to take off after a few years. This forgetfulness greeted by Toynbee had only occurred in his own wishful thinking. Other points of view are also interesting. In *The Natural History of Make-Believe* by John Goldthwaite,[8] a compendium of the main works relating to the fantastical and the fairy tale in Great Britain, Europe, and America, The Lord of the Rings trilogy is reduced (in 1996!) to the "fairy tale response to Conan the Barbarian" instead of being mentioned as one of the most influential works of this kind.

Humphrey Carpenter, Tolkien's authorized biographer, when speaking[9] about him during the BBC program *Bookshelf*, stated: "He doesn't really belong to literature or to the arts, but more to the category of people who do things with model railways in their garden sheds."

Others, in recent times, have taken Tolkien as an example of a whole literary genre, by now successful but vacuous and pernicious. Historian Felipe Fernández-Armesto, in a 2002 article, follows a title worthy of Edmund Wilson—"Fantasy is the opium of the ignorant and the indolent"[10]—with an equally scathing subtitle: "The popularity of *The Lord of the Rings* signifies our cultural impoverishment." Fernández-Armesto's complaint is that fantasy has become like a drug, the most widespread form of narrative in our age. In his opinion, those with common sense should view the phenomenon with suspicion. Reality is far more complex than narrative, given the strangeness of our world against which Middle-earth appears simplistic, from a moral point of view, while the Harry Potter train (leading to his magical world) is childish and predictable. Realism is more interesting, an unlimited source of stories and facts. In fantasy anything can happen; magic is a tool ready to use to get the hero out of a problem. This way, stories have no tension because characters' actions are unconstrained by reality. So it's hard to understand why audiences love fantasy.

Why doesn't he understand that? Because he could not understand how these fantastic worlds have rules and coherence as well, and thus, can create an environment where a story finds a structure that makes it worthy of being told.

But, for Fernández-Armesto, the rise of the fantasy genre did not cause the collapse of interest in history. Rather, historians have not been able to narrate the past in an interesting way, so people turned to create imagined ancient worlds instead. In Fernández-Armesto's opinion, we escape from history and true myth because we do not want to learn their hard lessons, but the fantastic too, at times, has hard lessons from which we can learn.

We will briefly touch on a "counter-criticism" that reviews Wilson's opinions. Marion Zimmer Bradley[11] (a feminist fantasy writer) underlines how Sam and Frodo achieve an idealized male friendship towards the end of their adventure, with a passion similar to that between Achilles and Patroclus in *The Iliad*, greater than the love for a woman can be.

Ursula Le Guin.

Wilson's contempt for Sam and Frodo is for Bradley just a demonstration of his "cataclysmic ignorance of the pattern of heroic literature." According to Marion Zimmer Bradley, Wilson may have been misled by the glimpses of comedy, seen in Sam's role in the opening parts of The Lord of the Rings: Sam sees himself as little more than ballast, leading some critics to think that he was a somewhat intentionally ridiculous character, in Sancho Panza's style. However, while Pippin takes on the role of the fool in some sections of the book, Sam does not play such a role, although Tolkien makes fun of him here and there. As for Wilson's opinion of fantasy, we have the words of the writer Ursula Le Guin,[12] who thought that Wilson was a good example of the deep, puritanical contempt of those confusing fantasy (which from a psychological point of view is a universal and essential faculty of the human mind) with infantilism and pathological regression.

Epic Pooh: Michael Moorcock's Opinion

In the essay "Epic Pooh,"[13] written in 1978 by Michael Moorcock and revised at a later time, the famous British author criticizes authors of fantasy for children and especially Tolkien. Moorcock is known for his success in the fantasy and science fiction genres; his most praised saga is about the anti-hero Elric of Melniboné, a tormented character whose nature and deeds are the opposite of Tolkien's heroes.

In Moorcock's opinion, the prose of high fantasy is like a lullaby, comforting and relaxing but without tension. This kind of prose is false but pleasurable, and this is exactly the reason why it's successful. The slightly detached sentimentalism in this kind of books is sad and lacking in spirit; if there's humor in them, it is unconscious. Tolkien's work is, obviously, associated with this kind of fantasy, while other writers are referred to in a more positive way.

The quotation from The Lord of the Rings trilogy, which goes to substantiate the lack of humor, may leave us perplexed, as it is the part with the announcement of Frodo's house being sold. The incredulous comments from the Hobbits can hardly be "involuntary" humor by Tolkien. On the contrary, it is a chance for Tolkien to give an insight into the Hobbits' mentality, sometimes a little petty in its materialism and its conformity. It's difficult to comment on the comparisons Moorcock makes in several quotations, as this is very subjective territory; in fact, he seems to believe that, invariably, the British high fantasy is artistically modest, covertly conservative and Christian propaganda, and that fantasy written expressly for children is better than that written for adults. Moreover, for Moorcock, authors such as Tolkien being entered into the literary debate is a sign of how much standards have dropped; the idea of The Lord of the Rings overtaking Joyce's *Ulysses* as one of the defining works of the twentieth century is unbearable for him. As for Tolkien's followers, who slavishly imitate his works, Moorcock thinks that they are not even capable of writing a sentence correctly in English, yet they are still successful, which is hardly surprising, when pop bands are manufactured and films based on sensationalism. The success of Tolkien and his imitators means that academic standards and intellectual level are dropping in recent times.

Maybe in this, at least, Moorcock is similar to Tolkien, because he regrets the fall of the standards of good old times?

As an example of style, we shall look at a passage Moorcock cites in the article as an example of prose more expressive than what we find in The Lord of the Rings. The following is excerpted from Susan Cooper's 1975 novel *The Grey King*: "They were no longer where they had been. They stood somewhere in another time, on the roof of the world. All around them was the open night sky, like a huge black inverted bowl, and in it blazed the stars, thousand upon thousand brilliant prickles of fire. Will heard Bran draw in a quick breath. [...] The stars blazed round them. There was no sound anywhere, in all the immensity of space. Will felt a wave of giddiness; it was as if they stood on the last edge of the universe, and if they fell, they would fall out of Time."

We will analyze shortly another critic's comments, explaining step by step why Tolkien, stylistically, could be considered less endowed than certain other authors; inversely, Moorcock gives several examples like this one but he does not go into detail, as if he believes that citations do not need explanation. To say that Tolkien's prose is empty is not enough, however: the reader, in addition to submitting to dull, scarce emotions and false narrative is,

Michael Moorcock.

in Moorcock's opinion, also deprived of drama, due to Tolkien's established belief in the need for a happy ending. Here, Moorcock quotes the essay "On Fairy-Stories" (1939),[14] where Tolkien argues that a good fairy tale should lead to the "eucatastrophe" or a favorable and unexpected conclusion, a ray of light and happiness (for example, the resurrection in the biblical gospels). No room for the idea of death.

Moorcock observes, however, that the unexpected happy ending can be anything but unexpected, since Tolkien's practice is always to use it. The observation may be questionable in light of Tolkien's much less joyful works such as *The Silmarillion*, published after the author's death.

Apart from the comments that go against the whole genre of "Tolkien's epigones," perhaps an interesting opinion that could be shared, but which goes beyond our discussion, in his corrosive essay Moorcock destroys The Lord of the Rings from a stylistic point of view. He trashes both the author and, as we shall see, his ideology, regardless of whether it is apparent or hidden in his works.

Is he right? How can one respond? The problem here is that the criticisms are based on personal, subjective, artistic opinions (while, as we will see later, several of the vitriolic attacks against the author's ideas are based on political divergence: Moorcock was left-wing, Tolkien was certainly not).

The Oxford scholar's style, looking to recover a feeling of the myth, epic, and languages of the past, certainly is not that of his contemporaries, and what is effective in the context of his work may obviously clash sharply in comparison with theirs.

Moving on to another critical point, we shall try to understand what Tolkien's happy ending really is. Is it similar to some Hollywood movies of the past, everyone laughing and happy in the end? Not exactly. Is the idea of death excluded from The Lord of the Rings? Not exactly. Even if we wanted to remove (as a posthumous work) *The Silmarillion* from the picture, Tolkien's "consolation" is not an ending where everything goes well and everyone is happy. Unexpectedly salvation or victory arrives, and perhaps, for the shrewd reader or a critic like Moorcock, the unexpected victory is anything but unpredictable. However, the ending is, in part, sad and gloomy. Something has been ruined forever; the greatest damage has been avoided, but nothing will be as before. After Sauron's defeat, the Elves leave Middle-earth forever, and take their magic with them. Frodo, carrier of the Ring, is incurably injured during the adventure, so is welcomed aboard ships sailing towards the West, leaving prematurely. The Shire has been saved, but not for him: someone must sacrifice him- or herself in order to keep others safe. Although the author avoids representing him as dying, Frodo's farewell to Middle-earth takes place unwillingly and, while it is an assumed Paradise, it is also reminiscent of death. After Sauron's defeat, it is certain that more evil will come sooner or later, because of the departure of the many supernatural beings, both good and evil, and the knowledge that the next epoch will be that of Men, non-fairy beings, who, of course, will be even more fallible.

Burton Raffel: Is Tolkien's Work Literature, or Not?

In the essay *"The Lord of the Rings as Literature,"*[15] Burton Raffel (professor, translator, poet) analyzes the text and tries to establish whether or not we can consider the work of the Oxford professor to be true literature. The Lord of the Rings, he thinks, is a magnificent work, but the term "literature" does not fit.

Raffel considers three aspects: style, characterization, and plot. As for style, the critic's examination focuses on both Tolkien's prose, and poetry, giving some examples. Here we see one:

"They found themselves in a small and cozy room. There was a bit of bright fire burning on the hearth, and in front of it were some low and comfortable chairs. There was a round table, already spread with a white cloth, and on it was a large hand-bell. But Nob, the hobbit servant, came bustling in long before they thought of ringing. He brought candles and a tray full of plates."

This was Tolkien; what follows is Thomas Wolfe, American writer of the first half of the 1900s: "She replaced the disreputable furniture of the house by new shining Grand Rapids chairs and tables. There was a varnished bookcase, forever locked, stored with stiff sets of unread books—The Harvard Classics, and a cheap encyclopaedia."

The difference, regardless of the relative value of the authors, is that Tolkien paints a clear and unambiguous scene for the reader, and it is evident in what he finds pleasure. After various adventures, the Hobbits arrive in Bree, where they find a seemingly safe refuge, but nothing about this is described to the reader, only the virtue of the function and meaning that is relevant to the story (the low and comfortable chairs, the fire in the hearth and so on). But although it is clear what Wolfe wants to tell us, he still leaves the descriptions open to interpretation: the varnished bookcase and the books inserted are just to set the scene, because they are new and untouched. The furniture is made by a cheap company but paints a decent image with its shiny new look (Grand Rapids, explains the critic, is a bulk product). One can say that the woman of the second text cheaply furnished the house, paying attention to outward signs of respectability. But the description allows us to visualize what the author is telling us, and not just to understand what he wants us to understand.

Therefore, according to Raffel, while Thomas Wolfe knows the tools for writing literature, Tolkien does not, although his work is more famous. As for Tolkien's poetry, Raffel finds it bad at an embarrassing level, as well as childish in many cases. He brings some examples and points out the inconsistency of meanings, the boredom and the lack of incisiveness of certain passages, the rhythm with no charm (criticisms similar to Moorcock's). The Tom Bombadil song "Hey! Come merry dol! derry dol! my darling!" is the worst in Raffel's opinion (and, moreover, full of borrowings from other ballads). The only appreciation is for the poem that introduces the trilogy: "Three Rings for the Elven-kings under the sky...." But even here, the poem is strong because of the magical intensity.

As for the characters, their qualities are communicated to us clearly and unambiguously, looking at the main ones (Bilbo, Frodo, Gandalf, Aragorn, Sam), but with a simplicity that has little meaning with respect to the actual complexities of human reality. Tolkien gives us an almost religious teaching. However, what is true in his world, where the author controls everything, does not have the substance to be meaning-ful outside of it. Anyone who reads Dante cannot ignore the Florentine poet's theological convictions, but is not obliged to believe them, while the qualities of Tolkien's characters do not tell us about human reality but rather the articles of faith that the author wants us to believe. The main characters of The Lord of the Rings would, therefore, be described as archetypes,[16] meaning that they are not very interesting, and their speech and actions are stereotyped. After his resurrection, Gandalf becomes more of a superpower than a significant character, someone who no longer belongs to the world of ordinary mortals.

Raffel offers us a comparison with Fitzgerald's The Great Gatsby: "Why, my God, they used to go there by the hundreds [in Gatsby's man-sion] ... the poor son-of-a-bitch." The speaker is one of those who went to Gatsby's parties to get drunk, and now he attends his lonely funeral.

Tolkien (at the end of The Lord of the Rings): "At last the three companions turned away, and never again looking back they rode slowly homewards; and they spoke no word to one another until they came back to the Shire, but each had great comfort in his friends on the long grey road."

A mysterious character with a poor past, Gatsby tried to be admired (and to win the heart of the woman he loved) by spending big fortunes on generous parties. In a nutshell, Fitzgerald shows bitterness for the cynical use that people made of the character's generosity, while the less able Tolkien "has demonstrated to us, again, that Friendship is a Good Thing."

Turning to the plot, Raffel criticizes the "Deus ex Machina," or the fortunate or fortuitous events that lead the Good to prevail over Evil (with both in capital letters): he understands that the author loves to show us Faith prevailing, but this kind of ploy "lessens the stature" of the trilogy.

So, Raffel is not always generous in his assessment, but he ends the essay by surprisingly announcing that there is another element to eval-uate, in addition to those previously mentioned, to decide the literary qualities of a work: imagination. Tolkien has plenty, which is clear to see, and this is a primary requirement of any literary work. Therefore, in the end, the critic concedes that the work of the Oxford professor can be considered literature, stating that he has shown the arguments against him as a needed answer to excessive adulation and flattery towards Tolkien.

Therefore, we have a final tribute to the author, but a rather tight criticism of many aspects of his work, written without the tricks and style of mainstream fiction.

I think this attack, carried out in arid academic terms, is rather futile and snobbish, and it is curious that in the end the swipe is fearfully held back in the name of fantasy, a quality that, ultimately, Raffel generously recognized about Tolkien. It may be that he was influenced by the thought that Tolkien's success was meteoric, destined to fade away; probably he believed that The Lord of the Rings was to be a temporary bestseller. It seems to me that the critic did not understand what Tolkien, in terms of content, language, and style, wanted to create. In front of an unconventional author like Tolkien, the comparison with what is considered to be a valid style in modern literature should be conducted with greater prudence; otherwise you risk a formulaic and sterile exercise, accusing Tolkien of not being "adequate," judged against the parameters of his contemporaries, when it is obvious that Tolkien did not want to follow them.

Moving to another criticism, in a 1969 essay about the style of The Lord of the Rings, English university professor Catharine Stimpson[17] claimed that the characters are one-dimensional, just good or bad, whereas female characters, of any rank, are described with the most abused stereotypes. Female characters will be subsequently discussed. As for the one-dimensional characters, some are, but others are definitely torn, or decide to change sides at the beginning of the story (Saruman, the magician who makes an alliance with the evil Sauron). We will revisit this subject at a later point.

The God from the Machine. Really?

As for Raffel's accusation that Tolkien relied on the arrival of a "Deus ex Machina" to save the day at the last moment, the use of this Latin expression here is not correct, as Raffel commits a very widespread error, broadening its meaning. In ancient theatrical performances, a god is commonly literally descended "from the machine," in the sense of using a contraption that lowered the actor from the rafters into the scene, to reveal a plot twist now tangled beyond the possibilities of the characters. It was used to resolve conflicts, reconcile souls, explain what had happened, and happily settle everything. In Tolkien, we have, instead, an unexpected event saving the situation, the joyful "eucatastrophe" that Moorcock mentions, and which he characterizes as a tool capable only of adding tedium to Tolkien's already drab plots.

Now we will look at some examples. The battle of Helm's Deep is about to end in disaster for the besieged troops of King Théoden (the king of Rohan, free from Grima Wormtongue's evil influence thanks to Gandalf), when a contingent, believed to be missing, arrives on the battlefield, a surprise that flips the situation. In the battle of the Pelennor Fields, an immense army attacks Gondor, capital of the most powerful human kingdom and stronghold for the Free Peoples. A first counterattack by Rohan's men (always led by Théoden, who meets his death there) tries to disrupt the armies of Mordor, but they, with new allies converging on the battlefield, seem to have the upper hand again, until Aragorn arrives by sea with reinforcements from the south, and manages, once again, to turn the situation around.

On both occasions Tolkien presents us with a partial view of the facts, so it appears as if the "good guys" do not have enough strength to cope, but then an unexpected contingent intervenes on the field, at the last moment, and manages to rout the forces of evil.

Maybe it's not really a "Deus ex Machina," but for those who analyze the topic from a military point of view, it may seem as if the reader was not given all the required information about the forces in the field to enable them to assess whether the situation was really as desperate as it appeared to be.

In my opinion, this is a criticism that makes sense in the way the two battles are depicted.

Another example: an exhausted Frodo must throw the Ring into hot lava in order to destroy it, but in the end, the magic, an evil influence contained within the artefact gets the better of him.

He cannot bring himself to do it. Gollum then arrives and, in a providential event, fights Frodo for the possession of the Ring, only to lose his balance, just at the moment he finally seizes it, falling into the abyss, completing the mission that Frodo himself could not accomplish.

Here too, the coup de théâtre that Tolkien inserts is to show that Frodo exerts himself, almost reaching his final goal, but, in the end, he is just as fallible as anyone else, who is just the instrument of a higher will. Does this plot device seem preordained, and, indeed, disappointing? Of course, this can be easily interpreted by the reader, me included.

We are reading an epic, however, and we do not expect the final outcome to be in doubt.

Frodo may be considered as one of the best possible bearers of the Ring but fails to make it to the end. Therefore, we have divine providence at work.

About Tolkien's Creatures

Middle-earth, as a panorama, is nothing out of the ordinary, says English professor Thomas J. Gasque[18] in his essay titled "Tolkien: The Monsters and the Critters." Gasque discusses the efficacy of creatures and peoples living in and giving substance to the world of The Lord of the Rings and *The Hobbit*. He comes to the conclusion that maximum efficiency is reached by the elements that are well rooted in tradition. Nevertheless Tolkien, according to this critic, finds some success with his personal creations too: he presents the first race, the Hobbit people, at the beginning of the story and manages to overcome the reader's disbelief, seeing as they are quite similar to Man and have the same "provincialism" about stories of incredible things that happen outside of the Shire. Tolkien seems very convincing about this created race of his and says that there may still be some Hobbits in the world, just that they do not wish to be seen.

The dragon that appears in *The Hobbit* is a well-known creature; Dwarves and Orcs are races that the reader can imagine. Other races are supplied to Tolkien by tradition, though sometimes the tales are inconsistent: for example, Elves, which are different depending on the source one reads (in some myths they are tiny creatures). Tolkien obviated the problem by taking from the legend exactly what he needed, making his whole world coherent and rational according to its own internal logic. At times, he uses another device, introducing into the conversation something that we are yet to see, like the Nazgûl, for example. Their nature is ambiguous: they were Men, and are now only ghosts. Since they remain quite mysterious, they are effective. As for the Ents, for Gasque they are not Tolkien's invention, but rather his creation (that is, something entirely new), first of all because there is no lack of precedents in the myth, and secondly because, like the Hobbits, they are humanoid creatures, which in this case resemble plants. It is impossible to blame Gasque: talking trees are not absent from classical legends. For example, we have Zeus's oracle oak in the woods of Dodona in Greek mythology.

In Gasque's opinion, Tolkien fails when he introduces creatures—Shelob and the Balrog, for example, or a magical being like Tom Bombadil, who is indifferent to the power and temptation of the Ring—that are outside the traditional pattern. Much of the characterization in Tolkien is accomplished using humanoid creatures, whose characteristics we already know, meaning we already know a lot about a character just by knowing that it is a Dwarf or an Elf. But these non-human beings, forces of nature whose psychology we do not know, remain foreign to us: they are incarnated allegorical principles (Shelob's gluttony; the nature spirit in Bombadil; the chaotic disorder of the Balrog, a fiery demon). Moreover, they are not tied to the plot, as none of the three seem to be interested in the Ring, none obeys any of the Middle-earth powers instead following their own nature or interests. Note here that we do not necessarily need to trust Gasque, as the Balrog that we see in The Lord of the Rings, while not fighting in the ranks of the Orcs, seems decidedly "lined up" on the side of evil as indeed the Balrogs are, undoubtedly, in other works by Tolkien (*The Silmarillion*).

Our critic goes on to point out, first of all, how unexpected and sudden the encounter with Tom Bombadil is, a rather long episode that does not seem part of the fabric of the story: it remains a digression from the main narrative, and a failure of Tolkien's narrative technique that he did not announce his existence or prepare the reader to meet him. Bombadil is not created, but suddenly invented, and fails to come to life.

The Balrog enters the scene when it is already overwhelmed with enemies and makes his weaker allies disappear from the scene, lightning-fast as a "diabolus ex machina," as Gasque defines it, paraphrasing the expression Deus ex Machina we have seen before. The reader, according to the critic, remains incredulous, even when Gandalf tells his companions to run away, because this is a strength they cannot overcome.

Therefore, the excitement remains superficial. According to Gasque, without explanation for this statement, even Shelob is a creature who is neither very alive nor very real.

Ultimately, Tolkien adapted many mythical creatures to his universe. Others he created from something that already existed and introduced, quite effectively, whatever their origin. Yet others came from his own imagination, with no organic connection to tradition, or were suddenly presented to the reader, and these were the least successful, perhaps because he didn't really believe in them, as Gasque assumes.

It is a subjective point of view and, therefore, difficult to discuss, despite the elements the author gives to justify his thesis. Obviously, there are others who gave a very different judgment, and here I mention China Miéville, both a creator of very bizarre beings and an admirer of those described by Tolkien.

My point of view on the three least successful entities, according to Gasque, depends on their effectiveness in the plot. Tom Bombadil slows down the pace; when the Hobbits visit him, it is more like a long break in the story, which, as it is, is already quite slow.

When Peter Jackson decided to do without Bombadil in his film version of The Lord of the Rings, many enthusiasts fiercely criticized his choice, whereas I admit I appreciated it.

The Balrog demands a certain amount of imagination to visualize, but this is one of the reasons why I, personally, found it interesting and stimulating. Saying this, however, I admit that this could be seen as just another flaw in the eyes of other readers. But how it is possible to underestimate it? It's a real monster of fairy tales, an ancient creature, rare and terrible, which materializes before the characters in an already desperate moment.

The Balrog is unknown to all members of the Fellowship of the Ring, except for Gandalf, who knows they are facing a formidable opponent. It is immediately clear to the reader that, this time, there will be trouble: the monster, in fact, is not deterred by Gandalf's warnings and request to stop, and it succeeds in dragging the old wizard into a lethal struggle, putting the rest of the Fellowship in flight.

The giant spider, Shelob, is a horrifying creature with some hints of originality, but its effectiveness derives very much from its form, that of an animal that has scared most of us, at least in childhood. A monstrous vision, certainly, but I do not find it to be that original, so I cannot appreciate Gasque putting it among Tolkien's "inventions."

Tolkien's strangest or most monstrous creatures (let's add to the list the Watcher in the Water, the creature that threatens the wayfarers, arriving at the doors of Moria, with its tentacles) are effective in giving strength and mystery to the author's fantasy world, along with the threats of various servants of Sauron and his flaming eye that scans the whole world for the Ring.

Without these unpleasant or alien elements, Middle-earth would feel a lot more homely, and would be a less interesting place, populated only by creatures that are well linked to legends and myth, and in any case more recognizable to the public, those that, in short, Gasque considers to be the best.

But monsters and horror are essential ingredients to make Tolkien's world a real fantasy world.

I can therefore say that I do not agree with this critic's ideas, excluding those about Tom Bombadil. All kinds of monsters are very welcome in Middle-earth.

About Sauron, the Character

Incidentally, we note that Sauron as a character has been criticized for being a non-physical and non-appearing entity, or, more precisely, appearing just as a fiery eye scrutinizing the world. Edmund Wilson depicted Sauron as a well-presented character that strikes fear in his opponents, but lacks further development. As observed by critic Richard L. Purtill,[19] "this is far more effective than any amount of direct description that might attempt to arouse feelings of horror."

This is quite believable; in fact, a rule of horror movies is that "the monster" must not be clearly seen. This way, film directors leave the audience with the task of filling the void with the workings of their own imaginations. Same thing in books. Horror writer H.P. Lovecraft with good reason described in vague terms one of the most horrible creations of all time, the alien god Cthulhu. We know that Cthulhu is a giant tentacled being and little more. After all, people who survive an encounter with him become mad. The real reason is that Cthulhu is beyond the human ability to describe. Sauron has no physical form, so we see nothing except the eye with its terrible gaze. Is the eye tangible as well as visible? We do not know for sure. With these features, Sauron is a hidden horror. An evil god seated on a throne could hardly be more effective.

In an essay by Christina Scull,[20] we have another interesting note about Sauron's strategy. Scull notes that evil in Tolkien's work is strong and sometimes smart, but it has a very restricted perspective. Both Sauron and Saruman want power and world domination, so they judge the actions of others by this criterion. In Sauron's case, he doesn't take the necessary precautions to be sure no one enters Mordor because he can't imagine his opponents want to destroy the Ring. Sauron expects one enemy leader to use the Ring and try to take a leadership position; he does not anticipate the free people wanting to get rid of the Ring.

Richard Morgan and the Orcs' Tragic Nature

Richard K. Morgan, a British science fiction and fantasy writer, is not a Tolkien fan and clearly states as much in his essay "The Real Fantastic Stuff," published online.[21] He seems to appreciate, however, the short glance into the Orcs' lives that is afforded the reader during the capture of Frodo, after the fight with the giant spider, Shelob. We have two captains, Gorbag and Shagrat, who must decide what to do with the prisoner, and a formidable treasure—Frodo's mithril mail—that will be enough to trigger a conflict between the two. Morgan, nevertheless, points out that these Orcs have feelings, hopes and fears: "We get a fascinating insight into life for the rank and file in Mordor. The orcs are disenchanted, poorly informed and constantly stressed by the uncertainties that lack of information brings."

Orcs are afraid of spies in their ranks and live in incessant terror, but they vent their worries anyway. They fear that their leaders are making mistakes, and that the war could go bad for their side. If defeated, their treatment at the hands of the victors could be unmerciful.

The critic argues that Orcs are capable of humor and hold great loyalty to their comrades; they take no more pleasure in war than the "good guys" of the story. Morgan admires this realistic part in Tolkien's narrative.

These Orcs seem, to him, "human," caught up in the terrible circumstances of their condition and little interested in the dilemmas of good and evil. This probably comes from Tolkien's firsthand experience of war, but the author did not exploit this vein of inspiration; rather, he evaded it. He preferred to let the Orcs fall back into stereotype. This is Tolkien's fantasy, and Morgan wonders, in the conclusion of his short essay, why people find it interesting.

There is not really much to think about, other than that the short text by Morgan points the finger at some "positive" aspects of the Orcs, often neglected by readers, such as the fact that they have a certain camaraderie within their own factions and that there is a certain tribal loyalty—although to be honest, this often leads to conflict between groups.

Morgan points out that this dark atmosphere strongly contrasts with the epic nature of Tolkien's work and is perhaps more interesting than other more well-known moments; not expanding the discourse about the Orcs would, therefore, have been a lost opportunity. One can certainly agree with Morgan in considering this passage interesting and noting how Tolkien has given us a look, devoid of antipathies, into the enemy camp; on the other hand Morgan seems to suggest that the book would be better if, instead of epics, there were a grim realism, a wallow in the mud of the trenches, imagining the uncomfortable boots of the anonymous fighters on our feet, things that Tolkien could have handled, as he knew the war, but which he preferred to only make a timid hint at before fleeing in terror. The answer could be (and must be, in my opinion) that Tolkien wanted to do something different, and that if he had chosen this path, he would probably have written one of the many books of our time, impregnated with realism, and not something unconventional, as The Lord of the Rings undoubtedly is. To Tolkien's greatest credit, he wanted to introduce a scene like this, something different in the context of the book, to give us the words of the anonymous masses of Mordor's troops for once.

Interesting Worldbuilding, Less Interesting Characters

China Miéville, a leftist (Trotskyite) "revolutionary" writer, commented on Tolkien's work in a 2002 short essay,[22] offering a critique reminiscent of Moorcock's regarding political aspects, which will be covered later. He does not simply criticize Tolkien's political ideas, but also his way of writing, the pomposity of it. Miéville argues that dialogue in Tolkien's works is pompous and clumsy; it sounds like the opera, but with no music. However, he does not give a totally destructive criticism of Tolkien's style: he finds it ironic that his triumph blossomed when The Lord of the Rings, sold as a pirated edition in the United States, was welcomed by the children of the "counterculture" of the 1960s, looking for hidden meanings.

This event caused astonishing horror for the English professor, himself furthest away, in terms of mentality, from the readers who built him up as a prophet.

Even if Miéville amuses himself by pointing out how Tolkien's success has become irresistible and planetary, thanks to a truly unforeseen factor, he nonetheless derides even the proponents of "serious" literature, overwhelmed by this book that shocked all conventions with its triumph.

While Moorcock attacks the commercial "garbage" associated with Tolkien, Miéville has a very different attitude, which is far from the somewhat aristocratic and snobbish contempt shown by others towards popular and genre literature, to which The Lord of the Rings belongs. Miéville also dissociates himself from the position of the Marxist critic, Lukàcs, who sees the fantastic as decadent and socially irresponsible.

As for the style, Miéville does not claim that it is all bad, even if, in part, he judges it terribly; he states that "it would be churlish to claim that there's nothing to admire in the book. The constant atmosphere of melancholy is intriguing. There are superb, genuinely frightening monsters, and set pieces of real power."

This is interesting. Miéville, a writer who likes to bring forward creatures who are not only monstrous but also extravagant, fearful, and terrible, recognizes a similar capacity in Tolkien, and is taken by the atmosphere created by the English professor, as well as by its evocative power.

Despite rubbing salt in the wound of Tolkien's political metaphors, he is, however, struck by the epic grandeur of the work and, at least at times, by the descriptive capacity he finds in The Lord of the Rings.

This testimony is an important truth in order to understand

Tolkien and his success: The Lord of the Rings is a work that can also be appreciated by those who see it differently from the author. Miéville also adds that Tolkien gave a fundamental contribution to the fantasy genre, because he was the first one who built a detailed secondary world. Before Tolkien obviously we had plenty of fantastic settings, but they were vague, intended to serve the plot's needs, with details added when necessary. By contrast, Tolkien built the world first. He built his world in great detail, giving it history, geography, and mythology. Then he wrote the stories. Miéville states that Tolkien's thoroughness remained as an example.

Miéville, as we shall see, reserves his most cutting remarks for the ideology that he sees at the base of Tolkien's work, and still finds something valid in it; he admires the ability to create fantastic worlds and invites the reader to throw themselves into them. Also, in this, he finds another reason for criticism, but not from a stylistic point of view.

Scottish writer Edwin Muir[23] wrote about Tolkien: "His good people are consistently good, his evil figures immutably evil; and he has no room in his world for a Satan both evil and tragic." But is this really the case? Melkor, Tolkien's "Lucifer," a kind of rebellious demigod, is actually a very similar character to Satan, and maintains his greatness after having embraced evil—by choice, not by obligation or predestination. The certainly evil figure of Smeagol-Gollum has a tendency towards good after Frodo shows kindness towards him; he tragically tries to redeem himself and fails. And positive characters are tempted by evil: Boromir and Frodo are two characters who are fascinated and influenced by the Ring and, in the end, succumb to it in different ways.

On the one hand, Frodo resists as much as possible, heroically extending the trial of strength to a presumably unattainable limit for any other common living being of Middle-earth (not even Gandalf dares to keep the Ring!), and, if in the end he fails, it is because the ability to resist forever would mean having a perfection that humans are not allowed.

On the other hand, Boromir, who tries to steal the Ring, believing he can claim the rightful chance to fight for his people with a winning weapon, in truth suffers from its charm, and so reminds us that the road to hell is paved with good intentions.

We need to add the magician Saruman to the list. He who should have been a bulwark against Sauron is instead seduced by him, at the same time deceiving himself that he can maintain some freedom of action to maneuver for his own ambitions. The characters who choose evil do so by using their own free will—that is, knowingly—and they have the possibility of abandoning it, but they do not.

After this fair defense in favor of Tolkien, it cannot be denied that the general impression of the conflict, as told in The Lord of the Rings, is of a forward attack with the presence, as we will see later, of a troop of countless evildoers, who are always present in the background, these Orcs appearing en masse, and who we will see speaking only on one occasion.

Without question, Tolkien's "villains" are predominantly malignant, without ambiguity, doubt, or subterfuge, and Sauron is, certainly, monolithic in his own wickedness, whatever the premise, acting both as leader of the evil faction as well as a perverse and satanic divinity, all of this without being a character of any real interaction. Indeed, it must be acknowledged that there is no enemy with ambiguity, for example cruel but beautiful and seductive, or able to justify himself with some motivation, at least partly founded. Sauron is not even corporeal; we never see him. The only seduction is that of the Ring, a metaphor for a corrupting power. Without compromising his own religious beliefs, Tolkien could have created negative characters with greater complexity or depth. In fact, it is a common religious warning to learn to recognize the insidious trap of evil, which is disguised in so many different forms.

The evil could, therefore, choose many masks, but in the end, the only one we see is that of the Ring. Not wanting to believe, like the most severe critics, such as Moorcock, that Tolkien was incapable of creating more complex villains, we must deduce that it is the author's choice to make them merely horrendous and terrifying when they are frightening and painfully petty or repulsive when they are not. I cannot say I appreciate this choice, but it is one that is common in fairy tales. The villain is an archetype (that is, the "classic," basic, evil character) or extremely stereotyped: bad witches, cruel queens, Orcs who eat children, and so on. And we know how Tolkien cared about the fairy-tale nature of his stories. I think it is important to remember that, aside from the judgment of Tolkien's work, fantasy has been strongly influenced by the more visible aspect of his books, the struggle between good and evil: for better or for worse, by the practice of writers who lack the same merits, endlessly repeating the story of The Lord of the Rings and by imitating it, rather than drawing inspiration from it. In my opinion, this was not the right direction for the fantasy genre to head in, but either way, Tolkien cannot be blamed for this later consequence.

The Evil

Talking about the representation of evil in Tolkien, we have an essay by Tom Shippey, "Tolkien as a Post-War Writer."[24] Tom Shippey is arguably the most influential scholar and critic of Tolkien's work. The essay is about the war experience as an influence on Tolkien and other British authors like George Orwell (author of *Nineteen Eighty-Four* and *Animal Farm*), William Golding (*Lord of the Flies*), the less famous T.H. White (*The Once and Future King*), and C.S. Lewis (*That Hideous Strength*). These works are fantasy, fable, or science fiction and written by authors touched by the war. The First World War was the central experience for Tolkien, the eldest of this group, but all of them were touched by World War II. These writers gave us a testimony about the nature of evil, something they had to know firsthand, except White. In Shippey's opinion, these writers turned to fantasy or science fiction because they did not manage to describe human evil and its origin by means of realism alone. Such a problem could not be dealt with by writing about contemporary political or social issues: these writers faced disillusion, the loss of faith in man's nature, horror beyond any literary fiction. Tolkien did not describe horror and blood too closely, nor did he pronounce any condemning sentence about human nature. Still, he wrote about the necessity of fighting evil. Anyway, the way good and evil were portrayed was a cause of criticism for The Lord of the Rings. Shippey quotes Edwin Muir's desire for more interesting evil characters. Still, the group of post-war writers to which Tolkien belongs could not use old literary tropes to represent the evil of the twentieth century they knew. Questioned about the merciless slaughter his good heroes fulfill, Tolkien observed that his protagonist has only willpower and no weapons to complete his quest. Moreover, the book is about Mercy (with a capital M) from beginning to end. Besides, as Shippey notes, the hero Beowulf could never reason with the troll Grendel[25]: that is, the enemy's nature makes any conciliation impossible. In The Lord of the Rings, some characters are good but bloodthirsty at the same time (Théoden is the example Shippey gives us). This behavior makes sense in the context of the real war Tolkien experienced and as a necessity of wartime. In this vision of legitimate and civilized war, fighters must do terrible things to fight evil, but at the same time avoid becoming a part of it themselves. Shippey finds a difference between his post-war writers and many of the critics who came from a sheltered academic environment. They didn't appreciate the war experience as reported by others, yet they didn't have to fight a war in person.

In the foreword to his book *J.R.R. Tolkien: Author of the Century*,[26] Shippey adds that Tolkien avoided fashionable gloom and nihilism, offering solutions to the problem of evil but not conforming to the modernist style and themes of his times. Doing this, Tolkien had to engage a political and public topic, rather than writing something private. But even private lives, Shippey argues, are touched by events that are public and political—and private deaths often are too.

Hot Air?

Fred Inglis[27] thinks Tolkien's writing style is moving. It's "round and full," but ... this is the product of "hot air." It's the prose of the sermon, the voice of the Church. There's no real-life experience in a narration of heroic deeds by high-minded knights, with a simplistic moral. Inglis quotes a segment of *The Fellowship of the Ring* in which Merry and Pippin reveal to Frodo that they had sensed his intention to quit the Shire. There's a slightly humorous tone in Frodo's surprise. He had thought he had managed to hide his intentions perfectly, and now he feared his intentions were transparent to anyone.

Tolkien tried to write a lively dialogue but without following the contemporary language. The result is not a living speech, but bookish and contrived. While the way people actually talk is different from what we see in books' dialogue, the artist's task is to balance that way with an art form, to create something that looks real enough. A task more difficult in prose than in poetry. The result is something that sounds too literary to be real and lacks the substance of authentic speech. Inglis thinks modernity separates people from real-life experiences: Tolkien's writing style, with its thinness, is well suited to this modern lifestyle. This is even more evident in action and heroism scenes. Everything is shrouded in myth or allegory, nothing has a corporeal reality, and nothing is tangible in the fights and heroic feats Tolkien tells us about. Whatever his qualities, Tolkien cannot make you feel the sweat and blood of the real thing.

A Lack of Femininity

On style: British critic Kenneth McLeish wrote[28] an essay titled "The Rippingest Yarn of All," in which he criticizes a "lack of femininity" in The Lord of the Rings. Criticism about the lack of women in the book, or the lack of strong roles for them to fulfill, is not scarce. But McLeish doesn't mean that we don't see Gandalf's or Merry's girlfriends. He finds a lack of gentleness, of grace in the male characters. For example, McLeish mentions the scene in Homer's *Iliad* in which Hector and Andromache and their baby son have a farewell before the death of Hector in a duel with Achilles. Another similar scene is Priam pleading with the Greek invaders for Hector's corpse after his fatal last fight. In *The Odyssey*, we have a long quest to go home, in which the main character, Odysseus, learns to use gentleness and flexibility to his advantage. He experiences personal growth: after that, he's not just a warrior. He became a complete man, integrating these new features into his personality. In The Lord of the Rings, McLeish notes, there's nothing like that. Gandalf turned from gray to white after his fight with the Balrog and his rebirth. But this is a revelation of latent features of this extraordinary character. Boromir's greed for the Ring is revealed and Frodo becomes an outsider, but there's no real character development. Another criticism from McLeish is about the over-simplification of moral and ethical issues. In the critic's opinion, this is a trait that Tolkien shares with many other British authors of his time. They were creators of dangerous literature, taking all moral and ethical problems for granted. The evildoers who challenge the status quo (the normal equilibrium) are defeated and eliminated, so the British Empire's certainties can be reaffirmed, again and again. Except for some strangers, like Freud and Marx, nobody could doubt the premises on which society worked: McLeish hints particularly at lower classes and women kept in their place. The First World War destroyed these certainties: so, in this critic's opinion, Tolkien's clinging to Victorian values is out of his time.

Tolkien's "cult" is more worrying for McLeish. He defines the fans as frivolous, wrong-headed, and "a lethal model for late-twentieth-century living." Moreover, McLeish states that in the nasty and brutal world of today, dressing up in Elven clothes and baking lembas (the Elven bread) means avoiding, not finding, life's reality.

Today, probably, we're more used to this phenomenon. Media industries act, on purpose and with great skill, to instill a passion for their heroes in the public. Therefore, McLeish's astonishment might sound strange in the present day. As for the lack of gentleness, other critics (as we will see) have noted that a gentle and "feminine" vision of power is, even in male heroes, what really wins the day, not simple strength and performance without consideration (Aragorn is an example of the first kind of power, Boromir of the second).

Bad Style, Bad Poetry

In the swollen ranks of those having a not so high opinion of Tolkien's verses we can include Scottish poet Alan Bold.[29] In Bold's view, Tolkien could not use the English language's qualities profitably, so he "bullied" it. He was derivative, anachronistic, too preoccupied with rhyme and conforming to the verse pattern's exigencies. Tolkien had no interest in modern poetry, so he was not touched by the modernism practiced by Pound, Eliot, and Joyce. But, as Pound wrote, you can't write good poetry in a style that is 20 years old, because the verses will sound as if inspired by books instead of real life, and hopelessly cliché. In fact, Bold states that Tolkien wrote his major works in prose because he was ill at ease with verse.

Incidentally, Bold's essay mentions the disease that allowed Tolkien to return to England to receive treatment. It was trench fever. This critic describes it as a "psychosomatic condition to which imaginative men were particularly prone." Is this some kind of innuendo suggesting Tolkien was not strong enough to bear the hardships and horror of war? Bold's essay hints at Tolkien being horrified by his war experience, the suffering in the trenches. Tolkien was not happy to be in the army, nor was he keen on doing his part in the war's carnage. But, if you search for information about the illness, trench fever is described as an infectious disease. In a more recent work by John Garth, *Tolkien and the Great War: The Threshold of Middle-earth*, we read that when Tolkien went to the medical officer when his unit was away from the front, he had a quite real raging fever—not something one could fake. Garth also states that Tolkien's friend Christopher Wiseman later (when Tolkien was in Great Britain) suggested that he pretend to be sick, but "he didn't need to pretend." So, it's challenging to assess Bold's statement without deeming it as a jab at Tolkien.

An Unsatisfying Hero

Janet Menzies, a Tolkien enthusiast in her adolescence, manifested some dissatisfaction with the style of The Lord of the Rings in "Middle-earth and the adolescent."[30] Menzies notes a revelation technique used by Tolkien when he wants to show a character's importance or supernatural strength. When Strider meets the Hobbits in Bree, they initially do not trust him. From his look, Strider could be a vagrant or a bandit. Strider reveals himself, standing up and immediately looking taller, with a commanding aura and a gleaming light in the eye, and says that he could have the Ring immediately if he wanted it. We notice the same technique when Galadriel reveals her own ring, and her appearance is suddenly majestic and terrible. "Giving brief glimpses of the true nature of a veiled character can be very eye-catching," Menzies writes. But if the trick is not used sparingly, it becomes annoying and ridiculous, and so it is in Tolkien's case.

About Frodo: Menzies states that he shares some Christlike qualities. He's innocent and meek, but he's not heroic. His introverted personality, his belonging to the Hobbit world, requires a profound transformation to be the hero of The Lord of the Rings. This critic thinks Frodo's change is not entirely believable, and the author had some uncertainty writing about him.

Tolkien's language is sentimental and patronizing when showing Frodo and Sam during their march to the Crack of Doom (where Frodo is supposed to destroy the Ring). For example, Sam watching his master sleeping is described as a Great War soldier in awe of his captain. This is not adequate when writing about these small creatures with leathery feet. Sentimental, Victorian language, in Menzies's opinion, is a symptom of Tolkien being unable to connect adequately with his subject.

Anyway, Tolkien made the wrong choice with Frodo; another character (Gandalf, Aragorn) would have been better suited for the task. The author had chosen a Hobbit because this was the readers' desire and because Tolkien wanted the bearer to be a nonentity. But this is detrimental to the story. A strong-willed character as the ring-bearer would have been forced to accept a great, terrible inner struggle. The reader would have enjoyed a fully developed character, using the ring and going through this intellectual struggle, following his enlightenment journey. This moral struggle would have elevated The Lord of the Rings to the level of great novels. As a result, we see the ring-bearers' experience as an external struggle, the problematic walk of Frodo and Sam: Tolkien avoided the challenge of having Frodo or another more competent character experience the inner tribulation. Menzies concludes that human conflict is not at the heart of The Lord of the Rings. The author worries about the changing world: this is evident in the tormented landscape of Middle-earth. The Orcs have conquered Moria, and Elven Lothlórien is fading away, while Ithilien has fallen. Even the Shire is industrialized and polluted before the story's end.

Maybe Janet Menzies has a point. But we need to note, about Frodo, that Tolkien wanted a humble hero for a reason. This option of powerful characters taking responsibility for the Ring was examined and discarded in The Lord of the Rings: even Gandalf refuses to be the ring-bearer. He doesn't want such a temptation. Nobody can win that terrible struggle, and surely no great hero can. Tolkien wanted the Ring destroyed by a providential event, a divine intervention, not by an almost godly character. So, the Hobbits are the humble heroes who can make the journey to the Crack of Doom. Sam and Frodo are nearly immune to any temptation by the Ring's power (Sam more than Frodo, probably). But even they can't fulfill the heroic deed; it's not a thing that human beings can do without divine help. In fact, Frodo can't resist the Ring in the end. At the last moment, he decides to keep it. Ironically, it's the creature Gollum, a corrupted Hobbit, who resolves the dilemma: he does it by stealing the Ring, tripping, and falling into the flaming chasm.

Aragorn or Gandalf would have failed, even sooner than Frodo did.

However, in Menzies's opinion, the lack of a formidable hero remains a shortcoming in The Lord of the Rings. While the book sure has its own standard of good and evil, morality is related to human behavior. By giving us the thoughts of his heroes, the author would have given the reader a connection to evaluate his own reaction to the book's events and challenges. Menzies doesn't find satisfaction in a story where the characters lack internal development. In her opinion, the lack of internalization is due to the strong influence religious faith had on the author. This is true for another famous writer, C.S. Lewis, a member of the "Inklings," Tolkien's discussion group at Oxford University. In Menzies's opinion, the personality of the individual has little place in the Catholic faith. Moreover, in ancient sagas, a man is defined more by what he does than by what he thinks. Tolkien gives us the exterior trappings of heroism, but his narration is unsatisfying, his characters lack an inner core. This critic thinks The Lord of the Rings is better suited to adolescents or children than adults.

Power, Politics and Knowledge at the Base of the Story

In her essay "Power and Knowledge in Tolkien: The Problem of Difference in 'The Birthday Party,'"[31] Jane Chance states that Tolkien shares some perspectives on power and knowledge with French philosopher and social theorist Michel Foucault.

Foucault (1926–1984) studied the effectiveness of knowledge ("monopoly of knowledge") and information to wield power, including the creation and imposition of norms of behavior and methods of surveillance. Chance finds an analogy between the nature of Sauron's power and the systems of control studied by Foucault. In particular, the French philosopher refers to the Panopticon, a building model ideated by Jeremy Bentham (1748–1832), English philosopher and social reformer. The Panopticon is a perfect prison or asylum, a rotunda with a central tower where a guard is situated. The guard can see every cell in the building from the central position; the institution's guests or inmates don't know when the guard is actually watching them, so they are continuously forced to behave as if they are under observation. Power is enacted without interruption at a minimal cost. Jane Chance states that this is the same way in which power operates in Tolkien's works. Sauron, with his searching eye, is an evident example of this. But Saruman or Shelob, or even Frodo and Bilbo, act the same way.

The power uses knowledge against people; free people try to use knowledge to find the truth. Truth is at the center of The Lord of the Rings because it brings liberation from power's hegemony. In Bilbo's birthday party scene, we see celebration of the individual: Bilbo talks with and gives gifts to people, offers fireworks, and then disappears. Bilbo's intellectual heroism consists in his social role (the gift-giving) and lack of self-indulgence. Giving the Ring to Frodo, Bilbo gives him a heavy burden, but resisting Sauron's authority is, at the same time, a boost to the determination to accomplish the bearer's duty. There are factionalism and divisions in the Shire, but with their ability to perceive the local politics, Bilbo and Frodo attract followers for the mission. Bilbo keeps the Ring for many years; he stays young and has an unexpectedly long life. This longevity is an effect of the Ring extending its control over him. But at the same time, the gentleness and generosity of this character enable him to resist the Ring's power. Although many Hobbits see him as a suspicious character because of his adventures, Bilbo's education and respectful ways permit him to exert influence and leadership on others.

In The Lord of the Rings, language and knowledge are repeatedly used as political tools against threats facing the community, but they can also be misused and be a menace. Wormtongue and Saruman use these means to expand their power. Other evildoers—Shelob, Gollum, the forces of Mordor—use raw violence: they are inarticulate, their strength is mindless violence. The leader that emerges at the end of the struggle (Aragorn, the king) is a tolerant, understanding, nurturing power. The emphasis is on the generosity of the master. Not just in Aragorn, but even in Frodo towards Sam (and Gollum, too); it starts a circular relationship of mutual utility. Social roles, the power of words and knowledge, shape the relationship between the characters and societies in The Lord of the Rings.

In Jane Chance's essay, we find an interesting discussion on the use of knowledge, information, and power in Tolkien's work. There's no evident proof of her assumption that the author's understanding of leadership is based on a "post-modernist relationship" between power and knowledge. If Tolkien was aware of Foucault's theories, or if the comparison is appropriate, remains to be demonstrated.

The Problem with *The Silmarillion*

In his essay about the critical response to Tolkien,[32] Wayne G. Hammond deals with the topic of Tolkien criticism. Obviously, many others have discussed the subject; Hammond notes that all the attention is devoted, usually, to *The Hobbit* and The Lord of the Rings. Early criticism is made without the information published in *The Silmarillion*. He notes that many reviewers had written their comments before publication of *The Silmarillion* cast a light on many details of Tolkien's legendarium.[33] Some ignored *The Silmarillion* and *Unfinished Tales* or gave them bad reviews. Many of them were quite harsh, lamenting a lack of all those elements that, in The Lord of the Rings, had made an enjoyable book. No landscapes, no likable rangers or wizards, no Ents, and a lack of women as in The Lord of the Rings. The female characters too majestic and fierce, like divinities or heroines. Critics thought the style was Victorian and excessively archaic. In Hammond's opinion, that was to be expected, because it was difficult for Tolkien to follow The Lord of the Rings with a similar success without repeating himself. *The Silmarillion* sold well enough anyway. It could be a proof of quality or an indication that Tolkien's fans bought everything written by him without judging the quality. The *Unfinished Tales* also received scant appreciation. Hammond quotes Guy Gavriel Kay, the writer who helped Christopher Tolkien in his work as editor of Tolkien's uncompleted manuscripts, saying that it's not a book to recommend to someone looking for an enjoyable read. There's not the same spirit. Tolkien's "magic" is not in it.

And yet, while criticism has been harsh, the readers have contradicted the critics once more because Tolkien's posthumous work still appeals to the public.

It's necessary to make a point here: readers and scholars want to read the works Tolkien couldn't finish before his death. They liked The Lord of the Rings, loved *The Hobbit,* and they want more. Yet, these books should be kept separate from Tolkien's other tales and essays appearing during his life. We don't know if and how he wanted to present this material to the public. Any criticism should take this into account. Moreover, *The Silmarillion* is, in part, a reconstructed work. Douglas Charles Kane, who wrote[34] extensively on the subject, states that this is "perhaps inevitable, given the state in which Tolkien left the work. However, there are number of areas in which he [Christopher Tolkien] may be said to have overstepped the bounds" of an editor. Later publications put this right, but still we need to remember that no editorial work can replace the hand of the real author.

A Different Take on Heroism

The essay "We don't need another hero: Problematic Heroes and their Function in Some of Tolkien's Works," by Thomas Honegger,[35] is about the relationship between heroism and the needs of society.

In the beginning, the behavior of Túrin and Beorhtnoth is examined. The first one is a character created by Tolkien: he's the tragic hero of *The Children of Húrin*. Beorhtnoth is a real historical figure quoted in the Old English poem *The Battle of Maldon* and the subject of Tolkien's *The Homecoming of Beorhtnoth Beorhthelm's Son*.

Túrin's bravery doesn't result in any improvement. His homecoming can't defeat the Easterling invaders, and he kills Brodda, the enemy leader who had taken Aerin, a relative of Túrin, as his wife. The hero's revenge precipitates this woman's condition. Not that it was ideal: she was Brodda's wife against her own will. But now she'll have to kill herself. Túrin's actions have effects that don't concern him alone, but does he care? This is why Honegger states that he failed in his social obligation (as a hero that should be of help to his people). Beorhtnoth's behavior is similarly detrimental. The Anglo-Saxon leader is facing Viking invaders: they are stalled in an unfavorable position until Beorhtnoth graciously concedes that battle will be held in open ground. Then he loses and dies, with the majority of his soldiers. His "sportsmanship" is costly not just to him, but to the community as well.

Tolkien was unequivocal in his disapproval. There's just a difference Honegger finds between these heroes: as opposed to Beorhtnoth, who dies because of his own failure, Túrin survives and learns something. His decisions will be more cautious in the future. When Túrin faces the dragon Glaurung he arranges for the safety of others as much as possible, and he makes use of any advantage the terrain can give him. Túrin is doomed anyway (because he was cursed by Morgoth) but against Glaurung he wins without causing innocents to pay for his rashness.

By contrast, Aragorn, the "social" and responsible hero, has wisdom as his primary trait. He follows Gandalf's advice and is aware that his success depends on many helpers and allies. He will give credit to Gandalf as the real leader and victor, and to all the people who fought on his side. The Lord of the Rings is very different from *The Children of Húrin* in its treatment of heroic characters. The harsh, gloomy world of this last book comes directly from the Nordic world Tolkien loved: there's no divine providence or salvation at the end. The Lord of the Rings is, to use the definition by Tom Shippey, the "mediator"[36] between the author's Christian belief and the heroic ancient literature he studied.

Still, we have Éomer's last stand during the Battle of Pelennor Fields as an example of a "Nordic" moment: after King Théoden's death, seeing his sister Éowyn lying nearby, he leads his men on a reckless charge until his force is surrounded. When he sees the black corsair ships coming, Éomer thinks everything is lost and gives orders to fight on foot to the last man (incidentally, the ships are carrying Aragorn and his reinforcements instead of more enemies). Still, Éomer is not another hero who creates more damage than good: the "eucatastrophe" of unexpected victory redeems his bravery. Honegger notes that Éomer is not expecting to be remembered, because he thinks everything is lost and everyone in Middle-earth will be enslaved. This heroic last stand in pure pagan, heroic style is not marred by rashness or a desire for personal glory, because Éomer is not putting the will to fight before his social duties, and he's not after future glory. Also, he's not giving in to suicidal despair as Denethor did.

The Fairy Story as Utopia

Critic Jack Zipes wrote a study[37] on fairy stories examining their social and political context. He thinks fairy stories are connected to reality in their drive to modify it: their content is far from being childish or absurd because it represents real hopes. There's an important element of rebellion and self-determination in fantasy; Zipes tries to find it even in modern mass media, films, television, books, and so on, to use them as an educational tool for young readers. His goal is to make them able to avoid society's manipulatory mechanisms.

The meaning of fairy stories comes from unrealized desires. Moreover, a fairy story has a utopian potential: even in Tolkien's work, Zipes claims to have found it. The fairy story in Tolkien is based on hope: consolation, a happy ending, the "eucatastrophe." In this happy conclusion, there's a fleeting vision of joy beyond the boundaries of this world. This vision is in the real world: here, Tolkien is not a conventional Christian. In his ideation, Fantasy in the form of a fairy story has a mystic ardor as a hope of freedom and as humanity's redeemer. It has the power to figure different circumstances and situations than the real ones: it's not simply a romantic regression to the past. Rationality gives fantasy no value; it bridles and inhibits desire. But rationality alone is not able to give expression and satisfaction to human needs. This is why fantasy has a social and political meaning. For Tolkien, it had a religious one, too, because he understood the necessity, in the modern world, to express Christian messages in a secularized way. In Zipes's opinion, Tolkien tries to secularize religion to fight against the dehumanization of the modern world. But he puts the small Hobbits in a divine role, at the center of his universe. There's no God in Middle-earth. The small person is the source of spirituality; fantasy finds its own contents and consolations. There's no paradise or afterlife. Humanity has claimed the power to change the world and get immediate gratification.

In his analysis of *The Hobbit*, Zipes identifies a traditional heroic figure in Bilbo, similar to other small heroes (David, Little Thumb) ready to fight a brave challenge. Bilbo is not a believable hero: he looks like a classic consumer; he'd like better to see his own fantasies displayed on the screen while he's enjoying a beer. When 13 Dwarves invade his house to enlist his aid, he doesn't want to go with them on an adventure. Gandalf comes to stimulate Bilbo's hidden adventurous side. For the Dwarves, the mage is like a famous football coach who says Bilbo will be able to carry out a decisive role, so they believe him. This is the utopian perspective of *The Hobbit*: Bilbo is a passive, dull character who doesn't want any risk. But there's a different person in him, with unknown powers that need to be awakened. He's a modest Hobbit until he permits his real potential to develop and unfold.

What kind of adventure is it? Why do the Dwarves fight against a dragon? Dwarves are miners; they are rude, energetic workers. They are the working class. Smaug, the dragon, steals treasures and keeps them: he's a classic capitalist exploiter. Bilbo is middle-class; he should be wary of giving aid to the Dwarves and have a propensity for connecting with the ruling class. But, this time, he identifies with the working-class struggle. With his description of the goblins, Tolkien identifies them as apparent agents of capitalism: they use slaves to manufacture their weapons, slaves who are worked to death in appalling conditions.

In the initial fights, Bilbo is afraid; he would prefer never having left his Hobbit hole. But the discovery of the Ring is a symbol of Bilbo getting his hidden talents back. He earns the Dwarves' respect. When the Dwarves refuse to share Smaug's treasury, which is in their hands after the dragon's death, they are, in reality, taking his place as grabbers and oppressors. Bilbo is unaffected by greediness; he donates the Arkenstone to Men and Elves to facilitate negotiations (Thorin, the Dwarf leader, is keen to get this gem). Things do not go entirely for the better, but, in his last words, Thorin will acknowledge Bilbo's generosity and yearning for friendship. When he returns home, Bilbo is quite different in the knowledge of his potentiality, his understanding of the need for peace and goodwill in the world, his ability to deal with several races that he didn't even know before his adventure.

The lack of women in the story and Bilbo's acceptance of his place in the old hierarchy limits Tolkien's utopia. Women are claiming no role here, and there's no possible social development in the world. God-given harmony must be preserved.

What are we to think? Zipes gives us radical theories about Tolkien's work, identifying progressive values in it and, at the same time, strong limits. In the commercial exploitation of Tolkien's work, Zipes sees opposing sides. On the one hand, the power is misleading the masses; on the other hand, Tolkien's work creates forms of community and communication for his readers beyond common social relations.

Not an English Fairy Story?

Roger King, in his essay,[38] held back from assaulting Tolkien with the ferocity of other intellectuals; still, he has some interesting opinions about Tolkien and his work, starting from the functions fairy stories have in the modern world: escape, recovery, and consolation, as expressed in Tolkien's essay "On Fairy-Stories." Recovery, the regaining of a clear view to see things free from an everyday perspective or familiarity, surely belongs to the fairy story with its world of monsters and supernatural beings. Still, fairy stories are usually also familiar on another level: locations and events of fairy stories are drawn from our world. But Tolkien's Middle-earth presents us with an unfamiliar world and previously unknown heroes: so in Tolkien's mythology, the reader finds an intellectual puzzle, a "literary Rubik's cube."

Moreover, recovery in fairy stories gives us a clear vision of good and evil. Roger King thinks that The Lord of the Rings presents us with so many characters and races that we don't know where we are in a moral sense, with the exception of characters obviously evil (Sauron) or heroic and good (Frodo, Bilbo). In this critic's opinion, Tolkien's work is confusing for the reader's moral sense of right and wrong. King's opinion on this matter is surprisingly different from the usual viewpoints about Tolkien's characters and their actions. His thesis is that, in a fairy story, good and evil are absolutes: the evil must be destroyed, the good will inherit the Earth. The Lord of the Rings works this way for some important characters. For all the others, there's not a clear destiny. For these reasons, Tolkien fails to achieve recovery in his work. What about escape? In both *The Hobbit* and The Lord of the Rings, there are some passages where you see a hostility against modernity that doesn't necessarily exist in fairy stories. An example of this is the Shire, ruined by industrialization. We find another in *The Hobbit*: the once-powerful lake town near the mouth of Forest River is shown as a much-decayed shell of its former self. Roger King gives us the example of other fairy stories: Dick Whittington, the Three Little Pigs, Jack and the Beanstalk. In these stories, city life is celebrated: strong brick buildings give security and rural poverty forces the characters to go to the urban market, where their troubles will be solved. Characters in fairy stories show persistence, initiative, and courage: they don't fear modernity, and they achieve success by their efforts. Tolkien's characters apparently just want to go hide in their homes in comfortable retirement. So the escape Tolkien gives us is only his own disdain for the modern world. Roger King does not judge the author's feelings, but he states that English fairy tales are different from The Lord of the Rings or *The Hobbit*.

Is this perspective a relevant critique of *The Hobbit* and The Lord of the Rings? Difficult to say, but Tolkien's success seems to indicate that, for a majority of his readers, it is not.

Not Worth the Effort?

Alessandro dal Lago,[39] talking about mythopoesis and sub-creation in Tolkien's work, thinks that "Tolkien's seriousness, together with his pretension of writing something that could be real, puts the reader in front of a radical choice: to accept them or to repel them as a whole."

This is because, as he says, the matter is very complicated: the Tolkien fan needs to read various narrative works by Tolkien, published during his lifetime or posthumously: maps, vocabularies, handbooks. Between Middle-earth and Arda, the languages and the histories, the reader has an immense amount of material to study in detail. Is this worth the effort? Dal Lago believes that this large quantity of material to explore forces the readers to make a radical choice, to accept or reject the challenge. In or out, with very little middle ground. This would be the reason why we have very different judgments and criticisms about Tolkien's work: it's love or rejection when critics talk about him.

This opinion could have been remarkable if expressed in the years immediately after The Lord of the Rings was published. But it's baffling to read this in recent criticism. Today, the imaginary worlds are the obvious fundament of fiction in writing and on the screen. Tolkien's Middle-earth was not the first, but it was so important that many others followed. The universes of *Star Trek* and *Star Wars*, George Martin with his books and the TV series based on them, Marvel's superhero movie franchise—all of these are examples of massive worlds that have been represented in books, comics, movies, and video games. Mark J.P. Wolf, professor of communication at Concordia University,

Wisconsin, wrote in his book *Building Imaginary Worlds*[40]: "Books like The Lord of the Rings are considered 'immersive' if they supply sufficient detail and description for the reader to vicariously enter the imagined world."

Another way of engaging with an imaginary world is by absorption, the process of filling one's mind with the names and particulars of a fictional world's places and characters. The third process is saturation: the presence of "so many secondary world details to keep in mind that one struggles to remember them all while experiencing the world.... Saturation is the pleasurable goal of conceptual immersion."

Tolkien was probably the earliest and most eminent master in creating secondary worlds, but authors, cartoonists, studios, and publishers have learned the lesson about imaginary worlds. These creations are massive, organized, detailed. They live in different media. Even the most ardent fan probably can't learn everything about one of these secondary worlds. The majority of the audience doesn't even try. Today, Middle-earth is just one of many worlds of similar complexity. Therefore, there are many reasons why Tolkien's worldbuilding divides critics' and readers' opinions, but it's hard to believe that excessive complexity is one of them.

The Flying Eagles Trick

Journalist Charlotte Haunhorst wrote an article on the German daily newspaper *Süddeutsche Zeitung*[41] titled "What is the hype about The Lord of the Rings?"

It is satirical criticism: Haunhorst looks at the Hobbit team of Sam and Frodo, marching towards their quest's destination. While the former is optimistic and spurs the other one to go forward, the latter is a whiny, self-pitying Hobbit. This is the story of The Lord of the Rings: if it sounds boring, it's because it is. Still, fans all over the world wrongly celebrate it. Tolkien wrote 1,300 pages to tell the story, but the movies by Peter Jackson are even "more unbearable" than the book. You can skip the pages when reading, but if you're watching the series of movies in the company of fans, you'll be condemned to watch the extended version. Twelve hours instead of nine. The end of the movies is a good example of the squandering of your time. Frodo and Sam are brought to safety by the eagles, escaping from lava spewed from Mount Doom. Haunhorst notes that, sure, the eagles could have swooped in earlier, sped the journey into Mordor. They could have spared Sam and Frodo all the wailing and crying, and that long march. Had anyone in the book thought for an instant, the Hobbits could just have flown. After the movie, the journalist writes, you just want to bang your head on the wall, but the better solution is to run away before you're forced to watch *The Hobbit* series of movies too.

This article is a bit of a humorous piece, part of a series named "hatred of art," where uncommon or controversial opinions are published. *Süddeutsche Zeitung*'s journalists are free to vent their rage. But it's not the first time that the problem of the eagles shows up. Is this a terrible plot hole? A possible clarification is that the eagles could come and save Sam and Frodo after the Ring was destroyed because its destruction has hollowed out Sauron's power, neutralizing the danger posed by his far-seeing eye, the Nazgûl, and their steeds. Before the Ring's destruction, the eagles' flight would have been noted and caused a reaction. Does this make sense for you?

Another Hope to See Tolkien Fade Away

Some of the most aggressive criticism against Tolkien was written over a rather long period starting with the publication of The Lord of the Rings trilogy and gaining momentum with the books' unforeseen commercial fortune, which was seen as an additional reason to attack them, and sometimes their readers too. In more recent times criticism has become more nuanced, and generally more positive. Somebody thinks, as we will see, that Tolkien's success forced the established critics to take him more seriously and acknowledge his worth, at the same time downplaying his thornier and more contrarian viewpoints. But, even in the twenty-first century, we have those who don't hold back in their negative criticism. Harold Bloom (1930–2019) does it in the introduction to his essay collection about Tolkien.[42] As he states at the beginning, his doubts are of an "aesthetic" nature. Bloom is not a progressive, a committed Marxist, or the proposer of some inventive critical theory. He's a defender of classical Western culture against the "school of resentment," a term he coined to group feminists, Marxists, post-structuralists, and followers of other literary theories.

Bloom states that the trilogy of The Lord of the Rings is Tolkien's delayed reaction to the Great War, and it is in fact a descent into hell. But there's an error about the author's life; strangely, the more a critic dislikes Tolkien, the more likely he or she is to get some details in the author's books or life wrong. Bloom states that the author lost nearly all of his friends to the First World War, and was wounded himself. Tolkien, however, was not wounded during his war experience. Anyway, several critics state that the war was a dramatic, life-changing experience for Tolkien; obviously this is fairly accurate.

Anyway, Bloom is in doubt about the language used to depict this descent into hell. In his opinion, The Lord of the Rings is "inflated, overwritten, tendentious, and moralistic." Tolkien's language is "acutely self-conscious, even arch." Bloom describes the opening of *The Return of the King* as a very difficult-to-read passage, and wonders how a mature reader can read such a long book written like that. He states that Tolkien has met a need in the counterculture period, but he doubts he's an author for the twenty-first century.

So, in Bloom's opinion, we have a writer who can't write, because his style is terrible. It's incomprehensible how the mature reader can stand it, which means, evidently, that The Lord of the Rings is not for a "mature" reader. Decades after Edmund Wilson, the refrain is very similar. Moreover, Bloom ascribes Tolkien's success to the counterculture of the 1960s. To imagine that he would not be successful without this fortunate push was maybe believable 40 or 50 years ago, but it's strange to see a recent critic reiterate the contention. As for Bloom's doubts about Tolkien's enduring success, the twenty-first century has now entered its third decade, with no decline apparent. Only time will tell.

2

The Anti-Modernist
and Political Tolkien

The Political Tolkien

It is a fact that Tolkien did not appreciate modernity, but we must wonder, to what extent? For many critics, his writings are imbued with his way of thinking and his political ideas, which are implicitly thought of as propaganda. The author claimed that his work was mainly philological and linguistical: the creation of a land in which to bring legends to life and give voice to the languages he had invented. Is it therefore possible to ignore those who criticized Tolkien based on these aspects? Absolutely not. We cannot avoid the debate by stating that the simple mythological and fantastic nature of his work justifies the depiction of a traditional society with traditional values. The Lord of the Rings is a modern work; it was not written at the time of *The Song of the Nibelungs* or *Beowulf*.[1] It has not sparked a new interest in mythology: there are not many people who are interested in mythology or epic outside of its scholastic and academic context. Generally speaking, those who have read and appreciated *The Hobbit* or The Lord of the Rings are not going to read *The Iliad* or the *Poetic Edda* or the legends mentioned above. There is, therefore, something different in Tolkien's work, and given the interest it arouses, it is normal for the message it transmits to be analyzed. In fact, this is what Damien Walter does, in his *Guardian* article.[2] He states that Tolkien's myths are like a dangerous double-edged sword. "Myths are a lens through which we investigate the mysteries of the world around us," he writes, admonishing us about the deeply conservative nature of the myths created by Tolkien and his friends, the Inklings. The story is narrated by just a single source (the Red Book of Westmarch, Bilbo's, and then Frodo's memories). The feudal society is ever righteous and victorious. The adversary Sauron doesn't get a chance to talk to us; everything we know is from the "good" characters' viewpoint.

Damien Walter thinks that it's no surprise to find in Tolkien's work the myth of a better world that was lost but that can be recovered by turning back to the past. It's the same myth of conservative political parties (Walter mentions the UK Independence Party, a populist political party in the UK). Tolkien's genius gave inspiration to new creators of myths, focusing this time on dystopian or anti-capitalist fantasies. So, in a way, today's world is still powered by myth.

On the other hand, John Gart notes[3] that, when Tolkien started dabbling in his mythical fantasies, he went in a sense ahead of his time. It was 1916, he was writing about the fall of the city of Gondolin, at the hands of the evil lord Melko and his troops. He exploits science, slave labor, machines, and terror to subdue his enemies, in a way that reminds us of totalitarian regimes even before they began to take shape.

Tom Shippey makes some interesting points[4] about the English cultural world between the wars. In literary contexts and universities, a disillusion had spread, cynicism and a disdain for authority. In his book *Children of the Sun: A Narrative of "Decadence" in England after 1918*, Martin Green (1927–2010) chronicled brilliant young people choosing decadence as a way of life. Shippey states they were relevant in English literature, spreading contempt of the older generations. They were privileged young men, snobbish and disdainful. In the group, Green mentions the group of spies from Cambridge (Philby, MacLean, Burgess: the first one had a career that inspired a book by novelist John le Carré). Green didn't much care for the Christian group to which Tolkien belonged. Shippey believes they had to separate themselves from the dominating circles and create their own group, trying to find a better reception in the mass market. They found it, C.S. Lewis rather quickly, Tolkien later but with more outstanding results. Both attracted criticism by the decadent environment because they didn't conform to their cynical worldview.

Moorcock Again

One of the critics who examined Tolkien's political leanings most severely is Michael Moorcock, in the long article we have previously quoted. Although Moorcock is aware of the phrases reported by Wilson (Tolkien claiming that there was no allegory in his novel), he does not give too much credit to those statements, believing that Tolkien's beliefs permeate through his books completely, as with C.S. Lewis and Charles Williams (both being friends of Tolkien).

The conservatism of these authors is deep and pervasive, in

Moorcock's opinion, although he does not agree with those who associate them with fascism. Instead, he finds doctrinal orthodoxy, profound hypocrisy, and, consequently, a hidden aggression directed against those who are not on the same side, disguised with good-natured attitudes, which are ambiguous and fundamentally false.

In everything they wrote, they have promoted—consciously or unconsciously—their political conservatism. Moorcock admits to reacting with antipathy towards Tolkien and Lewis, as he believes they spread a disgusting consolatory ideology, actually promoting misanthropy and selfishness. In post-war Britain, a country struggling with great difficulty after losing the illusion of being a great empire, Moorcock categorizes Tolkien, and with him other middle-class writers favored by him, as repressed to the point of never being confrontational, not even against their own politicians who betray their country. He finds in these writers the kind of sentimentalism that was used to make the sacrifice of war acceptable and, from an artistic point of view, accuses Tolkien of the "moderation" of feeling that leads to a failure in his work both as a real novel and as an epic. The Shire, a safe (mental) shelter surrounded by mysterious and fearsome landscapes, is part of that fear of real life experience, fear of which Moorcock accuses Tolkien and his social class.

For Moorcock, the most orthodox Christian writers, such as Gilbert Chesterton and Tolkien himself, were diverted from the pursuit of art because of their faith; they see the cornerstone of the community in characters such as the peasants, artisans, and the petty bourgeoisie, people who like order in contrast to chaos. Given that they are the ones who complain least about the state of society, in this kind of narrative, they are appreciated with sentimentality: bulwarks of sound common sense, against insidious intellectualism. So, Tolkien supports and confirms the values of a declining nation, and of a morally bankrupt ruling class. These are the people who made Thatcherism possible, putting their self-interest ahead of the country's problems. Humanity has been marginalized in favor of sentimentality.

This affirmation is associated with the political proposition that with more courage and open-mindedness, the damaging liberal reforms of the "Iron Lady" could have been avoided. Here, one can only make a note of Moorcock's hypothesis, but without being able to easily confirm nor deny it, as anyone has the ability to attribute sympathy or antipathy, based on *their own* political ideas.

Therefore, in Moorcock's opinion The Lord of the Rings is a book entrenched in infantilism. It's like Winnie-the-Pooh presented as an epic. "If the Shire is a suburban garden, Sauron and his henchmen are that old bourgeois bugaboo, the Mob—mindless football supporters throwing their beer-bottles over the fence."

Moorcock argues that The Lord of Rings trilogy is the kind of book written and read by a backward-looking class, the kind of people who love restraint in feelings, conventional behavior, pastel colors. These are the people who can't protest even when the government is betraying them; they can maybe write a letter to a newspaper. The good characters in the book are made this way, and the bad guys are a mystery because Tolkien doesn't reveal them. The reader can't get close, so we could even doubt if Sauron and his accomplices are really that bad.

The creator of Elric of Melniboné gives us a description of the political and mental world of Tolkien and his characters, sarcastic and humorous but perhaps not entirely in correspondence with the truth regarding the events of The Lord of the Rings. Incidentally, it is clear to see that Moorcock does not like conservatives. What about this tirade against the reactionary Tolkien? First of all, Moorcock's discourse often unfolds rigidly towards social classes, which can turn into genuine judgment of intentions against the person who is boxed into these schemes; Tolkien was certainly an anti-modernist, but in his own way. He defined himself as an anarchist,[5] although he was keen to point out that he was not of the type to plant bombs. As we will see, Tolkien was identified by a critic as an anti-totalitarian writer; he certainly preferred government to be minimally intrusive. He was not an imperialist: he did not recognize himself in the established order of his country or in the "empire." Nor did he consider himself a patriot.

Tolkien's hostility to industrialization and environmental destruction should not be underestimated: it may be as unrealistic as you want, but many (not necessarily those of a similar opinion) have found inspiration in him. As for political ideas, it's difficult to take a position on issues that, in large part, are specifically British. Anyway, Moorcock makes judgments about Tolkien as if he did not know who he was, without reference to what is known about him. The hypocrite who emerges from Moorcock's description is different from the real person we know from published biographies, however scarce the known facts may be.

We should also consider, in partial contradiction to what we have seen so far, a much more recent statement by Moorcock on Tolkien in an interview.[6] The accusation of fascism, from which Tolkien had previously been spared (framed instead in an orthodox and annoying conservatism), is this time asserted by Moorcock, who calls the Oxford professor a "crypto-fascist." The British author, described in this piece as "an equal and opposite force to J.R.R. Tolkien," narrates his life and evolution, the cultural environment in which it developed, and at some point, inevitably comes to Tolkien, who is disdained as follows: "I think he's a crypto-fascist.... In Tolkien, everyone's in their place and happy to be there. We go there and back, to where we started. There's no escape, nothing will ever change." This is the offending sentence, with an obvious reference to *The Hobbit's* subtitle, "There and Back Again." A short sentence from a very long article, in which Tolkien is not the main topic, of course. Apart from the accusation of fascism, which Moorcock had previously refrained from making, there is, not for the first time, a very superficial understanding of Tolkien's work. Did Moorcock step up his criticism with an unintentional exaggeration? Or was he willing to say just that? Or perhaps, with age, it has become less polished? One wonders if this was just attention seeking on his part ... it is impossible to know.

However, if we look at the argument, maybe *The Hobbit* is a fairy tale that is a simple prologue to the wide-ranging narrative of The Lord of the Rings, but, at the same time, it must be said that even in "There and Back Again," events take place that lead to profound consequences in the world of Middle-earth. Moreover, we need to consider that Tolkien modified *The Hobbit*, changing the meaning of many events to adapt this tale (in editions released after The Lord of the Rings) into the much more complex narrative he had undertaken. The Ring, initially, did not seem to be a sinister artifact of deadly power, for example. Still, even thinking of the original plot, Bilbo came back from his adventure wiser, and as a changed Hobbit.

However, the satisfied and stolid immobility, even if it can be considered the ideal of many typical Hobbits, is certainly not the fate of Middle-earth, as characters like Frodo and Sam know very well. The world is not limited to the Shire, and it is a rapidly evolving world. With all his ambiguity towards the modern present, and his nostalgia for earlier, better times, Tolkien is immune from crude accusations, such as those launched by Moorcock in this interview.

The same piece contains further consideration on the influence of The Lord of the Rings on fantasy: it made it bland, like everything else in the entertainment world. This is a concept that does not stray from the opinion already expressed by Moorcock in "Epic Pooh." Tolkien has had a strong influence on fantasy, which is still present today, but we cannot dispute that today, some of the most popular fantasy writers have their own, different style (George R.R. Martin and Joe Abercrombie, to name just two). In this out-of-line interview, Moorcock seems to show the weakness of his criticism: partly exaggerated and outrageous, partly perhaps opportunistic and maybe dictated by envy. In the opinion expressed by Federico Guglielmi[7] in his book, Moorcock is like a disciple who needs to kill the fathers. This is why he's so aggressive against older fantasy writers (Tolkien among them). But his words also demonstrate that he suffers from a "Tolkien complex."

I do not deny Moorcock's merits; he has been, more than any other, directly contrasted with Tolkien, so he has shown he's able to write something different and equally good. But he does not seem the most lucid or rational of critics.

Sauron and Stalin

Among the critics of Marxist tendencies, we may briefly mention essayist Nick Otty,[8] who considers Mordor, the domain of the evil Sauron, as a caricature of eastern communist countries (at the time of the Cold War). Otty wonders what drove the inhabitants of such an inauspicious place to even get out of bed in the morning. The most obvious answer is that in Sauron's domain, the subjects are constantly motivated by terror and harsh police tactics: this is also made clear in the only passage in which the Orcs talk to each other. And yes, we could interpret this as being reminiscent of Stalin's Russia. Although Tolkien rejected any direct comparison (Sauron seen as Hitler or as Stalin), it must be said that similar systems were in use in real-world dictatorships. As for the obedient gardener Sam, according to Otty, he is the "idyllic face of class warfare."

Bucolic Idyll in Tolkien

As for Tolkien's nostalgic love for the countryside, Moorcock (in the aforementioned essay "Epic Pooh") observes that it is shared by most Englishmen, and very present in literature. However, he thinks it is associated with an inability to enjoy urban life and, with that, an aspiration to be able to enjoy the bucolic landscapes again, through the eyes of a child. But, since the countryside can be reached quickly using various means of transport, this nostalgia, typically urban, is borne more out of reveries and a fear of change, rather than coming from a real need. Similarly, with reference to Hobbits, he thinks their inability to imagine another beautiful landscape outside of their own Shire borders on xenophobia. Furthermore, in Moorcock's opinion, it is the typical British middle-class sentimentalism, hiding from the country's gradual decline in dreams of a happier past, dreams in the form of rural fantasies. The aforementioned Catharine Stimpson in turn stigmatized Tolkien's work, pointing the finger at his incorrigible nationalism and celebration of a bourgeois pastoral idyll: people who live in peace in their rural coziness, but ignorant and wary of strange people and new ideas. Here, we return to the criticism of "pastoral" Tolkien, but mixed with another concept, nationalism.

Although not associated with the general critical contempt of Tolkien, China Miéville complains about his political leanings and his conservative and Catholic beliefs. He judges Tolkien as an enemy of modernity: not capitalism or exploitation, but modernity in and of itself, as he sees this as the triumph of a sinister "machine." Tolkien's lament towards the world of machines is, however, like a fairy-story feudalism, because the rural idyll he loves never existed in the real world before industrialization. Therefore, Miéville argues that Tolkien's anti-modernism is reactionary and backward looking. In Tolkien's works, the Hobbits of the Shire are inhabitants of an idyllic rural country, artisans and happy peasants. They are idealized by Tolkien, but at the same time the author is condescending towards them. Tolkien hates industry, and he wants the peasants to remain true to their ways; he loves to watch them, but from a distance. He's a professor in Oxford; he doesn't want to be like them.

We add to China Miéville's words those of a critic who, in turn, launched arrows against this supposed rural sentimentality, this "feudalism-lite," as Miéville calls it. In 1973, the essay "The Country and The City" by Raymond Williams,[9] an influential Welsh critic with Marxist tendencies, from the point of view of the "New Left" of the 1960s and 1970s, examined the contrast between the countryside and the city, questioning whether or not they were really opposed. Regarding fantasy, Williams observed that the country and the people who inhabit it are mystified; any real surviving features of the country are ignored. "In Britain, identifiably, there is a precarious but persistent rural-intellectual radicalism."

This attitude comes with hostility to industrialism, capitalism, exploitation of the environment, and consumerism and attachment to country values, way of life, and feelings. But at the same time this attachment to country ways is retrograde, in Williams's opinion. This attitude is retrograde; it is a partial and misleading response to what happened in history. In other words, even here those who take refuge in the false, deceptive "myths" lose their way to the true, profitable "revolution" of historicism. To the criticisms against the "bucolic" Tolkien, essayist Patrick Curry[10] answered with Tolkien's words, quoting the Elf Gildor, who tells Frodo that Hobbits are not the masters of the Shire: others have lived there in the past and others will live there in the future. Hobbits can fence themselves in and try to take shelter inside, but they will not be able to avoid the real world forever. This bucolic refuge, therefore, is not intended as a perfect and eternal world, or as a nation: it is a finite historical moment. As for the Hobbits' isolationism, Tolkien cannot be accused of xenophobia as, in defense of the Shire, it is necessary that they come out and, when they eventually go back, the experience will have made them stronger (Frodo's fate is more complex).

Obviously, these critics could be right in stating that Tolkien mourns a country idyll that never existed, but it can also be said that they are simply stating the obvious. Tolkien loved greenery in his life, recalling with nostalgia the places of his childhood, despite his family's situation being anything but serene in those years. As an adult, he continued to love nature and hated seeing it destroyed. It is reasonable to assume that he knew very little about the real life of a farmer, but his anti-modernist nostalgia can be seen as a symbol. It is a nostalgia for an imagined past, perhaps? But it is also the love of a period in which man should not fear the sinister threats of the unregulated power of the machine, or the secular and violent ideologies that bloodied the last century.

Escapism and Retreat from Reality

As we have seen, from a stylistic point of view, China Miéville admires Tolkien's ability to create fantastic worlds and entice the reader. However, the escape in these worlds comes under fire from Miéville, as he considers this to be escapism. If the function of his fantasy is "consolation," Tolkien's purpose is to cuddle the reader. His admirers, many of them from the political left, give escapism a heroic appearance by claiming that jailers hate escapism. But Miéville, like Moorcock, disagrees: the jailer hates real escape, but loves escapism. Tolkien is not escaping anything in reality; it would be naive to think otherwise. His world is amazing and seems full of possibilities, but Tolkien uses it to give the readers nostalgic daydreams. To imagine an idyllic past is consolation for capitalism, not opposition. "Troubled by the world? Close your eyes and think of Middle-earth."

Without malice or minced words, Miéville rubs salt into the wound. I am tempted to cut it short by pointing out that Miéville's radical ideology, Trotskyite communism, is a vague and unattainable promise of paradise to be conquered by revolution, little different from escapism as he himself explains it. However, here we are, talking about Tolkien and not China Miéville. Fortunately, in his essay on the fairy tale ("On Fairy-Stories"), the Oxford professor clearly states his opinion on escapism, disputing the scorn heaped on the word "escape." Escape is a function of fairy stories: there's no harm in it in the real world, unless it fails. If escape is impossible, there's no reason to think just about the jail, or the guards. If a man thinks about something else, what's the problem?

Tolkien adds that the prisoner's escape is not the deserter's escape. We could say that the function of fairy tales, as he conceives it, is escaping from reality in order to obtain rest and consolation, in order to sustain living in a world where we consider ourselves strangers, whose values we do not share. Tolkien's consolation would, therefore, be an instrument of daily resistance, an anchor to be used in order to remain resolute in our own values and help us face the difficult task of playing our part in a world that runs in a direction we do not like. Tolkien knew how to resign himself to what he could not change but did not stop opposing what he did not love.

The Rigidity of an Immutable World?

If we think of a classist and conservative Tolkien, we must also mention John Molyneux, a British academic, politically aligned with the Trotskyites. In his short essay "Tolkien's World—A Marxist Analysis,"[11] he speaks of the social structure of Middle-earth, citing its decidedly medieval aspects, both economically and technologically (there is no technology, energy sources are primitive, firearms are missing) and on a social level. In Middle-earth we have kings and queens, princesses, knights, and so on. The position of a character comes from his or her ascribed status (heredity, class, and lineage) rather that from achievements. This is taken for granted: although Aragorn must prove that he is up to the task, it is he who is predestined to the throne of Gondor rather than Boromir or Faramir, despite the fact that their family has guarded it for centuries. He will love Arwen, not Éowyn, because Arwen is of a comparable lineage, while Éowyn will fall back on a catch (Faramir) more suitable in regard to high birth. The inflexibility of this social structure is never questioned in Tolkien's work. So, for this critic, the social order in Tolkien's secondary world is fundamentally immutable; furthermore, there are no social upheavals of any kind and there is no real problem (apart from Sauron, of course). No pestilence, and famines are mentioned solely as distant events: in Middle-earth, everything is fine. No one suffers from poverty. Middle-earth is a very optimistic portrayal of a medieval world because, in reality, this world would not be fascinating, and, in addition to this, the inhabitants are not very liberated at all. Molyneux notes that the character of Melkor—one of the Valar, practically a demigod—becomes somewhat reminiscent of Lucifer in the Bible, a sort of fallen angel, condemned to evil: this is because, not being in harmony with the world around him, he resolves to create his own (thus rebelling against Ilúvatar, or God, and tradition). This implies that there are some roles that cannot be questioned and are immutable destinies. Fate's hand seems to play on everything. For example, the role of Smeagol-Gollum: trying to take the Ring at the last moment, he would inadvertently succeed where Frodo had failed, by destroying it. Gollum has a very important role; he is fated to play a part before the end of the story. Several characters (Bilbo, Frodo, Gandalf) could kill him, but they show mercy; all of this goes to fulfill his destiny. Unerring premonitions and prophecies are an important part of the plot. Trying to avoid their inevitable fulfillment just makes it easier in the end, just like in a Greek tragedy. This fate is arguably comparable to the will of God, whose vision is represented as Ilúvatar's condemnation of Melkor's desire to alter the harmony of the world around him. For Molyneux, then, there is no freedom in this conservative view: human beings are not in control of their society or their lives, and never will be. In Marxist terms, they are alienated.

The unsavory aspects are not lacking, however, but not in same way as in our world. Both evil and exploitation exist in Middle-earth: they are put in place by the armies of Mordor, a fact that allows them to avoid any internal (socio-economic) tension: the oppression exists, but the oppressor is the enemy!

Concurrently, there is the rather incongruous presence of the Shire, in juxtaposition to the feudal world that surrounds it, apparently more like an idealized England (not ruined by machines) and with a social structure halfway between oligarchic and democratic. Tolkien describes a beautiful and pleasant world, or at least one that is much more favorable than the true feudal world. However, it is a world paralyzed by social stasis.

This structure allows Tolkien, according to Molyneux, to carry out a critique against industrial capitalism, based on an idealized view of a pre-capitalist past. The critic recalls a line of thought, referred to by Marx as "feudal socialism," belonging to an aristocracy that sought the support of the working classes, denouncing exploitation by the bourgeoisie and dreading the coming of catastrophic change. It's a satire against the new emerging class (the bourgeoisie) coupled with nostalgia for the past, which, at times, is effective but never manages to fully understand the march of time. Tolkien is not considered a "feudal socialist" by Molyneux, but still, he believes that the author certainly puts the past (good) in contrast with the present (evil). Quoting Marx, he finds a description of this fear of the future, mixed with a nostalgia that may not be far from the Oxford professor's way of thinking: the bourgeoisie puts an end to all feudal, patriarchal, idyllic relations between servant and master. It leaves no other connection between men other than a naked and raw interest: religious ecstasies or chivalrous enthusiasms sink into the icy waters of selfishness. Molyneux thinks this is the key to Tolkien's grip on the public: he appeals to a remote world that is somehow familiar to us, presenting it as an idyll, leaving poverty, hunger, and oppression aside, and contrasting it with the vulgar world of industrialization, pollution, and greed. But in real life "this abstraction is completely impossible, of course, and what one ends with is either tragedy (Pol Pot) or farce (Colonel Blimp,[12] new age Druids) or some mixture of the two (Mussolini perhaps) but in fantasy, indeed in literature and art, it is perfectly possible."

I guess the reader does not need clarification as to why Mussolini or the neo-pagan movements appear in this sentence; as for Pol Pot, exterminator of the Cambodian people, he interpreted communism as the duty of returning to pure, agricultural roots, and, in order to obtain this result, he devised a system of eliminating educated people. Moving on to why Colonel Blimp, the old-fashioned and stereotypical British cartoon character, may have been mentioned: he is quick to anger and obviously a colonialist. Maybe Molyneux has come, via the tortuous way of Marxist criticism, to understand something of the spirit of Tolkien's work, although certainly with little sympathy for the author's point of view: an opposition to modernity, combined with nostalgia for something that belongs in the past, albeit a past that is largely symbolic and imaginary, or only present in its values and ideas. Molyneux also brings our attention to an important detail: this vision, in the way it is presented to us, is not a functional, political idea, but, at most, an artistic image. We must point out here that Tolkien never claimed things to be otherwise. He was apolitical, and with little interest in the government and its workings.

Class Struggle in Middle-earth?

On the class-conscious Tolkien, we have seen a series of criticisms that deserve further scrutiny: the fact that there is social separation and some who are condemned to evil. It is debatable whether or not the work of our author is a nod to a bourgeoisie worldview, but it is hard to deny that there are "bad guys" without hope or choice, bearers of absolute evil, and, at least seemingly, those who are irretrievably corrupt. It is easy to create a line of defense for Tolkien by pointing out that, after all, the humblest people are the ones who save Middle-earth, but it is also true that Tolkien's world seems to be divided into castes: some beings are endowed with instinctive nobility and an affinity for beauty or magic (Elves), others are capable of hard work and great feats in their own right (the Dwarves), while others are humble commoners, such as the Hobbits, and so on. These characteristics are generally associated with all members of a specific race (perhaps it is the humanoids who are the most versatile). The ones in the worst position are the Orcs. As Miéville curtly puts it: "Orcs are shits by birth."

In short, some are superior, some are inferior, and some only know evil. Evil which, in Tolkien's work, is typically that of a Catholic matrix—as expressed by St. Augustine and Boethius—meaning evil that is "absent of good" and cannot create, as creation is only that of divine right. This is evil that corrupts, perverts, and destroys (as a matter of fact, even the Orcs are not "born" from evil, but are the product of corruption in primarily good creatures). Tolkien mentions that the Orcs are not hopelessly bad[13] because, in the end, they are sentient creatures of God and ultimately they must be potentially good and godly. The Dark Lord has shaped them into a corrupted race, but their souls are not created by him, because this power was never delegated to Melkor. Therefore, they should have free will, but in practice we see them in action and only performing evil deeds, ordered by their commanders. Tolkien uses these creatures as convenient cannon fodder, representing the advance of evil and exterminated without mercy or remorse when evil is rejected. We do not see female or infant Orcs, nothing of the "civilian" life of this species. Therefore, we can cite Tolkien's social and religious background as justification, or possibly hypothesize a will on his part (this being anything but anti-modern) to see, imagine, and visualize the enemy as hopelessly evil, the enemy of nature, the enemy of a traditional way of life, a willing servant of evil criminals. Are these justifications, or rather arguments? To each his own. As for the idea that the world of Middle-earth never changes, obviously this is not the case. If it is true that Tolkien's world has well-defined social classes, it should also be true that many things may change throughout the course of the books. The story evolves with large-scale events, whole races disappear, and, in the long term, even the shape of the world mutates. However, we must reiterate that, in the midst of all of this, the roles of various lineages and races change little if at all. It is a fact that there are rigid social and existential differences. Some sentient beings are born only to be slaves of an evil power; there are predestinations, whatever we wish to call them, with advantages and disadvantages, insurmountable divisions. If a Hobbit is born Hobbit, or humble worker of the land, he can become mayor of the Shire, but he will never become a nobleman or a wise Elf. He will not be a magician, he will not be a king, and although Hobbits are human, though small, none of them will ever be a Númenorean (the strongest, most beautiful, tallest, and oldest living human race). It must, however, be recognized that the view of the world in these works is fundamentally that of the Middle Ages and fairy tales (with kings, knights, princesses, and so on) to which Tolkien makes a profound variation by elevating the modest Frodo and Sam to the rank of great heroes. Do we call it classism? I do not know. In fact, I think it is inadequate to define such a world, based on myth and fantasy, even if written in the modern era.

Tolkien's Manichaeism[14] is, however, an undesirable characteristic, for which it is more difficult to find justification. As we shall see later, John Yatt points out that the Fellowship of the Ring and the armies of the Free Peoples encounter enemies, occasionally terrifying and formidable, but always loathsome, slimy, or repellent. Many critics, such as the aforementioned Catharine Stimpson, have emphasized the inflexibility of morality in The Lord of the Rings: the good are infallibly good, and the evildoers remain bad. It does not always apply to individuals, but it applies to certain races.

Militarism in Tolkien's Works

As for militarism in Tolkien, let us return to the criticism of Moorcock, according to which Tolkien approved of a mental attitude, a class conformism, by which armed conflict can be considered just and acceptable, even when it is, in fact, the contrary. As we have seen, others have found massacres too casual in the events described in The Lord of the Rings. To answer these accusations, let us ask ourselves two questions: Was Tolkien a militarist in his life? And did he approve of the war in his writings, where conflicts are, so often, described?

In answer to the first question, I note that Tolkien, despite the pressures of the time, enlisted to perform his duty in the First World War as late as he could, after he graduated and got married. He did not think he had the physical courage, he disliked military discipline and the world of barracks, and he did not want to leave his wife or risk his life. Tolkien saw the horrors of the Battle of the Somme firsthand; hundreds of thousands of British soldiers died to move the front forward a few kilometers. C.S. Lewis[15] says that the author's military experiences influenced his writing in certain details, such as the eerily quiet front lines before an attack, the civilians on the run, the friendships, the sudden joy of unexpectedly finding tobacco; moreover, Tolkien told him that his love for the fairy tale grew during the period of the First World War. However, there is nothing in the Oxford professor's private life to suggest a love for war, which by now has become a tragic triumph of machine over humanity, where humanity always comes out defeated. In his letters he clearly states that he is not patriotic, and although it was clear that, in the Second World War, he wanted the defeat of the Axis powers, for him, the conflict was won, not by the Allies, but rather by machines. As for the second question about how war is acknowledged in Tolkien's writings, it is evident that he approved of the war against Sauron as a conflict of a defensive nature. A hard conflict, no doubt, as we have seen when discussing the Orcs, the cannon fodder of evil. The enemy is certainly dehumanized and killed without remorse (this term "dehumanized" must obviously be understood in the context of a world where various humanoid races exist). But war takes place because aggression is unleashed by Sauron, an entity that represents evil itself, and by Saruman, a sage who should have supported the Free Peoples with his own moral stature, and instead became second-in-command of the evildoers, under the illusion of maintaining some autonomy. Tolkien certainly talks about war against cruel dictators. Saruman is a tyrant, and let us not forget that, towards the end of The Lord of the Rings, he imposes a dictatorial regime, even in the Shire, destroying trees and raining down fire and brimstone, before being definitively neutralized. Sauron's reign is also a ruthless dictatorship. In The Lord of the Rings, this empire is not explored in its entirety. Sam and Frodo enter a corrupt and lifeless landscape; the author, obviously recognizing the need for a logistical structure that nourishes and sustains the Dark Lord's armies, mentions distant lands, where workers, reduced to slaves, produce what is necessary. Not a technological nightmare like Saruman's tower but an authoritarian system, an image that has often been associated (although Tolkien always said he did not want to create metaphors) with the totalitarian regimes of the time.

This does not exist in the opponent's camp. With all their faults, fears and, in some cases, rivalry and weaknesses, people under threat do not compete for the power or pleasure of fighting, but to defend themselves. In The Lord of the Rings, the arguments against the war are repeated. Let us recall, for example, Sam's contemplation of a Haradrim's corpse, killed in an ambush. He looks at the enemy soldier, who comes from a distant land in the service of Sauron, and wonders who he was and where he came from, and if he really was evil or if he had just been pushed with threats and lies in order to participate in the war, although he may have preferred to stay home. Let us remember the words of Faramir, the second son of Denethor, superintendent of Gondor: he says that war is a necessary evil, when a terror threatens to devour everything. He does not admire weapons for their ability to kill or soldiers for their honor, but, rather, for what they defend.

Peter Kreeft,[16] a philosophy professor from the United States, says that Tolkien is neither militarist nor pacifist, but defends the glory of a just war, a position that today, in truth, can be much disputed since even a "just" war is questionable. This philosophy is "not a moral compromise; it's just as moralistic, as idealistic, and as absolutistic, as pacifism or militarism."

This interpretation appears solid. It's a rejection of any accusation of militarism addressed towards Tolkien.

Still Class Questions: Comparing with Another Myth

Militarism and classism in Tolkien must also be interpreted in comparison with other models that the writer, undoubtedly, used for inspiration. Considering the need for the humble Hobbits to win against the enemy, we can see that Tolkien's work is more progressive and modern than that of the myths par excellence, namely *The Iliad*, where we see another "popular" character struggling with a heroic story, notably written for nobles, the audience of the time. I refer to Thersites, an Achaean fighter of dubious origin: in *The Iliad*, his father is not mentioned, so he is considered a plebeian. He is also lame and has crooked legs; he is, in other words, very ugly (the opposite of the Homeric ideal, having an excellent mind associated with a visually attractive physique). Thersites is presented as a quarrelsome man, and words of ridicule against the Achaean heroes are attributed to him. He accuses the leader, Agamemnon, of being greedy for gold and slaves, criticizes him for his attack against Achilles, and encourages the other soldiers to go home. Odysseus quickly intervenes to restore order. Thersites is harshly reprimanded and given a beating. It is an episode with a very modern flavor, which has given rise to different interpretations, given that Homer puts significant criticism into the mouth of this objector, and yet he ridicules him at the same time. Thersites is presumably used to describe the decline of morale among warriors at the time, caused by quarrels between the commanders, but it is also an extraordinary interlude in

The Iliad's epic tone. On the one hand, it exposes a protest by the "people" (in this case the troop); on the other we have a complaint carried out by an unpleasant, ungainly character, immediately ridiculed in general laughter. Tolkien also presents us with ugly and ungainly characters, in the form of the Orcs, slaves of evil, who are solely present in the story to be massacred. But there are other characters of lesser value, such as the Hobbits, humble peasants who will go on to prove their importance, being an essential component in the destruction of the Ring. In his worldview, with good opposing evil, Tolkien has, if nothing else, much more regard for the humble, who stand on the side of good, than is typically found in other mythologies he studied. The story of The Lord of the Rings is centered on the *sanctification of the humble*, and with this aspect, departs from (pagan) mythology that is a part of the inspirations for Middle-earth.

Is Tolkien's Success Due to Counterculture?

In his essay titled "Tolkien and the '60s,"[17] Nigel Walmsley assumes that Tolkien's success developed in parallel with the popularity of LSD. The primitivism, the counterculture of those times, the use of drugs found a relationship with the rich, imaginative world of Middle-earth. *The Hobbit* and The Lord of the Rings had enjoyed just moderate success before 1965, Walmsley states. Everything changed when Tolkien's work became more fashionable and widely recognized as a cultural text of this period. It was easy to read and understand, with a clear moral and a wonderful setting, infused with ethnicity and the charm of a remote, mysterious place. Even the Hobbits' lifestyle—vivid clothes, long hair, love for smoking a pipe, and the enjoyment of simple things like natural food—went together with the alternative culture of that era. In Walmsley's opinion, this curious convergence did not last long. Years of turmoil and harsher protests were coming. So, changing culture had helped boost the popularity of The Lord of the Rings, but youth culture in the West soon left it behind.

So, is Tolkien's success indebted to drug use?

About Walmsley's essay, we can read an opinion by professor Shaun Hughes,[18] from Purdue University's Department of English: Tolkien was anachronistic even before going out of sync with counterculture, but the popularity of his work didn't diminish. The Lord of the Rings and *The Hobbit* maybe are no longer attracting middle-class youth in conflict with society, but they have found a wider audience, so their success is no longer in question.

The Traumatized Author:
Tolkien and the Reality He Faced

Tom Shippey highlights the extremely modern concept of the Ring as a power tool that can't be used for a good purpose but also can't just be left aside or abandoned. So The Lord of the Rings is not a quest but precisely the opposite, because the Ring is to be rejected and destroyed. It is something the Free Peoples need to get rid of, something they must keep from falling into the wrong hands. There are people like Boromir, son of Denethor, who desire the Ring and think that true-hearted Men will not be corrupted. They are wrong. Boromir, as we know, will betray the Fellowship of the Ring trying to steal the Ring from Frodo, but nothing good will come from his actions. Today, Shippey states, no one doubts Gandalf's words about the Ring (and the power). That's because we learned from the modern world's tragedies to distrust absolute power. The phrase from historian Lord Acton quoted by Shippey—"All power corrupts, and absolute power corrupts absolutely"—is from the late nineteenth century, but it finds its widespread applicability in modern times. We have the raw, sly face of power in works like *Animal Farm* or *1984* by Orwell, *The Lord of the Flies* by Golding, and others. Moreover, the good intentions for benefit of all humanity in the twentieth century have brought us the concentration camps and mass exterminations. Tolkien's view on power is modern, and shared with other authors, albeit anachronistic in the setting of Middle-earth. The triggering experience is the modern world with its automatic, industrial, large-scale massacre. The perceived cause is the presence of "something irreducibly evil in the nature of humanity," but there is no easy explanation for this. The literature of the past does not help at all. Today's evil is prosaic, hollow, and bureaucratic. Old vices like wrath or lust are replaced by solitude and sloth. We have absurd, bureaucratic situations in books like *Slaughterhouse-Five* by Vonnegut, or *Catch-22* by Heller, with evil hidden by skilled and unscrupulous use of language, or horror behind a routine work in *Heart of Darkness* by Joseph Conrad. This is different, Shippey argues, from everything we have read from the Middle Ages. This is one of the reasons why Tolkien is deemed as a modern author in Shippey's book, *J.R.R. Tolkien: Author of the Century*, where this critic claims he's to be considered modern even in style.[19]

Now we need to examine this thesis. Was the "old" evil less upsetting in its reality or its representation? We have copious evidence of massacres and tortures realized in a casual way from the ancient, medieval, and subsequent but still pre-modern times. Their description is sometimes full of horror, in other instances quite normal, business-like.

Impalement and crucifixion were used on a large scale to inflict a slow, torturous death to the enemy and, at the same time, to create a staggering, intimidating image as a warning for viewers. We can see representations of mass hangings during the wars of religion: death administered as a daily job; business as usual. During the Thirty Years' War some regions in Germany were almost depopulated. The First Crusade saw, with the conquest of Jerusalem, so great a bloodbath[20] that Christian soldiers "waded in blood." The recovery of the Holy City was followed by an unrestrained massacre of Muslims and Jews.

Slavery or torturous death was a very frequent outcome for those surrendering on the battlefield.

Whole populations all around the world have been forced to convert to their conquerors' religion. Continents have been depopulated (North and South America) during a long process of conquest during which the natives almost disappeared, replaced by colonists and, in part, with slaves brought from other continents using common sailing ships with no particular technology. It's true that records of "old" atrocities often lack the traumatic tones used by the writers Shippey mentions. Quite the contrary, old descriptions of terrible events are often simple, blunt, matter-of-fact, as if the witness did not expect anything better. But a painting like *The Triumph of Death* by Pieter Bruegel the Elder shows a nightmarish, barren landscape in which every act of torture and violence is enacted, including a crowd being forced to enter some kind of enormous coffin, evoking mass murder devices. The painting may have been influenced by the Black Death plague, or it's simply a moralizing work in the tradition of the medieval Danse Macabre (Dance of Death), representing the universal destiny of humanity: death. If Bruegel is too modern, we have a good example of dramatic artistic rendition with Dante Alighieri's *Divine Comedy*.

Anyway, if we admit there's something different in evil as the "traumatized authors" have experienced it, with respect to the "old" kind of evil, we must ask ourselves what this difference is. It could just be a matter of perspective: after the illusions of positivist ideology based on scientific progress and rationality, the wars of the twentieth century have been a rude awakening about man's true instincts. In addition to having to come to terms with the unchanged nature of man, people had the experience of modern technology applied to war and politics. There's no heroism left on the battlefield, no showy uniforms or banners. Modern explosives and automatic weapons have transformed the war into a meat grinder where there's no hope of survival based on skill or bravery: life and death in the modern battle is a matter of statistics, and probably dumb luck matters more than valor. While in pre-modern times the act of killing in battle, or mass murder for any cause, had to be carried out by single people on a one-on-one basis, modernity has industrialized the process of killing with the use of weapons activated by a finger (machine guns) or with impersonal acts, like in the bombardments by artillery or planes. Development of bureaucratic organization in states has made possible persecution on a previously unimagined scale. While indoctrination in the past was made by single performers, usually priests, talking to a small flock, in modern times the printing press, the radio, and more modern media have spread the range of murderous ideology to every corner of the world.

So evil has changed, or it has just modernized itself? Tolkien was certainly a "modern" author because he lived in the real world of his times, and talked to ordinary people who need to face evil in very difficult times. However, the "traumatized author" thesis must not lead us to think that Tolkien was something different from an opponent of modernity: rather the opposite is true because "trauma" comes from evil reinforced by modern weapons, industry, communication, and organization.

Lucio del Corso and Paolo Pecere[21] state that Tolkien's narrative never comes to terms with the issue of the reality it refuses. Reality is bad, so what could we do about it? Refusal of allegory in Tolkien's works is avoidance of real problems in the real world. If Tolkien's fairy stories have a great potential as utopia (as stated by Jack Zipes), they refuse "modernity" without looking it in the face. And so, Tolkien's utopia is an artist's dream: there's no road map to get there.

John Garth, writing about Tolkien's experience in the First World War,[22] notices a change of style in the British writers and poets who took part. They discarded the old language used to describe battles and war deeds. The old sanctimonious style of glorifying acts of valor was insufficient to write about what they had seen. Garth quotes the first lines of *Anthem for Doomed Youth* by Wilfred Owen: "What passing-bells for these who die as cattle? — Only the monstrous anger of the guns."

This poem positions the mechanical massacre's reality in opposition to the old customary funeral ritual for the fallen, made of bells, prayers, and candles. Tolkien did not compose any poem or writing about his own war experience. He went against the current: his works talk about mythical wars with the same ancient style of the past, considered inadequate and obscene by other writers who had seen the battlefield. This influenced the reviewers negatively, because that kind of romanticism and traditionalism was out of fashion after the war. But he was not attracted by war. Garth argues that Tolkien's style does not mean that he remained unaffected by what he saw in the trenches. On the contrary, the war pushed him towards fairy stories. He could see that the world was rapidly changing, so that kind of aesthetics he liked was going to disappear, along with many other things. But he felt it was necessary to preserve the values that kind of language expressed. Garth's intention is to show in his book how Tolkien was influenced by the Great War, so he finds connections between the conflict and the author's ideas. So the flamethrowers become a possible inspiration for dragons; out of the author's experience of the Battle of the Somme comes the attack on Gondolin (in *The Silmarillion*); the bleeding of Tolkien's riflemen battalion, and other massacres of those times, are inspiration for bloody battles. Whether these insights are totally correct or not, it would be absurd to think Tolkien was unaffected by the war, or wanted to glorify it. There's a wealth of information about Tolkien's disgust at military service and the horror of war.

We have another reason to doubt that Tolkien insisted on a stultified celebration of war and heroism for its own sake. The proof is in his criticism of ancient myths: Garth quotes the rash heroism in *The Homecoming of Beorhtnoth Beorhthelm's Son* and in the *Beowulf*, courage that becomes thoughtless sportsmanship and creates useless danger. Tolkien's own examples include Fëanor and Théoden, both defeated and killed because they went too far in their attacks. Garth reminds us that Tolkien was reluctant to reveal his thought, but reading his work we can find hints. Reckless bravado is not glorified; the right thing to do for everyone is to stand one's ground and do one's duty.

Incidentally, critic Alexander Bruce[23] states that Gandalf's brave stand against the Balrog in the mines of Moria is the exact opposite of Beorhtnoth's rashness, because he stays in the fight not for its own sake, but for the common good. He doesn't endanger the group he's responsible for (like Beorhtnoth did). He understands the need to stand and fight to give them time to escape.

Tolkien brought the war topic up, however, in a letter[24] quoted by Garth: his plot was not influenced by the world wars or by the atomic bomb. He admitted that the landscape's features are sometimes inspired by war memories. Garth has given us some examples and found similarities between war as Tolkien knew it and the books he wrote. Tom Shippey adds several more. When Frodo talks with Gandalf about the new menace from Mordor,[25] he complains that such a big problem happened in his time. Shippey notes that these are the same words used by Neville Chamberlain after the Munich Agreement in 1938.

We need a quick note about what happened there. British Prime Minister Chamberlain took part in this diplomatic meeting among the United Kingdom, Germany, France, and Italy to discuss Hitler's claim to Czechoslovakia's border regions. The concerned country had no say in the matter. An agreement was reached by the transfer of a strategic border region where the population was mainly German. It was the "appeasement" policy, the attempt to avoid a direct clash with Germany through concessions. Chamberlain and Daladier, the French prime minister, were applauded for obtaining "peace for our time," but shortly after the agreement the remaining territory of Czechoslovakia was occupied. After only a few months the Danzig crisis started: this time, the German claim was against Poland and, as we know, the Second World War ensued. It's quite possible that Tolkien was influenced by these real-world events. In Gandalf's reply to Frodo, we read that nobody would want trouble in "his time," but you can't decide about that: Gandalf rejects any hypothesis of "appeasement" with Sauron.

Another example is the Rammas Echor, a great wall surrounding the Pelennor Fields. This fortification was intended to protect Gondor's capital, Minas Tirith, but it's incomplete or in disrepair when the enemy comes. King Denethor orders that the Rammas Echor be manned and defended, but it's easily breached and overcome. Tom Shippey finds an obvious resemblance to the Maginot Line, the fortified line built by the French. While it could be debated if the building of the Maginot Line was really an ill-advised idea, no one could refute Shippey's opinion that, in the end, it did not serve to defend France. Shippey examines the peace proposal by the Mouth of Sauron in *The Return of the King*: the terms used by Sauron's emissary are modern political and military definitions—withdrawal, transfers of sovereignty, disarmament, payment of tributes. Anyone having some knowledge about the world wars will find resemblances in Tolkien's words. This can't be coincidence.

But, in Tolkien's own words about The Lord of the Rings, there's no particular meaning in the story in itself. Even the idea of a struggle between good and evil is not supported by the author because there's not an absolute evil.[26] The story remains a mystery, the meaning is in the choice individual characters make.

Andrew Lynch notes[27] that Tolkien's style, despite his war experiences, doesn't conform with the prevailing mood of First World War writers. Tolkien's fantasy epic is more similar to Victorian medievalist literature. Alfred Tennyson (1809–1892) is the relevant author in Lynch's opinion. He wrote of Arthurian chivalry more as a symbol of heroism than as a realistic representation of warfare, narrating legends but avoiding some of the harsher realities of medieval times. Fiction set in medieval times had to deal with this chasm between fantasy and reality, talking about the war in more positive terms. In Andrew Lynch's essay, the thesis is that The Lord of the Rings is more a late Victorian medievalist poetic (a style that is thought to be dead by 1916) than a modern twentieth-century text or a medieval one.

From Tolkien's own words, we know that he was influenced by his experience in war, but also by the destruction of the country where he lived in childhood. But he never admitted there was a connection between his own war experiences and The Lord of the Rings, which remains just a tale. Tolkien retells his war experience without any rhetoric, speaking of the "animal horror" of life in the trenches, but in his writings, as Lynch notes, war is "a theater of heroic action," and its necessity is recognized. This way war can be terrible, but it's also an ennobling experience. It's also to be noted that only two characters on the "good" side will die in The Lord of the Rings: Boromir and Théoden. The war has its more modern aspect in the Hobbits, who display a less heroic, more pragmatic form of courage.

Some critics have examined the Great War's influence on Tolkien. John Garth wrote a book dedicated to Tolkien's war experience and its possible relationships with his works. Tom Shippey, as we have seen, made a comparison with other writers deeply affected by their traumatizing experience. However, as Lynch notes, Garth has highlighted the differences between Tolkien and other writers involved with the Great War. Tolkien still talks about glory, honor, and heroic deeds—subjects that Wilfred Owen would have refused. The way Tolkien dealt with war was transforming it into a medieval conflict, with weapons from that era: swords, axes, bows. Military duties come from feudal obligations. We have field battles and siege warfare, cavalry charges, and individual combat. Lynch finds some formal similarities—the use of parataxis (that is, sentences without subordination), for example—with medieval texts like Le Morte d'Arthur by Thomas Malory. But there are some differences as well. Medieval writings narrate single events of the fighting and deal with the outcome of the fight, with just some occasional references to the atmosphere of the battlefield. Tolkien's battles are wider landscapes, symbolic clashes where the confrontation is between good and evil; the representation is spectacular and romantic. Medieval accounts sound archaic because they are, Tolkien uses an archaic style to raise the literary resonance of his descriptions and revive the heroic potential in his contemporary generation. In Lynch's opinion, the author tried to make his war scenes lofty, solemn, and meaningful by the use of sentence inversion, archaism, formality. Battles and fighting are always important subjects in his narration and, as such, emphasized by a particular style.

But, in Lynch's opinion, Tolkien's reaction to the horrors of war, while different from some poet-soldiers, is not isolated. Quoting historian Jay Winter, Lynch states that loss and mourning caused many people to turn to older culture and tradition to come to terms with their suffering. In this context, Tolkien could have chosen a connection with the previous century rather than accepting the modern world as it is. His problem was the rift that had destroyed any continuity with the past, not a nostalgia for the Middle Ages per se. So his work is a defense of the English identity, a link with the past in the context of the typical, natural landscape he loved. Tolkien's nostalgia is the utopian dream of a past that exists only as a narrative, so it will be always beyond reach and can't be a lived experience (and can not, therefore, be told as such). On the other hand, this nostalgia is never sated, so it gives endless possibilities for narrative, in search of reconnection with this imagined past. So we have characters who can be a link with this always disappearing world. Warriors who remember their lost comrades, mages who preserve ancient knowledge or wisdom. In Lynch's interpretation, heroism in Tolkien's work is always the difficult struggle to reassert an old order over an ignorant, unaware present world. In this, the essayist finds a relationship with Tennyson's work.

War, in both writers, is more an ideological and symbolic struggle than a story of military deeds. The enemy is morally and physically filthy, to be driven away with force; the longing for peace must take second place in front of the necessity of this cleansing war. Tolkien's warriors on the "good" side are fighting in the name of feudal relations or by free will; the enemy is made of nameless slave-soldiers, draftees, machines. Mordor and Isengard are places of squalor and total deforestation. In a real war, in real life, Tolkien knew that Orcs "are on both sides,"[28] but in The Lord of the Rings, aesthetics and morality are on one side only. Lynch concludes that Tolkien goes against his own political ideas and personal experience when he attributes all the terrible features of modern wars to the evil side and bestows an aura of medieval idealism on the good guys. This critic doesn't deny that war had an effect on Tolkien, but argues that the worry about industrialization was complementary and probably stronger because, in the process of tying again the present with the (utopian) past, Tolkien gave the war a dignified place again.

A Camouflage of the Horror

Essayist John Goldthwaite launches another accusation[29] on the rejection of realism by Tolkien in the description of his battles, believing that there is a conscious embellishment, a camouflage of horror to maintain the heroic aspect (the criticism is, at this point, both stylistic and of merit): when Aragorn reaches the battle of the Pelennor Fields, in order to intervene in the clash, with his fleet of captured pirate ships, the tone is epic, and all the honors that glorify the hero and the future king are cited. Very bad taste, according to Goldthwaite. The essayist thinks Tolkien "regressed, it seems, into a compensatory dream of how a war ought to be fought, not with bodies piling up stupidly in trenches—that was all wrong, you see—but in the grand manner, with stirring rides and deeds of valor." This is precisely the unreal tin soldier militarism that led to the First World War bloodbath. What could be said in Tolkien's defense? Certainly, it is not his style to describe the most bloody and hideous details, but it is also not to glorify the conflict. Those who have read the books know that there are many points in which the fighting appears disastrous, crazy, and deadly.

Patrick Curry: The Readers Have Seen Something … and the Critics?

One particular position, also worthy of our attention, is that of Patrick Curry. Arising from an ecological interpretation of Tolkien's work, he presents a vehement response to the views of some critics from different backgrounds. This essayist expressly[30] announces his intention to use postmodernism to defend the current value of Tolkien's anti-modernism against his Marxist, materialistic, psychoanalytical, and structuralist critics. He offers us a very radical but interesting interpretative theory. Curry, an independent scholar and critic, strenuously defends Tolkien's work from the attacks (and silent contempt) of the critics, and, moreover, he believes that the Oxford professor, through his work, launched a real cry for help against the evils of today's world.

Postmodernism: Let us try, for a moment, to understand what it means, in simple terms. Various ideologies, which dominated the world from the Enlightenment onwards, brought us a narrative, sometimes expressed from opposite sides, identified with ideas of progress, triumph of reason, goals for humanity, and so on: so we have capitalist liberalism, communism, faith in scientific progress (positivism). Fascism also has its own modernist and progressive component. The modern world presents us with different, yet finalistic ways of thinking that propose future objectives to be achieved, depending on a shared history, an idea of unanimous progress towards positive utopian results. Modernity has entered into a crisis because of war, with the failure of ideologies or, at least, the realization that, taken to the extreme, ideologies do not solve the problems of the world and do not make our lives better. Postmodernism is born with this crisis, with the multiplication of means of communication, which, little by little, has increased the number of accessible points of view by creating a decentralized culture, with globalization and the birth of mature capitalist societies, not without conflicts and disputes. In fact, postmodernism challenges modern ideologies and considers them with skepticism, without necessarily rejecting them completely. The interpretation of the story loses its finalism, and even science is discredited. In art, postmodernism freely uses past forms of expression, or ones borrowed from other cultures, traditional or not.

In the area of postmodernity, Curry sees Tolkien as a creator of new myths, a creator of nostalgia who manages to push men to act, and not as someone who just sadly indulges in memories. This nostalgia "joins up with a growing contemporary sense, represented in postmodernism, of history's sheer contingency—the liberating perception that it-might-have-been-different, and therefore could be different now."

Curry groups commentators hostile to Tolkien into the category of "modernists," linking them to the cult of reason and science (including politics, as most critics tend to be left-wing). Curry sees, in literary circles, a sort of clique that evaluates both Tolkien's work and the preferences of those enthusiasts who admire him, not according to their own literary tastes, but rather by following snobbish and ideological criteria. While they say they desire the emancipation of non-intellectuals, in actual fact, they despise them. Nostalgia and childishness are two of the main accusations made against the writer and the fans. "As Tolkien ... noted, the connection between children and fairy-stories is an accident of history, not something essential; 'If a fairy-story as a kind is worth reading at all, it is worthy to be written for and read by adults.' But being Grown-Up is a recurring theme in modernism, with its teleological fantasy of collectively progressing towards the truth.... The Lord of the Rings and its readers are thus doubly stigmatized, both individually/psychologically and collectively/socially."

As for nostalgia, this is an important element for Tolkien: not a simple fantasy of a pastoral world, perhaps never existing, but an extreme, radical nostalgia. Maybe it's similar to the "utopia" as depicted by Jack Zipes (see above) but also a desire to find meaning in a world that is headed towards annihilation. "Now Tolkien gives us to understand, as strongly as possible while still writing a story and not a tract, that nostalgia pure-and-simple will not suffice. In Middle-earth, it is the Elves whose nostalgia is the strongest—both in the sense of yearning for the past and attempting to maintain that past now, in places like

Lothlorien and Rivendell. But the Elves, despite their valiant resistance, plainly offer no real solution to the central problem of the Ring. Yet it is also true that his work is suffused with the 'pastoral fantasy' of a better world, equally memory and longing."

.Thus, intellectuals despise "readers for whom Tolkien's work is large and alive, and who are therefore better-placed to understand it than his narrowly scholarly dissectors. It is the latter who deserve pity and scorn." They put Tolkien's work "through the structuralist text-grinder" to destroy its meaning. In Curry's opinion, the idea of the scientific study of literary texts is "a lingering nineteenth-century faith or superstition."

Patrick Curry is an ecologist, one who considers the destruction of the natural world as an unstoppable tragedy that unfolds before his eyes, and claims to have seen many people take to the streets and fight to defend the environment, driven by Tolkien's "unreal" and "bucolic" fantasies. For this reason, according to his point of view, when the protesters of a new road project are called "hobbits of Middle-earth" and ridiculed, he asks himself: "Who are really the fantasists, the indulgers in nostalgia, the reactionaries here: Tolkien and his readers, or his modernist critics?"

Curry denounces the ideologies that, from the Enlightenment onwards, wanted to "demystify" myths and fantasies, putting faith in "reason" at the center of everything, which, in the form of this or that ideology, or simple faith in science, should have taken us to some utopian goal.

Curry condemns Tolkien's modernist critics for their bad faith. Marx (ideologue), Freud (father of psychoanalysis), and Saussure (semiologist and linguist) would be some of "the very avatars of modernism, whose 'grand narratives' of modernity—secularised versions of divine revelation—were supposed to supply essentially complete accounts of our progress towards the realisation of the truth. But there have been too many broken promises by now, and too many terrible 'successes.' The human being has become a stranger not only to the cosmos and the Earth but to each other, and him- and herself."

For "terrible successes" we can imagine that Curry means ecological disasters, frightening weapons, murderous and oppressive ideologies. For him, progress is mystifying and fundamentally destructive. He consequently presents us with a polarized and politicized interpretation of what Tolkien said, stigmatizing the haughty reaction of dominant ideologies. "But the modernists are right, in their own twisted way. The Lord of the Rings really is a text whose predominant available meanings powerfully contradict their own values; and whose popular success, as a sign of widely shared doubts if not repudiation, makes it, from their point of view, all the worse. In the intention of its author an anti-modernist text, attacking industrialism, secularism, and the myth of Progress, The Lord of the Rings falls into the traditions of what Jonathan Bate calls 'romantic ecology,' Don Elgin 'the ecological perspective of comedy' and Meredith Veldman 'Romantic Protest.'"

These elements in Tolkien's work exist concretely. This becomes clear when the fortress of Saruman, the sorcerer, is described. He thinks with a mind "of metal and gears" and is now no longer interested in things that grow, only in machines: he destroys the nearby forest to feed his furnaces. Saruman, destined to be destroyed by the Ents, the guardians of the trees, is a transparent reference to industrial development and deforestation (and more generally, destruction of the environment).

In any case, Curry sees modern elements in Tolkien: the role of the protagonists being entrusted to the anti-heroes, the peaceful Hobbits; the reluctance of the warriors, such as Faramir and Aragorn himself (I could also add that, the more martial Boromir comes to a bad end); war being seen as a necessary evil at best; power (embodied in the Ring) as inevitably corrupting; and the absence of an explicit religion.[31]

"But Tolkien's very syncretism offends modernist purism. Ironically, therefore, it is his critics who belong to the past, and Tolkien the future." Modernists would therefore be hostile to the myth (and its rebirth) as it is a foreign concept, or even against their reductionist practices (ideological or scientific) and imposing transformation on society and the environment, without ever accepting limitation. Tolkien's work, however, invites readers "into a compelling and remarkably complete pre-modern world, saturated with corresponding earlier values, which therefore feels something like a lost home."

Curry speaks of a necessary re-mythologizing of the world: a discourse that we can see as evocative, given that it is certainly true that some enthusiasts see, in Tolkien's work, something mythical and sacred.

Moreover, I believe that, as far as ideologies and even the world that revolves around what we call science go, Curry exposes many flaws; but his speech has its limits, as the Pandora's box of scientific possibilities has now been opened and there is no easy turning back. Or, rather, it's impossible. Anyway, Patrick Curry appears to be a staunch defender of Tolkien. Still, he must be considered, if not with suspicion, at least with circumspection, given that Curry goes beyond the intention of the author himself. His counterattacks against Tolkien's detractors are very smart and sometimes pleasing to read, but it seems that Curry wanted to make the Oxford professor the ideologue of a revolution, or the idol of a new philosophy.[32] Even Tolkien's forced enrolment in postmodernism, a movement that manifested itself after the publication of his main works, is to be viewed with skepticism, although it is clear that he was an anti-modernist. In any case, Curry gives us a clear interpretation of the political and cultural stakes involved and allows us to better understand the hatred that many critics have nurtured towards Tolkien.

Interlude: The F-word

J.R.R. Tolkien should be an unlikely target for an accusation such as being a fascist. During the Second World War, his son Michael Hilary Reuel served in the anti-aircraft artillery. Another son, Christopher John Reuel, was an RAF pilot (Christopher later became the literary executor of his father's work). Tolkien himself couldn't go into active service; still, in 1939, he accepted a proposal to work, if necessary, as a cryptoanalyst for the Foreign Office in case of necessity (see notes to letter 35).[33] We should also remember a very terse answer (letters 29 and 30) he gave to a German editor, negotiating the translation of *The Hobbit* in 1938. Asked if he was of Aryan origin, Tolkien answered that if the meaning of the question was to discover if he was of Jewish origin, he "regretted" having no ancestors of that people. He was proud of his German name, but if inquiries as the one he received were to become the norm, in no time, a German name wouldn't be a source of pride anymore. As one might expect, the prospect of a German translation was shelved after that. Nevertheless, between the many and various charges against Tolkien, you can find some statements about him being a fascist. How can this be?

First of all, the word is often misused. Then, there are people of culture who associate many heterogeneous concepts with fascism.

British journalist and writer George Orwell wrote[34] (*Tribune*, 24 March 1944) about the complexity of finding a definition for the term "fascism," noting that some differences existed between the fascist states: not all were anti-Semitic, or warlike, or enemies of capitalism. While one could understand, during wartime, what the fascist nations were and what they were doing, the word was ceasing to have a meaning in other contexts. In internal (British) politics, Orwell noted, the term "fascist" was applied to many categories—to conservatives in general, for example, even if they were not appeasers. Or to socialists, for different reasons: some capitalists thought fascism and socialism were the same, while some anarchists and communists thought the socialists were not far enough left. Pacifists and war resisters were accused of pro–Nazi sympathies. Many people regarded the Catholic Church as pro-fascist. Supporters of the war were likewise vilified. And the list went on. The conflict was still raging when George Orwell wrote this, so it's easy to understand the confusion: the people who wanted to fight could be seen as militaristic, thus similar to fascists, but everyone could accuse those who were against the war of being friendly to fascists.

In Orwell's opinion, the word "fascist" had become meaningless; it had fallen to the level of a swearword.

So, Orwell seems to think that this word should be used with more circumspection.

Italian semiotician, writer, and philosopher Umberto Eco seem to think differently. In his piece "Ur Fascism"[35] he writes about the instincts and cultural habits that could manifest themselves again in a new party or political entity, not Nazist but Nazist-like, in Europe or elsewhere. Eco differentiates the various movements he's talking about: Nazism was neo-pagan and anti–Christian, racist; Mussolini's fascism had no official ideology of philosophy but created a liturgy, with its rites and uniforms (the black shirt), which in a way was the "archetype" of fascist regimes and movements. Fascism blended together different and contradictory elements: the survival of monarchy together with a violent militia, respect for the Church together with state-mandated violence, the promise of a revolution having the financial support of the conservatives. Still, in his essay, Eco states that it's possible to delineate the typical feature of the "Ur-Fascism," the primeval or eternal fascism (a term Umberto Eco invented). If one of the elements is present in a political movement, it may develop into fascism.

What are these features? First, the cult of tradition, as a syncretism of different times in human history in which unalterable truths have been pronounced. As a consequence of traditionalism, a rejection of modernity. Both fascists and Nazists appreciate technology, apparently, but, under this pretense, there is irrationalism, rejection of the enlightenment, the cult of blood and soil. From irrationalism, the cult of action for action's sake follows. Then, the distrust of the intellectual world. Other aspects of Ur-Fascism are the disapproval of critical thinking and disagreement; the fear of difference (and, consequently, racism); the appeal to a frustrated middle class, frightened by an economic crisis, or by the restlessness of a lower social group. Another feature is the cult of struggle (the whole life seen as a continuous battle), of bravery, and heroic death.

There are 14 points in Eco's essay, but we can stop here. Let's try to draw some conclusions. We've seen two very different intellectuals and their different opinions. Orwell was not happy with a generic use of the word "fascist," while Umberto Eco made it a paradigm. So it seems that even if there are people not happy with it, "fascist" can be, and will, be used as a vague, ill-defined term. Therefore it's no wonder some critics said that Tolkien was a fascist.

Fred Inglis vs. J.R.R. Tolkien

Fred Inglis, a professor who graduated from Cambridge, wrote a book[36] aimed at analyzing novels written for children and understanding the teachings and experiences children can obtain from them. Speaking of Tolkien's work, Inglis states that it started something like a cult for the readers: this is interesting because it started with a book intended for children (*The Hobbit*) and developed without any marketing manipulation. The Lord of the Rings cult is born from the charm of old rural life present in the book, which has a strong appeal in both the United States and Britain. Inglis thought this cult status was diminishing (he was wrong), and deplored that it had taken the shape of a craving for any merchandise related to characters and themes in the book, and the birth of many Middle-earth societies on American campuses. Inglis's opinion follows those of other critics: Tolkien's style is thin, lacking substance, far from real-life experience. The world of Middle-earth lacks concreteness and is an allegory with extraordinary adventures—sword fights, travels to the Crack of Doom—all told as a myth. Still, it has found success as a mystical romance written in a classical, pastoral style. These heroic deeds belong to the past; they are unreal, unreachable today. As Inglis writes, Tolkien "offers to his ardent audience a desperate glory without either physical or moral effort." Strong criticism is implicit in the words chosen by Inglis, because they recall the bitter verses of "Dulce et Decorum est," by war poet Wilfred Owen. After showing the death of a soldier under a gas attack, Owen ends his poem showing children "ardent for desperate glory" intent on listening to the "old lie": *dulce et decorum est pro patria mori* (to die for one's mother country is sweet and fitting). As Owen mocks the confident patriotism of his era, Inglis deplores Tolkien's rhetoric of warrior courage.

Still, Inglis is not surprised by the strong appeal Tolkien had on the counterculture, because it shares the same resistance to anonymity and blankness imposed by the industrial society. Inglis says that Tolkien is a fascist but "in a non-hostile sense." Fascism appeals to real human needs. People menaced by modernity and machines turn to fascism, as individuals and as groups. Fascism gives people ceremonies, fealties, tribal structures. So the Elves, Orcs, Men, and Hobbits of The Lord of the Rings, with their rites and communities, belong to a "non-historical, romantic fascism." The book shows us ancient battles where technology plays no role, but you can see Mordor and Mount Doom as the headquarters of a "dirty, rough-spoken, brutal proletariat." At the same time, Gandalf flying on the great eagle is like a "US Marine general in his Cobra helicopter." Inglis refers to his present to find examples, so we don't need to underline that the Cobra attack helicopter entered the fray in 1965, about 10 years after The Lord of the Rings was published. The rich prose and ideals of chivalry in The Lord of the Rings, Inglis states, look like a nemesis for modern Socialism. Tolkien's masterpiece is a charm against the problems of personal and political life. It's acceptable for a child to read the book with enthusiasm, but an adult entering its cult will trap himself without a way out in a "grander version of Mistletoe Farm."

We need to note that this is a reference to a two-book series by writer Enid Blyton, started in 1948. *The Mistletoe Farm* is a simple story of people living on a farm: some of them are city kids discovering the country for the first time. Blyton was very popular, but her books were deemed as repetitive and of mediocre quality. Therefore, Inglis here compares Tolkien's The Lord of the Rings to a children's book author of questionable worthiness. This critic acknowledged some quality to Tolkien's work, but he thought it was just consolation for the readers, for their powerlessness in the modern world. Many writers after Tolkien have created similar fantasies, reacting to a feeling that the world's magic has been stripped, the individual deprived of the chance of making a difference, of the very sense of personal identity and role.

Creators of myths, historical romance, and fairy tales, these authors belong to what Inglis calls Tolkien's commando. They ensure the continuity of the national identity. They create a view of history for the petty-bourgeois, the people without power who want to belong to this imaginary, beautiful mystification. Readers of these tales will pass on the same values to their children.

In a new essay[37] Fred Inglis reiterates the concept already expressed in the previous book. He initially states that, confronted with a bestseller of Tolkien's size, it's easy to think of the decline in taste, as if a book that sells a vast number of copies must be worthless. Critics laugh, or they say the problem must be in the industrial society, where literature can be produced quickly and at a low cost by many producers. And the readers? They are men and women of today, lost in the wasteland of industrial, modern cities, condemned to loneliness and jobs without creativity. Inglis ironically alludes to intellectuals who take refuge in an ivory tower or utterly disapprove of this cultural landscape (depending on whether they are right or left). But, he continues, in human sciences, it's impossible to refuse to understand a phenomenon. And to judge a phenomenon, its meaning needs to be determined. Inglis states that Tolkien's monumental work is a residue of Arthurian revival in Victorian times or the Gothic style in architecture and poetry—think the country houses of architects Voysey and Lutyens. Things from the good old days. Tolkien writes in this tradition, but he doesn't write about dead things. His work is nostalgic, so it creates profound emotions. A memory of a lost social order that gave happiness in a way the present world fails to do. Nostalgia represents the past as a series of moments or images without development: Inglis states, for example, that the modern form of nostalgia is the television advertisement. The images of nostalgia are a series of moments without narrative or commitment to any future action. But it's useless to consign this nostalgia to "the rubbish bin of history" (as Inglis writes) because it will insist on coming out again. Tolkien, safe in a privileged environment where the English mentality is protected against modernism, creates his nostalgic material to fill a space in people's social identity, so incomplete in the modern world. A mythical, atavistic English tradition, made of idealism and adventure, manliness and womanliness, will always demand this kind of nostalgia. In this tradition, we can find Vaughan Williams and Britten (both composers), John and Paul Nash (architect and painter), Winston Churchill, and Lord Reith (director of the BBC). And, obviously, Tolkien. His work provides an outlet to live emotions and thoughts that have no relationship to the real world. So, The Lord of the Rings is a political fantasy that the new elites give to the people. People who are neither autonomous nor free, because the power doesn't want self-aware individuals. Middle-earth is a utopia, a classless society, outside of history: the individuals are members of a city-state without a real city. In the Shire, there's abundant food even if we rarely see people intent on working in the fields. There's no need for individuality: the individual freely associates himself with a militia that pursues a noble purpose. He gets a noble, archetypal leader in Aragorn, a father figure in Gandalf. The book's plot is full of emotions, but the characters have no emotional depth. They are what they are; they live in a structure that forces them to follow an inescapable route. Inglis sees Tolkien's characters as petrified in their roles, innocent because they live in a simple, fixed world, the world of a reclusive "pre-sexual Oxonian born before the First World War." In Inglis's opinion, Tolkien gives us an elementary world in which there is no psychological depth or individual decision because that is the author's personal world. The perfect, simple world of community, rites, and immersion in a whole people's larger dimension is an attractive counterbalance to contemporary individualism, even against rationality. But fascism is founded on this longing. Inglis admits that Tolkien is no fascist (the speculation he made in *The Promise of Happiness: Value and Meaning in Children's Fiction*), but still he could be, like Wagner, a creator of myth and ideals for use by fascism. The influence of feelings created by Tolkien, Inglis writes, has found its moment in the Falklands War in 1982.

The essay ends with this last jab. Inglis's position on Tolkien is harsh: if the Oxonian writer is not fascist, his work still creates the stones used to build the structure of an oppressive, reactionary, aggressive society. While he criticizes Tolkien's style, Inglis also admits it's powerful. But it's also an instrument to influence the powerless classes of the modern world.

Joseph Pearce had commented[38] on Inglis's text, noting that when a German publisher had asked Tolkien about his origins, the answer was uncompromising. That's because Tolkien knew that the real question was about his being a Jew or not. But, as Pearce notes, "The lack of evidence, and indeed the overwhelming weight of evidence to the contrary, has not deterred some critics from labelling Tolkien as a fascist." While there's no direct charge leveled at Tolkien in this essay, in Pearce's opinion, Inglis assumes The Lord of the Rings "is a proto-fascist myth."

In Pearce's analysis, Inglis failed to find the meaning of Tolkien's work. We see a longing for something lost, a sense of displacement, but this is a desire to be reunited with God. It's not a desire that can be fulfilled in this world. It's the opposite of ideologies, offering a quick solution for our needs here and now. "To Tolkien, and to Frodo, Galadriel and Gandalf, there is no heaven on earth; nor would they have listened to any demagogue of left or right, be they Hitler, Mussolini, Marx, Mao, Lenin, Sauron or Saruman, who suggested otherwise."

Comrade Tolkien?

For any Italian Tolkien reader, it would have been hard to miss the so-called "appropriation" of his fantasy world from the right, and the left's reaction to this. In fact, it was the younger element of the right who was interested in Tolkien's work, and gave the name "Campi Hobbit" (which can be translated as "Hobbit Camps") to some recreational and cultural meetings (held between the late '70s and early '80s) for the purpose of reviving an environment that needed updating with new themes. Did this reference to Tolkien's work make sense? Yes and no. It is certain that Tolkien offers interesting ideas for conservative or traditionalist movements, but some of his themes (the struggle of free peoples against tyranny, for example) appealed to hippies and the youth movement of the '60s and '70s counterculture all over the world.

Italian leftists first snubbed Tolkien, and then contested the far-right appropriation, in some cases trying to enlist the author himself in their own ranks. Anyone, having read Tolkien's books, can easily conclude that he cannot seriously be accused of being a fascist, although this error may have been made outside of Italy too (see the statement by English professor Fred Inglis and the aforementioned Moorcock interview). Sure, Tolkien can't be considered left (let alone extreme left). But all of this started before real criticism about Tolkien was available. To be honest, it went on in isolation even after a real cultural debate had started (in English), until recent times. This Italian controversy around Tolkien's belonging is therefore singularly provincial and sterile, and if it can be understood in the context of the scorching '70s, it seems senseless to drag it out to now: yet this is precisely what is being done. This diatribe, however, underlines an important characteristic of our author: Tolkien's work, and here I refer mainly to The Lord of the Rings, has elements that appeal to everyone and are appreciated by an extremely vast and varied public. We will come back to this at a later point.

Professor Marco Tarchi, one of the promoters of "Campi Hobbit," wrote that The Lord of the Rings was, for him, "the handbook of the rebels, of the desperate, the marginalized, that find there 'another dimension' of intellectual experience, apt to blend the mythical with the current events. Alienated by progress' contradictions, young people from right and left, anarchists of all kinds, protesters, found there a profound aspiration for change, for the construction of a different world."[39]

Reading The Lord of the Rings was an inspiration to find new values, extraneous to consumerism: in a way a common ground for radicals and protesters from different factions. A passion for Tolkien's work was the instrument for breaking the cultural isolation the right suffered.

Gianfranco de Turris, an expert in fantasy literature, a journalist and a writer, working for the Italian national radio (RAI), gives us his opinion on the cultural affinity of the right towards Tolkien in the introduction to an essay collection, Albero di Tolkien.[40] De Turris states that Italian critics are unable and unwilling to understand Tolkien, even in the face of his enduring success. In Tolkien's work, the plot, characters, and worldbuilding are undoubtedly important. Still, the fortunes of The Lord of the Rings are built on something else, as Tolkien's son Michael knew when he wrote that his father gave an answer to people of all ages disappointed by today's values. The ugliness that has been given them as a substitute for beauty, adventure, excitement, and joy makes the very soul of people wither and die.[41]

In de Turris's interpretation, today's hegemonic culture (the "left") can't go beyond the author's ideological values to appraise his work. The rationalist and progressive approach of Italian culture must repel anything non-compliant: for example, anything related to escape in fantasy and imagination, or anything spiritual. This is why Tolkien was sidelined by the Italian cultural elite. A gradual recovery of rejected authors began to occur in the last 20 years (*Albero di Tolkien* was published in 2007, so the start of this recovery as indicated by de Turris should be in the mid-eighties). However, this critic states that the new respect for Tolkien is just about those aspects harmless for the dominant culture. On the other hand, another segment of the reading public, albeit small and minor, respected Tolkien's work: they loved the myth, the symbols, the epic, and the sense of the sacred.

Gianfranco de Turris.

De Turris states that identifying this minority with "the right" is inappropriate. But he accepts the term (usually preferred by his political opponents) for the sake of clarity. Anyway, this smaller cultural world obviously gave Tolkien's art value, and adopted it without ulterior motives.

So, no exploitation of Tolkien's work from the political right. Is this really the case? Or is the opposite true? Suppose we limit this argument to the initial appreciation of Tolkien's work (to which de Turris refers). In that case, he's correct, because the Italian far right party expelled Marco Tarchi, although he was a popular young leader. His effort to bring some fresh air in was, apparently, unappreciated by the older officialdom. Still, the same party (and its later incarnations in new acronyms) in the following years used Tolkien and symbols from his world as propaganda tools, maybe without the revolutionary emphasis you can perceive in Tarchi's words.[42]

Anyway, as de Turris notes, if the "right" was reading Tolkien, and the right was fascist, as in a syllogism, Tolkien became a fascist for the Italian left. Thus, the left-leaning Tolkien lovers could not read his books or had to do it secretly. In this paradoxical situation, the more relevant and dominant critics from the cultural world condemned Tolkien and his work, but people of every political belief read it and liked it. In the seventies and eighties, The Lord of the Rings sold hundreds of thousands of copies. In recent times, as de Turris states, Tolkien has been rehabilitated, but the critics forget he was a traditional Catholic, a monarchist, a conservative. Tolkien is being redeemed, but also mystified, forgetting who he really was. In de Turris's opinion, he should be compared to other traditionalist and conservative intellectuals like Borges, Pound, Eliot, Céline, Mishima, and D'Annunzio.[43] His values are timeless, profound, mythical. Readers of any level of knowledge can understand them in all the world's cultures.

In the essay "Tolkien fra Tradizione e Modernità" ("Tolkien between Tradition and Modernity"),[44] de Turris states that Tolkien's worldview was based on the spirit, in direct opposition to the materialist world of machines, which tends towards secularism and homologation. De Turris refers here to French mythographer Georges Dumézil's trifunctional hypothesis: the social division of roles in all the Indo-European cultures, since pre-historic times. Dumézil (1898–1986) observed in those societies the existence of three classes, one of which is subordinate to the other two, in contrast to the homogeneity of democracy. The subordinate class is the producer (farmers, breeders, and so on). The superior classes are the warriors and the priests and sovereigns. The trifunctionalism is also reflected in the roles that divinities fulfill in the various cultures. De Turris states that Dumézil's non-materialist spiritual hierarchies are in accordance with Tolkien's worldview and most profound opinions. He was an anti-modernist and did not believe in democracy or any state intrusiveness in personal lives. Therefore, the war he described in The Lord of the Rings is not a struggle between good and evil but a defense of traditional values against modernity. The Ring is a symbol of wicked and dictatorial power; the evil lords' strongholds (Mordor, Barad-Dûr, Isengard) are places where science has defiled nature, where flaming forges create weapons and new monsters.

Mordor is not an allegory of a political entity (Nazi Germany or the Soviet Union). It represents materialism, hyper-capitalism (today also called "turbo-capitalism"), and massification created by modern technologies. Tolkien has revived values and symbols that seemed forgotten; this is why he enjoyed (and still enjoys) an immense success.

Italian professor Stefano Giuliano analyzes[45] the possible use of Dumézil's trifunctionalism on the part of Tolkien. There's no way to know if Tolkien was aware of this theory, or if he took it into consideration when creating Middle-earth. Still, this is possible, because many of Dumézil's publications are about philology and were widely debated. Giuliano notes that the main characters of The Lord of the Rings often call to mind those we find in the mythological material to which Tolkien referred. For example, Gandalf has some traits of the wizard Merlin or the god Odin, while Aragorn is a character who needs to fulfill his own destiny and become a king, like Arthur. But every character is strongly distinguished by a peculiar ability. This is where Giuliano finds a possible relationship with trifunctionalism. For example, Gandalf can use magic, is a wise man, and gives his friends and allies advice. If necessary, he's also able to fight, but his primary ability is in the first of Dumézil's functions: the sacred. Aragorn can be wise, but his prominent ability is to be a warrior, so he belongs to the second function: strength, bravery, war-making. When Aragorn finally becomes a king, he adds together all the functions because he is a leader (first function) and a sacred healer (a nurturing ability, belonging to the third function). Giuliano admits that Middle-earth societies are not very detailed by social roles, so it is not always easy to apply Dumézil's theory to Tolkien's characters.

Whatever ideological significance Giuliano and de Turris give to Dumézil's hypothesis, we need to note that a link between Tolkien and Dumézil's ideas is contested. For example, Italian writer Federico Guglielmi[46] states that, in The Lord of the Rings, the traditional hierarchy with its social partition seems overturned by the Hobbits becoming main characters and heroes of the tale. Sages and warriors must rely on those small, forgotten little men. This feature is absolutely modern and defies any hypothesis of a world divided into castes.

Symbolism

Italian journalist Sebastiano Fusco wrote an essay[47] on the use of traditional symbols by J.R.R. Tolkien. Isildur's sword is one example: a symbol of regality, it plays a role in the transformation of Strider into Aragorn. The sword is the symbol, but its possession is not enough. The man who wields it needs to be skilled in its use, to be a hero. He's elevated above the "common rabble." By the sword, a king can give the investiture to a knight, a status that is another symbol of a superior man because the horse gives him more height. This is the first example of the depth of Tolkien's knowledge of these symbols, and his ability in their narrative use.

Another is the struggle with the Balrog, the monster that dragged Gandalf into the abyss. This event happened during the passage through the mines of Moria, in The Lord of the Rings. The Balrog is like Gandalf's shadow, having similar strength: an identical but opposite power. Gandalf will emerge from this struggle as Gandalf the White, after going through a mysterious transformation. In the essayist's opinion, this is an alchemical transformation: Gandalf is enshrouded in flames, then he falls into the water and fights against the Balrog on the earth. This is the alchemical itinerary that dissolves the dark part of him, preparing for a resurrection, an ascent to the skies. After his purification, Gandalf emerges on top of a mountain. Then he is brought away by an eagle, a symbol of spiritual enlightenment. Every page of Tolkien's works is rife with examples similar to these, Fusco writes. He states that Tolkien uses traditional themes in a precise and knowledgeable way. Facts and plot are organically fused with symbolism. It could be by deliberate intent, or maybe it is an automatic effect of Tolkien's cultural disposition. Quoting Julius Evola, Fusco states that traditional meaning's natural use could be spontaneous but unknowing.

So, reading Tolkien is like welcoming something ancient and precious. Proof of this is the rejection of his work by the deniers of spiritual freedom.

The aforementioned Italian writer Federico Guglielmi (who uses the pen name Wu Ming 4), in his book *Difendere La Terra di Mezzo*,[48] replied to Fusco. First, Guglielmi states that whoever wants to find symbols, will find them. He writes: "It's obvious that if the presence of a royal sword were enough to make of Tolkien a traditional symbolist, then the primacy attributed to him by Fusco would be contended by thousands of novelists and film-makers." The elevation above the common people has no meaning in the context of a story where the protagonists are humble farmers, the Hobbits. Moreover, no further development of alchemical elements is present in the story, and there is no testimony of any interest in alchemy on the part of the author. So, it makes no sense to pretend that an informed use of alchemical references is present in Gandalf's fall into the fiery abyss, or in his body's further transformations. About the eagle, Guglielmi notes that the animal is associated with celestial divinities. When we see Gandalf lifted by the eagle, we should think of divine intervention instead of the spiritual development of the wizard's character. (Incidentally, we need to note that Gandalf will really undergo a transformation and will be back as a more powerful character, but this has nothing to do with the eagle).

Fusco writes that every page in The Lord of the Rings is crowded with similar symbols: Guglielmi answers that, in all literature, every phrase could be full of symbols if you abstract words from their narrative context. In short: if you want to find them, you will. And if you say that the author can make an unknowing use of symbols, that's quite convenient, because you can avoid giving us proof of a real intention on the author's part. In short, Federico Guglielmi refuses to recognize the symbolic interpretation's validity when it doesn't conform to the story context.

A Tolkien-loving President

In the book by Pecere and Del Corso[49] we can read an unusual participation in the political debate about Tolkien: an interview with Francesco Cossiga (1928–2010), who was both prime minister and president of the Republic (1985–1992) of Italy. Asked about the comparison between Tolkien and some right-wing intellectuals (Julius Evola, Mircea Eliade[50]), Cossiga answers in the affirmative, adding Carl Jung to the possible parallel. Tolkien was undoubtedly a traditionalist in the sense that he respected moral values and believed in them. Tradition is the source and the "storage" of moral values. On the other hand, Cossiga affirms that fascism is not strictly traditionalist, being influenced in its origins by positivist and socialist ideas formulated by Auguste Comte and George Sorel.[51]

Who absolutely cannot be an admirer of Tolkien's work? A Marxist, in Cossiga's opinion, because tradition is a continuity in history, is the tomorrow that needs a yesterday to make sense. Marxism wants a "new man" and a break in the continuity of history instead. Cossiga thinks the Italian right wing needed Tolkien to fill a vacuum, in the sense that fascism did generate some relevant writers in France, but none in Italy. Appropriating Tolkien doesn't make sense because fascism is more related to communism. Still, the Italian right takes advantage of Tolkien because it has no culture of its own. So when it finds ideas apt to support the right-wing cause, the Italian right takes them. However, when intellectuals and readers from the right embrace Tolkien, in fact, they break the fascist legacy: "I don't know if they realize that, though. Can you imagine in a Tolkien's work a squadrista[52] in black shirt intent on beating a political opponent?"

In the same book (*L'Anello che non Tiene*) we have an interesting criticism of symbolic interpretation applied to Tolkien's work: the intro-duction to The Lord of the Rings by Elémire Zolla, a writer and teacher of mixed British, Italian, and Alsatian origin. Writing about the cor-rupted Hobbit Gollum, Zolla depicts him as a being drawn to the roots, the deep, where the plants' seeds are. Therefore Gollum was condemned to an utterly material knowledge; he can't see the leaves, the flowers, or the branches that live in contact with the air. That means a living being has a form that gives it purpose; the observer that can only see mat-ter will not understand it. The goal of the seed is the flower, but Gollum can't see it anymore.

An esoteric interpretation, inspired by theories, traditions, and myths, can completely override the literary text. Gollum, as written by Tolkien, is no more. An alchemic vision has taken his place.

Is The Lord of the Rings really a container of disguised meanings, totally distinct from the story it tells? Or should the symbols be inter-preted in relationship to the text?

Del Corso and Pecere give their own interpretation about the cold reception the Italian cultural world gave Tolkien. In their opinion, it has nothing to do with politics, since a lot of famous Italian writers are right wing, or even fascists, and this didn't stop the critics from study-ing them. Tolkien was different because he was from a literary tradi-tion with a long history in Britain (MacPherson, Coleridge, Keats) but no equivalent in Italy. Medieval or Celtic legends and tragedies and fairy creatures found no match; difficult social and economic conditions and the pressing issue of regaining national independence influenced modern Italian literature into a prevailing realism, with few exceptions (Italo Calvino, Dino Buzzati).

Tolkien as a Creator of Fascist Mentalities

In 2003 Austrian critic Guido Schwarz published[53] *Jungfrauen im Nachthemd—Blonde Krieger aus dem Westen* (*Virgins in Nightgowns—Blonde Warriors from the West*). This book is part of the strong thread about the "fascist Tolkien," but it has some peculiar characteristics. Schwarz in fact criticizes society in general, using Tolkien's work as a tool: talking about the books is meant to be of help for the reader, to reflect on their world, external or internal (at a psychological level). Schwarz separates the readers into two groups: the first one is made of those people who are searching for an ideal world in which to seek refuge. They don't want to face reality. Schwarz doesn't say that this is necessarily bad, but this is not good for the community, because it is divisive. The second group is made of the people who dislike Tolkien's books and the world depicted therein. Schwarz tries to provoke a reaction, thinking that a debate or dispute can be beneficial, hoping that the readers are open to questioning their opinions and developing their critical thinking.

The critic himself is a Tolkien fan, but not fascinated as he was at the time of the first reading. He hopes to bring the readers to a less thoughtless and uncritical enthusiasm regarding Tolkien's work. In the place of the fantasy book, the real world needs to be seen.

With The Lord of the Rings Tolkien gives us something like paradise. The king protects us, women are only virgins or mothers, men dedicate themselves to their honest work wearing simple clothes. There's no fear of strangers, but no freedom of choice either, and no chance to speak against this kind of society. When we read Tolkien, a desire awakens in us for a clear, simple set of rules, a small structure or society where you can live separated from everything else; the other countries are on their own, and we sure are better than they are. We only use first names (our world is so small that they are enough), and in our beautiful villages we live with a lot of horses and without cars. There's no pollution because there are no factories (maybe they have been banished to poor countries); therefore everything is beautiful. There's no violence. What does that have to do with fascism? Nothing, at least not directly, but Schwarz says he will show how these thoughts can lead to fascism. Tolkien gives us a worldview in black and white, one that eliminates the gray. Fantasy literature in general does the same, in this critic's opinion. In the extreme, this worldview can be fascist, but Schwarz leaves the judgment to the reader.

People say that fantasy literature gives them a small opportunity to escape from everyday life, so they are not interested in ruining this sanctuary by studying its background. Schwarz understands this worry, but studying the background didn't ruin the pleasure of reading fantasy for him. It's also important to analyze fantasy stories because they influence people, mostly the younger folk. Schwarz works with a psychological approach, examining the thinking processes and motivations of the reader, and in this case of the writer as well, with the aim of uncovering the ideology he inculcated in the readers' minds. Schwarz's critical method can help the reader not to discover a new world, but to develop a more analytical view of his old world.

Reading Humphrey Carpenter's biography of Tolkien, Schwarz was impressed by the biographer's description of his subject: he got the feeling that Tolkien was buried in his own work, a lonely man with no connection with the real world. Sure he wanted to express himself in it.

We, as the readers, have to face his ideology; we can choose to do it consciously or unconsciously.

Schwarz makes connections between the bucolic world Tolkien knew when he was a child and the Shire, between the loss of his mother and the dream of a serene life in a safe country. He knew his mother as a non-sexual being (that is, not as his father's wife). And in an act we can scarcely imagine today, he renounced seeing his fiancée at an age when people think almost exclusively about sex, because this was the will of his tutor. Maybe this is why he transformed women into creatures that dance in the meadows, somehow out of reach. He even transfigured his own wife into a creature of this kind. Maybe Tolkien had sex with her just to generate children, for the rest it was just like having a housekeeper, something that is different from the modern definition of a relationship. Tolkien's friendship with men is another trait of his character. The important things were discussed with men; women were not taken seriously. This is a fascist way to relate with women, Schwarz states, and it comes from fear of losing control. Asexual women (mother, sister, nurse, virgins) are those who pose no threat to the fascist man. Independent women with a strong will, at ease with their own sexuality, provoke a strong reaction in the fascist man just by their own existence. They are to be driven out from the mind; if possible, they must die. Tolkien, in Schwarz's opinion, created a world where only one kind of woman is present, the one who gives no trouble to the fascist man.

Let's take a look at Schwarz's definition of fascism. He bases his analysis on the definition by Klaus Theweleit, a sociologist who examined male socialization based on hardness, machismo, and self-sacrifice.[54] German men of the first half of the twentieth century were influenced by the military institutions to learn a style of "annihilating" violence against their enemies but, also, against women, because they were unable to express intimacy or love. These men identified themselves with their work, or their status as soldiers, with a tendency to see anything extraneous or foreign as a threat. This kind of man could tolerate non-threatening women as virtuous mothers or sisters or nurses. Yet, erotic or sexually promiscuous women they see as menacing or castrating.

It's no surprise if Schwarz, using these criteria, examines Tolkien's personal life as we've seen above, taking a peek at his bedroom and drawing some conclusions. Still, Tolkien received no brutal military-style imprinting and was not the ideal military man. Moreover, while it's true that Tolkien spent the majority of his time with his male friends, we have sources (for instance, Humphrey Carpenter's biography) showing a strong link between him and his wife, Edith. He helped with domestic chores, was a loving dad to his children, later in life spent some years at Bournemouth because Edith loved the place (he would have preferred to stay in Oxford, allegedly). Is this really a portrait of the "fascist man" who considers his wife little more than a housekeeper? But let's move on.

Regarding the relationship between Tolkien as a man and his participation in the war, Schwarz thinks he enjoyed it because in his books there are so many battle scenes. Tolkien knew the horrors of war firsthand, yet he had some kind of mechanism in his mind that protected him from processing the experience in a critical way. How can a person cope with war trauma? One could sink into desperation, go to a therapist, retreat into private life trying to forget everything. Or get involved with veterans associations and meet to tell stories, forgetting the worst parts. But one can also retreat into himself and create his own world. A world where war does exist but it's the good that wins. A world that you create and then explore, like in a dream. Separated by the real world, still close enough to it, so that others can enter, can be invited in.

In Tolkien's world, we have the mysterious and wise Elves. They still control some enclaves in Middle-earth, and live in beautiful places like Rivendell, a big country house that has no fields around it but is "obviously" regularly supplied by a catering service. The Elves are the English, the noblest people of all in Schwarz's interpretation, but he likens their perfect appearance to the specimen of Nazi superman. They have all the desirable qualities and never really die, because even if they die, they are reborn. Schwarz thinks this is un–Christian: the Elves have no responsibilities to take for their actions in life; they are just born again. Anyway, we need to note that after the end of the world, the Elves still are going to be judged.

Another race, completely different from Elves, is typically English: the Hobbits. While they have no Elven qualities, they stand out for their philistinism: they love their little cozy country and don't want to hear about anything that comes from outside. Their lifestyle is Tolkien's Anglo-Saxon (or Germanic) ideal; it works by having no real hierarchy (except for their clans, and some ineffectual public charges). Well, everyone would like to be a Hobbit and live without a care in a peaceful paradise, so this is a powerful fantasy: in Schwarz's opinion, a sort of desire to return to the womb. A fantasy that Tolkien himself possibly had, or he was able to arouse in his readers. If you are in the womb maybe you perceive that something else is out there, but any influence is filtered so you may ignore it. In fact, the Shire is protected, by Aragorn and his mysterious rangers. Tolkien puts the Hobbits in the position of children who, unlike real children, are not curious, except for some bizarre and rare individual.

As to the Ring, it is an instrument of dominion, Schwarz notes. What people desire is domination over other people and money; this is why the Ring makes its bearer greedy. The power of this tool makes an individual omnipotent, omniscient, and gives a kind of immortality. Not real immortality, but something like stretching life over a longer span, like a piece of chewing gum. The Ring is part of Sauron himself; he's the only one who really can benefit from it. Mighty and wise characters (Galadriel, Gandalf) understand the Ring's true nature and refuse to use it. Any bearer will believe he has enormous power, but in reality he doesn't: actually, he's dominated by it without being aware. So it's not strange that many people want this Ring; rather, it's strange that Sauron was so careless and wore it to battle, and lost it.

The Ring is like the dark side of the Force in *Star Wars*: absolute evil, it wants to dominate and corrupt everything in the world. If Sauron had managed to get the Ring back, Middle-earth would have fallen under his dominion. Schwarz imagines the Elves sailing west and escaping, and a future of horror and torture for Men, Hobbits, and all the rest. Since it's not possible to kill and torture everyone, Sauron's future world probably would have consisted of a surveillance regime, with a big central jail, factories, smog everywhere, a central administration in Mordor, and ubiquitous spies. Something similar really does happen in the Shire, where a dictatorship is established: we discover this at the end of The Lord of the Rings, when a small group (the four Hobbits of the Fellowship) come back and act as a liberation army. This regime has brought new horrible buildings, pollution, intimidation. Every good is collected by a central authority to be redistributed, but, in reality, a majority of it is sent away. For the Hobbits in the Shire, there's just scarcity and oppression.

It's not strange that this story was imagined during the Second World War when the union of the Allied powers managed to bring Hitler down. You can imagine the Black Riders as SS or Gestapo officers; the Elves sailing west are like people fleeing from Europe, hoping for a visa and a more secure life in the United States. Schwarz thinks the Ring is the dark, evil side in each of us, but Tolkien didn't admit it, even to himself. In Gollum, this separation does exist: Smeagol is the good side of this unfortunate Hobbit who perceives the evil in himself, so he tries to fight against the Ring's influence. Gollum stays enslaved and continues to fret about the Ring; he wants it back. Schwarz states that by biting off Frodo's finger and getting the Ring back Gollum completes his choice for evil. He has gone down his circular, ring-shaped path, back to evil, but Tolkien eliminates him immediately after, with the fall into the Crack of Doom. As Gandalf says, Gollum hated and loved the Ring, and himself.

In regard to Bilbo sparing Gollum's life (in *The Hobbit*), Schwarz thinks that Gandalf's dialogue with Frodo about this fact is the key to the book's meaning. Compassion determined the course of events that saved the world because Gollum is destined to destroy the Ring while trying to steal it. The good guys may kill, but only bad guys, and only in defense. This is a Christian principle, the love for life. So Tolkien has a fascist view of the world, but he is also a Christian. What at the end prevails? The Christian or the fascist? The reader has to decide. But it's not charity or love to decide about fate; it's a hierarchical principle. As Gandalf says, not even the wise can see all intentions. There's a superior will, someone who decided that Bilbo, not an Orc, found the Ring. This is Tolkien, who can decide the course of history and even rewrite it as he wishes. Tolkien himself wrote that inspiration comes from something above him; the story grew and he let it expand. So what is the principle that moves everything, Tolkien included? Hierarchy or charity? Schwarz can't give an answer.

Let's go back to the Ring: if it's so dangerous, we can simply destroy it, right? Well, no: the Ring can be destroyed in just one way, by bringing it to Mount Doom. Tolkien doesn't love allegory, but here he uses one: the Ring's indestructibility is also the evil's. A big victory is possible if the Ring is destroyed, after many tribulations. A terrible defeat is possible if Sauron gets the Ring back. But even in the case of victory, evil will be back, because Sauron is just an agent, not the cause of all evil. Today evil is banished, but sooner or later it will come back again. What we can do is just to fight evil as best we can in our time. And we can easily imagine, writing just after the end of the Second World War, what Tolkien means by Sauron or Morgoth.

In his single-minded lust for power, Sauron is a leader lacking imagination. He can't understand that his adversaries think in different patterns from his own, so he's easily distracted by the ruse of the attack at Morannon, the Black Gate. This attack is launched as a cover for Sam and Frodo, who are trying to approach Mount Doom and destroy the Ring. Sauron, in Schwarz's opinion, is searching for quick success and quick fame; this is another bad thing because he thinks only for one legislative period. If you're elected for four years, you don't need to worry about what is coming after that. A king may think differently, with no time limit. We think democracy is the better form of government but this imperfection is true. Tolkien is a monarchist, and so are the leaders in his books. Schwarz admits that this view of the world has an undeniable appeal.

Simple-mindedness and a need for immediate results, are these really Sauron's traits? The Dark Lord is a strange specimen as an example of democracy's shortcomings. One could think instead that his goals could be dramatically permanent, just as those of the far-sighted Aragorn. But let's go on. Schwarz thinks that there's a "certain way of producing reality" that, regardless of the political or economic system, is the fascist way of thinking, or creating desire. So fascism is to be fought not only as a regime that could be back but as a way to create the perception of reality. This is why Tolkien is important, and Tolkien's criticism too. The problem is taking the thought to the extreme: one side is right, so the other has to disappear. But good and evil are codependent; they both need to exist to make sense.

Tolkien doesn't think so. We can see it in the tragic march of the three Hobbits to Mount Doom. Gollum leads Sam and Frodo and, at the same time, he fights with himself. It seems we have a dialectic, finally. But Gollum never really has a chance. A compassionate reader will feel sorry for him. His drama is a cautionary tale: Tolkien tells us not to get involved with the bad because, even if there's still something good in you, evil will win. And you'll be ruined because of this. Gollum betrays the Hobbits, leading them to the ambush by Shelob, the giant spider. Tolkien lets evil win over him and destroys his fleeting hopes of redemption. Boromir dies from a similar fate, but there's a difference. There's time for repentance, so the warrior from Gondor dies a hero's death and will find peace. The author gives better treatment to the nobleman, but the warning is clear: who comes to terms with evil dies. You can only serve the good or the bad side, to choose both is not possible. Nevertheless, some are tempted and therefore are lost. In Schwarz's opinion, Tolkien had something of an animistic perspective about this need for sacrifice. Those who let themselves be swayed by evil are like human sacrifices, needed for the rest to be saved.

The Shire's liberation at the end of the story is where we can see another form of evil: Tolkien doesn't name it, but it's socialism or Stalinism. Everyone, except some fools, is able to tell they were happier before. The new government brought some nasty folks to build a bigger mill, but the grain to be ground has not increased, so this doesn't make sense. They are not working on grain, anyway. The people inside hammer away, create stench and smoke, and throw out rubbish, as if this were the goal of everything.

At the same time, Tolkien critiques capitalism too: he hates the idea of increased production, to be paid with more pollution and destruction of nature. Both political and economic systems are disapproved: the truth is that Tolkien hates the modern world.

Schwarz's book is a commentary on Tolkien's world, fictional and real; it's impossible to analyze everything here. The definition of fascism that the author uses, and how he links Tolkien to it, is quite peculiar and maybe is more related to a kind of authoritarian personality, rather than expressly fascism. Some of his claims come out of the blue, in my opinion at least, with no attempt at a demonstration; other considerations are perceptive and accurate. Regarding Schwarz's psychological approach, Thomas Honegger states that it "simply cannot be taken seriously."[55]

Anyway, a quality that separates this critic from others is how he treats the reader. Some left-leaning, intellectual critics seem to doubt people's ability to think on their own and to decide what books to read without the correct teachings. We don't know if Guido Schwarz is one of that same kind inside his own mind, but the method he uses is different. Some critics scold the reader, as if to say, why are you reading that kind of trash? Schwarz doesn't interfere with the reader's freedom; on the contrary, he says that he likes Tolkien's work too. But he thinks the reader needs to be aware of the deeper meaning of these most enjoyable fantasy stories or, at least, what he deems to be the deeper meaning. Whatever a reader may think of his book, Schwarz claims that his intent is to stimulate debate, without posing as the repository of the truth.

Lost in Translation?

J.R.R. Tolkien gave great importance to his works' translations and drew up regulations about how the work should be done. In 1956, Tolkien expressed his displeasure with the first foreign translation, the Dutch one. The problem was rewording names ideated by Tolkien in another language. A Swedish translation fared no better. Tolkien deemed it necessary to write detailed guidelines to follow for the translation of his works.[56]

In other countries, like the Soviet Union, unauthorized, clandestine translations were the norm. In Italy, a new translation provided an opportunity for a new political battle.

The first translation by Vittoria Alliata di Villafranca was published in 1967; the translator was an Italian noblewoman, then a 17-year-old girl. A new publishing house commissioned the current (2019) translation by Ottavio Fatica, teacher and translator. Even before publication, this new text was the subject of controversies and complaints, as journalist Vanni Santoni notes in an article.[57] Fatica's translation lacks metrics and rhyme; it is quite different from the epic mood everybody knows from the previous translation. In Santoni's opinion, the new edition has a benefit: Elémire Zolla's preface has been replaced by Tolkien's original one (the second edition's one). Anyway, Fatica's translation is generally more faithful to Tolkien's original text.

The clash between the translators showed itself in various newspaper pieces, interviews, and web pages, each criticizing the other one's work.[58] Alliata claimed that her translation used a style more understandable for the Italian reader. She states that her work was approved by Tolkien himself, so it doesn't make sense to write a new one. Federico Guglielmi (author of *Difendere la Terra di Mezzo*) claims that this new version is approved by the Tolkien estate.[59]

This fight about translations has a political side. Cesare Catà sees in the new version[60] a new interpretation for The Lord of the Rings, almost as a modern Young Adult book. Alliata's translation was maybe less precise and lacked the individual way of speaking as devised by Tolkien for his various characters, but it sounds like a middle way between chivalric romance, Italian poetry, and the Nordic sagas. Fatica's new text is fluid and accessible but it doesn't mirror Tolkien's simple but solemn style. While in his piece this critic states that he prefers the old translation, he thinks both have positive and negative features.

But in the end, the stylistic choice changes the mood of Tolkien's work. Alliata's translation can't be sold anymore (her contract is expired and not renewed). Many readers who knew Tolkien through her work learned with dismay about this new version in which everything, starting with the names, was changed, and even the cover shows a disconcerting barren landscape. In Italy even translating Tolkien has become a political battle, traditionalism against modernism, and right against left.

Still on the Conservative Tolkien: But What Does This Mean?

Kreeft notes in his aforementioned[61] work that Tolkien is anti-modernist and anti-progressive, but he's not necessarily a political conservative. The author notes that the meaning of the terms "conservative" and "liberal" does not always remain constant over time, and it was certainly not Tolkien who particularly augmented political themes. Some of his populist beliefs, or the philosophy of "small is beautiful," are very far from the idea of modern politics as something bureaucratic, statist, specialized.

With the term in fashion today, Tolkien could be almost defined as "anti-political."

As the American kind of conservatism has a tendency to be ally of big business and the military, forgetting the environment, Kreeft argues that Tolkien would not be drawn to this kind of politics.

American liberalism would have been equally foreign to his way of thinking, because it means big government and no regard for morality, family, religion, or the sacredness of human life. Tolkien's Hobbits are typically bourgeois, so no affinity to the left is possible. But they are not staunch businessmen; they are simple peasants. Their society has nothing of the capitalist world.

Kreeft thinks Tolkien "is more of a European conservative, or old conservative, a Schumacher Small is beautiful conservative, a Chestertonian distributist."

To understand these lines, it is useful to know that Ernst Friedrich Schumacher was a British intellectual of German origin, who gave birth to the concept of "small is beautiful" with a book that bore precisely that title, and which highlighted the importance of individual insertion into economic and social life, as well as environmentalism. Schumacher set interest in people and their needs as human beings against the dominance of anonymous market forces. Gilbert Keith Chesterton was a theoretician of distributism, thus advocating for redistribution of wealth and the fight against social exclusion and poverty. Incidentally, he was also the creator of Father Brown, a detective priest character. Schumacher and Chesterton fit into a democratically Christian social and political mindset, and, in fact, both were influenced by the Catholic Church's social doctrine.

Having made this laborious detour to understand Kreeft's thought, we find confirmation in Joseph Pearce's opinions. He thinks[62] that, since Tolkien's work is fundamentally Catholic, it is logical to see the communities in The Lord of the Rings shaped by Catholic ideas. Pearce states that influence from Chesterton was at the peak of its strength during Tolkien's formative years, from the start of the twentieth century to the beginning of the First World War. In England, intellectual life was strongly affected by Chesterton's theories, so Pearce thinks that distributist ideas (from Chesterton and Hilaire Belloc, a French-British author) strongly influenced Tolkien. Belloc proposed distributism as a natural alternative to capitalism and socialism, because it was a traditional way of life for Catholic Europeans. To Chesterton's and Belloc's theories, Pearce adds the influence by the encyclical by Pope Leo XIII, "Rerum Novarum" ("about new things"). Tolkien's use of myth is consistent with these philosophical principles, Pearce states. In Tolkien's sub-creation theory, free will is given to Man because he has to make a choice: to obey (or not) the purpose of his creation. The right choice is self-limitation; the wrong one is an unlimited thirst for power and self-gratification. The same is true in marriage: faithfulness, and denial of self-indulgence, is the right choice. A belief in God means abnegation, acceptance of limits. Pearce thinks this applies to both the individual and society. We can be sure that Tolkien sometimes felt the same way, because in letter 186,[63] quoted by Pearce, he states that we should not do something just because we can; the topic of the letter was atomic power. Reading Humphrey Carpenter's biography, we can learn that Tolkien was not a rich man until his later years. He was generous with his family and, anonymously, a charitable man.[64] Is this enough to conclude that Tolkien was a distributist? In the *Letters*, Chesterton is quoted (Belloc is not), but there's nothing about economic theories. Tolkien did not believe in politics; we have no source about his interest in Chesterton's or Belloc's theories, except for an unverifiable source[65] claiming he was a subscriber to a magazine influenced by Chesterton's ideas.

Strangely, Kreeft states that Tolkien would be a proponent of the redistribution and social theories proposed by the most progressive part of the Christian political world, yet he cites a passage from letter 52[66] that should push him to a very different conclusion: "The most improper job of any Man ... is bossing other Men. Not one in a million is fit for it, and least of all those who seek the opportunity." In addition to this declaration of hatred for any form of organization that oppresses the individual too much, in various points in the letters, we also find obvious traces of intolerance towards the tax authorities, those whom the Oxford professor did not particularly like, but who are an essential part of any social policy of redistribution of wealth. Any distributist policy, to use the correct term, implies a profound interference of the state machine (so hated by our author) in people's lives. In letter 52,[67] Tolkien defined himself as an anarchist, in the philosophical sense of the term: one who wants to abolish state control, not one of the "whiskered men with bombs." Alternatively, he preferred a non-constitutional monarchy. Evidently, he could tolerate the king, but not the parliamentary, bureaucratic, and governmental apparatus. Famously, he would have liked to get back to the use of personal names: that is, living in such small communities that everyone would know everyone else. So, although he seems to agree with the idea that "small is beautiful," there's no basis to figure Tolkien as a Christian Democrat and advocate of welfare. Kreeft and Pearce, with their adherence to strong Christian values, make the same mistake as others did, by "enlisting" Tolkien in their own ranks. But the Oxford professor is hard to categorize with precision, as he follows his own, very particular way of thinking, not necessarily favorable to the Catholic culture of social reform that these critics seem to like. If the Hobbits of the Shire are the example of the society Tolkien would love, they don't look always sympathetic to each other. Actually, some are greedy and petty people. Anyway, be that as it may, nobody is too rich or too poor in the Shire, even if some are land-lords and others are servants. Tolkien's society seems to be small and beautiful; everyone gets at least what he needs to live. It's not too different from the political dreams of Schumacher or Chesterton, but the author doesn't linger on the details of such a wonderful state of affairs.

One could be tempted to paint Tolkien as a liberal, based on his hatred of state interference, but, other than his desire to become financially successful with his published works, he has no real flair for business so cannot be described as ruthlessly capitalist. Moreover, his sorrow at the destruction of the environment and his aversion to machines present a more complex portrait. I would, therefore, refrain from aligning Tolkien with any specific line of political thought: perhaps he himself summarized his own approach in Treebeard's famous quote from The Lord of the Rings: "I am not altogether on anybody's side, because nobody is altogether on my side."

However, it may be that the political definition that Kreeft has tried to give, however erroneous, is at least closer to Tolkien's mind than the ferocious characterization presented by the English leftist critics (the classical example: Moorcock) who, as we have seen, believe Tolkien to be associated with a greedy, oppressive bourgeois class, with all its unpleasant features: hostile to an open society, malevolent, fundamentally hypocritical.

The Structuralist Critic of Middle-earth

Structuralist British critic Nick Otty[68] wrote a "guide" to Middle-earth with several entries. Structuralism is a modern analysis method whereby the text is interpreted by the meaning of single words and elements to reveal the underlying structure. For example, under the entry "Evil," Otty analyzes the specularity of the two powers, Evil and Good. The reader knows that Sauron is Evil and his hypothetical victory will destroy all good things, but he's never informed with regard to how Trolls and wolves and Orcs think about good and evil. Both sides have hierarchical structures (Gandalf the good wizard is better than a Hobbit; Saruman the fallen wizard is more terrible than Smeagol the fallen Hobbit). In Nick Otty's opinion, nothing is differentiating the two symmetrical structures, Evil and Good. If the reader alters the words that define evil, he can find himself in the identical hierarchy of good.

Moreover, if you observe the inhabitants of Mordor, they work in fear and toil under an ever-menacing garrison of heavily armed guards, so one could think they hope for liberation. But in The Lord of the Rings, these oppressed folks merit nothing better than destruction by arrows and swords or being crushed by Ents. A profusion of prejudices characterizes the evildoers: they live in marshes, dark places, or in industrial landscapes and wastelands; they talk in foreign languages; they come from the east or south (west being the direction of the undying lands of Valinor). Otty notices another detail: evil beings talk—in languages Tolkien invented to operate in a xenophobic way—with guttural sounds; they use certain letters and sounds to increase their unpleasantness. But apart from the look and sounds, there's no real reason why these creatures are evil. In Otty's opinion, there's no real indication of evil beings' true nature and why we should avoid them. At about this specific point, Patrick Curry noted[69] that it is unclear what Otty means, except that it's not kind. But Curry specifies his own opinion: "Is it any less clear why in Middle-earth Mordor should be eschewed than, say, fascism now?"

About industrialization, Otty hints that it's linked to evil in some way. Rarely do we know something about Middle-earth's economics. The Shire is an unreal place, where enriched landowners spend their time eating, drinking tea, and smoking pipes. There's no detail on the way this agricultural plenty is obtained and managed. Mordor is very different; it resembles some of the industrial wastelands of the 1930s. But all the work and pollution there seem to produce nothing. When Lady Galadriel grants a vision in her mirror to Sam and Frodo, Sam sees the Shire being attacked by evil: this evil has the form of industrial development wiping out the Shire, quite similar to a lovely spot of rural England. When we have a vision of evil in Middle-earth, its shape is the shape of industry and technology.

The Russian Case

If some critics think Tolkien's fortune starts with hippies finding mysterious messages in his books during the 1960s, we must remember that the phenomenon could not influence some countries. Russia was one of these. Russia, at the time, was part of the USSR, the Soviet Union, a country that some suspected to be the blueprint for Mordor. Critic Vladimir Grushetskiy[70] states that Tolkien's work gradually gained appreciation in Russia: the first translation of The Fellowship of the Ring was published in 1982, and immediately several clubs devoted to Tolkien were independently born in Russia. Live-action role-playing games started with the name "Khobbitskie Igrishcha," and there was widespread enthusiasm. This is at last in part explainable with the former condition of Russia as a totalitarian state: everything that people could read in the past had to be compliant with the "socialist realism" genre. So *The Fellowship of the Ring* was the only part of The Lord of the Rings published, in abridged form. Tolkien's books had been readings for the dissidents during the USSR years. The state banned them because of suspected references to the Soviet totalitarian state (darkness coming from east, for example).

Tolkien's books broke the state's ethical norms. His words about the "prisoner's escape" from reality had a special meaning for Russian readers: it was the choice of a different reality preferred by the fugitives. Although it has very few examples in Russian literature in the way Tolkien meant it, the world of Faerie became the dimension of choice for many, in a time of chaos during which the old order collapsed.

However, as Grushetskiy states, many readers didn't go further than *The Hobbit* and The Lord of the Rings or didn't get the deeper meanings. Because of the expensive rights payments, information and criticism are not available, and pirated editions with faulty translations are in circulation. Whatever the difficulties, Grushetskiy thinks that Tolkien can find the right tone to teach children about human values and duties. But he also feels that critics manipulate the perception of the author's intentions following their own point of view.

Critic Sergey Kuriy poses the question: Are there political allegories in The Lord of the Rings? In his article,[71] he tells us that, although the meaning of the book is very clear, a myriad of different interpretations came out of it. The contrast between East and West gives us the temptation to see in this struggle free and democratic Europe against Sauron or the Islamic fundamentalism. Then what do we have in the West? An earthly paradise! These blessed lands are precisely where America is. Moreover, the Elves, with their special position in the world and the right to a promised land, are similar to the Jews. Maybe the fall of Mordor is an allegory of the decline of the Soviet empire? After all, Ronald Reagan had defined the USSR as "the Evil Empire." Kuriy remembers that in the first edition of *The Hobbit*, in 1976, the text was changed so Bilbo didn't go east with the Dwarves, but north. Today, after the fall of the Soviet regime and the debut of political correctness, Tolkien's books are accused of racism and discrimination against women. Orcs resemble the Mongols, people from Harad are African Americans, and there are few women in the books. It's difficult to argue.

But Kuriy is just kidding. We know that a mythical paradise where they brought wounded Arthur is really in the west, that medieval

Europe was menaced from the east. The book, in other words, follows real, old northern mythology and is not clumsily shaped around modern world events. As Tolkien said, if the book were an allegory, Sauron and his followers would be enslaved. The author of this article, writing from the old Soviet Mordor, doesn't believe Tolkien's books are allegories, or that hints of race and political issues should be transformed into their modern equivalents. This satiric piece from Kuriy is typical of the Russian attitude towards Tolkien's work. They enjoy it and at the same time they seem unfazed by the controversial points. Nevertheless, some took the matter seriously, and wrote their own works set in the same world, ignoring the obvious problem of intellectual property. Indeed, no writer can add to the legendarium. After Tolkien's death, as we know, his son Christopher began the long and difficult task of preparing for publication the copious unpublished material, but no work by other writers was ever added to the "canon." So all fan fiction and books by contemporary writers about Middle-earth are published without the Tolkien estate's approval. Paleontologist Kirill Yeskov wrote a retelling[72] of The Lord of the Rings: the story is told from the opposite viewpoint. In this alternative tale, Mordor and Sauron's forces are not evil, and facts are different. In other words, The Lord of the Rings is the story written by the victors, so Yeskov gives us another, different truth. The Ring war is the result of a clash of cultures: On one side, we have feudalism and an archaic aristocratic world; on the other, there are technological development and an industrial revolution. Aragorn is an unscrupulous adventurer, so maybe Boromir was eliminated in a power struggle over leadership of Gondor. Gandalf is a warmonger, the mind behind the western people's maneuvers. Yeskov's book is titled *The Last Ringbearer,* or *Последний кольценосец* in Russian. In a similar vein, N. Vassilyeva and N. Nekrasova retell *The Silmarillion* in their *Black Book of Arda*[73] (Черная Книга Арды). In this narration, Eru and the Valar are tyrants while Melkor is not evil. Last but not least, a commercially fortunate sequel to The Lord of the Rings was published by Nikolay Daniilovich Perumov.[74]

Tolkien against Totalitarianism

Jessica Yates wrote an essay[75] examining Tolkien criticism regarding the political message of The Lord of the Rings and the debate about Tolkien and fascism (yes, again) in British fanzines. Yates notices that some of the criticisms are cursory and can be refuted simply by a more accurate reading of the book. Tolkien's letters are another useful instrument to answer negative criticism, but they have only been available since 1981. Another topic of Yates's essay is the discussions she had when replying to critics in various publications, sometimes creating interesting developments. While many authors of negative criticism are generally well known, having been quoted in several books, Yates has managed to find some rare criticism (positive and negative). The negative ones start with Tom Davis, from Birmingham University. In 1973, writing on the occasion of the author's death, Davis noted dishonesty in The Lord of the Rings because Tolkien was writing as a modern author to a modern audience, but he acted like he was not. The book is about the east-west confrontation. Its moral outlook is European. In the East lives a race of androids alchemically created. They are ant-like creatures with no soul, but, conveniently, they speak as an urban lower class. So, in The Lord of the Rings, we are told about a proletarian eastern society that needs to be wiped out, without recognizing these people as individuals. Davis states that Tolkien's work is simple-minded and useless because real fairy tales bolster children's maturity, while The Lord of the Rings is about arrested development. "It appeals to the childish in adults." In fact, Hobbits are treated as children but given real swords to use in combat. At least, Davis notes, the book offers a rare opportunity for literary criticism to be validated.

Yates examined the following letters refuting this criticism, and answers by Davis, who replied defending his own opinion and insisting that Tolkien offered a solution to the Cold War analogous to bombing the enemy to oblivion, because the Ring's destruction does something similar. Obviously, as Yates notes, Tolkien hated aerial bombardments, and the loss of the Ring in the book doesn't destroy the enemy, but rather makes a negotiated peace possible with other races of Men because they now are free from enslavement. About Davis, Yates concludes that it is impossible to discuss his views. Yates answered personally another critic with better success in 1980: the article was by Andrew Stibbs, titled "For Realism in Children's Fiction." In Stibbs's opinion, Tolkien's chapter "The Scouring of the Shire," where the returning heroic Hobbits drive out the invader of their homeland, presents us with a snobbish view of Sharkey and his ruffians. Stibbs also lamented the use of non-realistic fiction for children (a wrong way to educate boys and girls). Yates managed to have a constructive dialogue with Stibbs, defending fantasy as a tool to improve young readers' development. Another critic, Robert Westall, tackled a problem that takes on great importance in this book. In a 1981 article, Westall warned against depicting people as irredeemably evil in children's literature. Westall promotes the awareness of the presence of good and evil in everyone, rather than a "hunt" for the bad guys. In The Lord of the Rings, which he mistakes for a children's book, good and evil are separated, polarized, stereotyped. Sauron's servants are totally evil, and the Dark Lord has only two emotions: fear for himself and nonsensical hate for the enemy. Tolkien doesn't acknowledge the Orcs' courage: they are there to be massacred ceaselessly. The good characters are pure; if they are wrong or do bad things, it's because of the Ring's influence. Then, as in the cases of Boromir and Denethor, they need to die to redeem themselves. Tolkien's world is merciless, in Westall's criticism: be good or die. The only character that knows evil and good together in his soul is Gollum, but he too is destined to perish in the flames. Westall states that changing a derogative term (he uses as an example "dago," the insulting term identifying south European peoples) into "Orc" still permits hatred of people perceived as alien or deviant. Yates replied, stating that Orcs are not a substitute for a race of this world, and they are brainwashed: they are the ones who hate others that are different. Moreover, Tolkien didn't specify if Gollum was eternally damned. Yates notes that in *The Silmarillion* Tolkien showed the wars between Elves and Dwarves as a useless waste; this is a good example of the author's thoughts about race relations.

To Yates's reply, we could add that Frodo, too, is swayed by the Ring's power at the very end of his quest, but his penalty is "just" that of losing a finger to Gollum's assault.

In this essay, Yates gives us also her opinion of Tolkien's vision about freedom. Noting that Tolkien has been accused of being a fascist (by Fred Inglis, as an example), Yates gives us several instances regarding oppression by communist regimes: the Chinese in Tibet, the killing fields in Cambodia, Serbian aggression in the breakup of former Yugoslavia. It's clear, in Yates's opinion, that racial persecution or aggression with the aim of territorial expansion is not the exclusive preserve of fascists; evil is not equivalent to fascism. Tolkien raises the question: What do we need to do when evil shows up? He believes that a Christian's duty is to fight it. Yates concludes her essay by saying that if you love *The Lord of the Rings* you can't accept totalitarianism.

Yates is right, as should be obvious to anyone who reads Tolkien's letters. Dislike of the words "state" and "government" is clearly stated in letter 52 (already mentioned) where Tolkien writes that he's some kind of anarchist or, as an alternative, he would like an unconstitutional monarchy, given his hostility to politics and parliaments. He wanted abolition of control, so this doesn't mean he desired a tyrant king. He wrote: "give me a King whose chief interest in life is stamps, railways or race-horses." Tolkien was not only anti-totalitarian; he wanted the smallest government possible.

In the political analysis[76] by Alessandro Dal Lago, a mythological villain well known to Tolkien is examined in an unusual way. Dal Lago poses the question: who is Grendel? The answer is that he is an outcast, rejected from the human race by the will of God, living in swamps, observing and hearing from a distance the celebrations in the king's house. He's restless. He wants to belong; he is attracted by humans and their pleasures, but he's cut off from them. Like Satan in Milton's *Paradise Lost*, Grendel hates a hostile world, and he is forced to be a rebel against it. Dal Lago categorizes him like an Orc, the race Tolkien despises so much, builders of weapons, tools and machines, living in darkness. This is an industrial, a worker class, belonging to the modern world the author hates. Tolkien's critique of modernity comes from his quiet corner in Oxfordshire, protected from the turbulent modern world he sees as pathological and dangerous. We can find a similar perspective, in Dal Lago's opinion, in George MacDonald with his goblins and in H.G. Wells's ferocious Morlocks (in *The Time Machine*). Therefore, the outcasts are the working class, a group that authors like Tolkien, in their deep conservatism, fear and hate. Dal Lago is interested in exposing the mindset of the author of The Lord of the Rings; he's not interested in the Italian "battle" about Tolkien. In his opinion, the appropriation from elements of the literary left is just the attempt to prevent the conservative interpretation by Italian scholars.

Tolkien the Conservative? Or Tolkien the Artist?

Tolkien certainly did not appreciate modernity, nor was he at all progressive. It only needs to be established whether, and in what way, he was conservative (or reactionary, etc.). His fantasy world was characterized by not being modern (in its narrative) and gives the reader the impression of a perhaps idealized past. It is possible that a socialist or communist intellectual could have seen Tolkien as a reactionary, as we have seen several times. However, Tolkien did not write about a recent past (Edwardian or Victorian England, for example), claiming that things were better then. He spoke of a very distant period or, rather, a period out of time; he speaks of an era that can, in no way, be recovered, a symbolic past, a mythical world on which the shutters have been drawn. There is nostalgia, a desire for something irretrievable, with no political indication of how to recover it. In some respects, the criticisms of Moorcock and Miéville can be partly considered, but they do not fully hit the target. Furthermore, denouncing the destruction of the environment, as Tolkien did, is not normally attributed to conservatives or the right wing, because they are in line with industry and capitalism. Was Tolkien a conservative? Yes, but not exclusively.

Insight into Tolkien's conservatism can be gleaned from one of his letters,[77] which is addressed to his son Christopher who then, in 1944, was training to become a military pilot in South Africa and would one day become the curator of his father's work. Tolkien deplores that his own son had to take part in the conflict and thinks the air force is something monstrous, but he understands that his son has a duty to fulfill. Maybe his feeling about the air war is "only a kind of squeamishness, perhaps, like a man who enjoys steak and kidney (or did) but would not be connected with the butchery business."

Tolkien admits that if he accepts the benefit of fighting with such weapons, then he can't refuse them. But, as he admits, he still does.

In protest against "the machine" and nostalgia, Tolkien expressed his feelings as any artist would, and was aware of the limits of his protest and the lack of a coherent ideological basis. He allowed the protest to emerge in his work. Not being a political activist or a scientist, however, he was not the one to decide what modernity could or could not be contrasted with. He did not say "how to do it." It therefore seems excessive to classify him as a petty bourgeoisie, who did not dare raise his head in protest. In his own way, he did just that, but as an artist. He expressed his own feelings, while not intending to make a complete political speech.

3

Race Issues

The Case of the Orcs

China Miéville appreciates certain aspects of Tolkien's work. What he does not appreciate, however, is the morality: Tolkien created the pattern for many fantasy tales where morality is absolute and political complexities disappear. This is convenient but abstract and unreal. Elves are the aristocracy of this world, Hobbits are the link with nature, and Orcs are evil. The good people are beautiful, the evildoers horrible. War means glory; heroic death is noble. So, with a sort of genetic determinism a conservative world is created, ordered and clean. While Moorcock criticized Tolkien as a representative of a certain social class, and a defender of his values in his writings, Miéville paid attention to what is represented in the text and found class divisions in Tolkien's secondary world. Certainly, the good ones are all fair skinned and often blonde (but let us remember, however, that there are also bad guys with fair skin). As for the Orcs, Tolkien gives a description that, according to today's standards, would be, at the very least, indelicate: in the *Letters*[1] they are described as "squat, broad, flat-nosed, sallow-skinned, with wide mouths and slant eyes: in fact degraded and repulsive versions of the (to Europeans) least lovely Mongol-types." Their weapons are often curved, similar to scimitars.

In an article in *The Guardian*[2] by John Yatt, the outcome of the battle of Helm's Deep is analyzed. On the one hand, the men of Rohan are described thus: "Yellow is their hair, and bright are their spears. Their leader is very tall." On the other, Isengard's Orcs are described as savages. This racial difference between the white man and the "dark men" (the Orcs) has brutal consequences after the battle. "10,000 orcs are massacred with a kind of Dungeons and Dragons version of biological warfare" while the wild men surviving the battle can freely go home. As those who have read the book doubtlessly know, there is no use of any biological warfare in the Orcs' defeat (and death), but the meaning of this note is clear enough. Yatt also notes that warriors coming from the south and the east to participate in the Sauron-led war present themselves with dark faces and eyes and long black hair; in general, they look quite evil. The columnist concludes that The Lord of the Rings is racist, immersed in the idea that race determines behavior: Orcs are evil by birth—they have no choice. They also have several characteristics diametrically opposed to the white characters. So, the Orcs' representation is a trite catalogue of clichés and stereotypes with obvious allusion to people of color. Tolkien's Manichaeism, or the clear division between the good and evil of this world (in this case, the secondary world of Middle-earth), seems to have left the Orcs hopelessly on the wrong side. According to this critic, they have almost every undesirable characteristic, in the eyes of the white characters, although Tolkien has never professed racist ideas (judging from his letters, it's quite the opposite: the one I mentioned above is the only one that can be seen as ambiguous). Finally, Yatt notes that these repellent opponents are certainly not reminiscent of the epic of other myths, such as *The Iliad*, where nobles clash on both sides (Yatt may be right regarding *The Iliad* but, obviously, in many other myths, monsters and monstrous folks are there in good numbers).

Returning to the Trotskyite critic John Molyneux, he points out, like others, that the existence of races is a fundamental fact in Tolkien's work. He notes that Orcs are and remain bad; they have no redeeming qualities. "At no point in the entire narrative do we encounter an Orc who is anything other than a merciless enemy."

As a consequence, the reader's sentiment about the Orcs is never a positive one. On the contrary, the most obvious feeling is a sort of delight when the Orcs are defeated, routed and massacred by the good guys.

China Miéville.

Although he judges this to be obvious racism, Molyneux notes that it is not emotionally registered. It doesn't feel like racism. He noted the same reaction in other people, who hate racism but don't react to this treatment reserved to Orcs, and love The Lord of the Rings. The reason for this would be that, first of all, in Tolkien, racism is not the denial of the humanity of those who are discriminated against in real life, as races actually exist in his books. Furthermore, the cruelty that the different races within this book face does not necessarily indicate racism; the Free Peoples of Middle-earth are fundamentally correct in their actions. If they kill Orcs, it is only because they meet them in battle (and they are killed, rather than enslaved or tortured), and the Free Peoples are an example of overcoming differences, even racial ones, in the name of a common cause: see for example, the friendship between Gimli and Legolas, or Gimli's admiration for Galadriel.

So, in saying this, does Molyneux let Tolkien get away with it? No, not at all. As one might expect, according to the critic, the fact that races do exist is a precise political choice and an ideology on Tolkien's part. He then goes on to note that the whole narrative is built around an East-West separation, where the West and its people evidently have the moral high ground. The different communities of the East and the South are described in a very schematic way, and are on the side of evil, be it by will or by constraint. The differences between the factions are such that if our critic did not already know that The Lord of the Rings was conceived before the Second World War, he would have thought that the Cold War had led Tolkien's pen.

The contraposition between light and darkness could be an explanation as to the colors used to recognize moral traits: white as a symbol of light is good, black as the symbol of darkness is bad. In the words of Italian critic Giovanni Agnoloni: "I think that, in Tolkien's works, there's no room for racism. His harsh opinion on Adolph Hitler, as emphasized in his Letters, excludes whatever possible racist angle in his mindset. This definitely is not one of the aspects of 'Shadow' evoked in Tolkien. Light and Shadow, a collection of essays that focuses on several different antinomies between 'luminous' and 'obscure' in his Legendarium, including spiritual, philosophical, psychological, historical and ethical ones. I believe that the latter ones were particularly important to Tolkien, who, as a fervent Catholic, uncompromisingly refused the Evil in all its manifestations. I tend to think that the (generally) 'white-skinned' appearance of good characters—I am particularly thinking of Elves— is rather (iconographically) connected with the angelic figures of the Christian tradition, whereas the dark-skinned enemies are just another manifestation of 'demonic' forces. But another reason could also be the impression left upon the author by the Nordic sagas that, as a scholar, he knew in depth."[3]

Verlyn Flieger[4] states indeed that light, and the relationship of the sub-creators with it, shapes the world of Middle-earth. Referring to *The Silmarillion*, she argues that the use of light comes from Tolkien's Christian belief. Light is given by the Valar, and it's a sign of Providence. The first action of Melkor against Elves and Men is to strike against the light.

Where Is Racism in Tolkien's Works?

Oğuzhan Yalçın, from Turkey, in his thesis[5] tries to find racism in Tolkien's work. After examining the critical reaction (and the statements about Tolkien, the racist), Yalçın defines races as a false classification of people not based on any scientific truth. So, race is a political concept, a tool used to an end. One of the components of racism is prejudice, an opinion formed without previous knowledge. The use of power in conjunction with prejudice generates habits, procedures, social policies that subjugate a race in favor of another. Institution and social structures may be involved in racism. Examining Tolkien's work, Yalçın finds that Middle-earth peoples have different qualities and features, but the author never treated a race in a contemptuous way. Skin color or culture is not a reason for punishment or discrimination. The elder race of Elves is superior in many ways, but we see Men not very different from them. Moreover, Gimli, the Dwarf, enjoys a relationship of mutual respect with Galadriel, the Elven queen. The Elves in turn will need cooperation from other races to face Sauron's menace. Men are mortal; this is the "gift" from Ilúvatar, making them restless and destined to another world beyond Arda. While the Men in the west remained uncorrupted, the Easterlings are influenced by Morgoth. Differences between Men are born from their behavior and choices, not from racial differences or prejudices. Therefore, it's the necessity of defending their homeland that forces Gondor's Men to fight against other people (like Easterlings, Southrons, etc.). There's no hatred or a feeling of racial superiority at the base of this conflict, and obviously after the War of the Ring this opposition is going to end. The Hobbits are not, apparently, the most gifted people of Middle-earth. Still, they are going to take Gandalf himself by surprise with their persistence and courage. Another example is the town of Bree and the Prancing Pony Inn, where everyone is welcome. In the town, actually, Men and Hobbits live together. Another old race is the Dwarves, resilient, laborious, and stubborn. They are the craftsmen of Middle-earth. With regard to Orcs, Yalçın thinks Peter Jackson's movies depicted their appearance in a way to arouse the condemnation of critics and intellectuals because they look darker than the books would validate. Anyway, blackness has no negative connotation per se in Tolkien's world: the evil powers love the darkness and fear the light. Orcs' unattractiveness and lousy smell are due to the evil that corrupted them. And besides, they are not a separate race: the Orcs are Elves and Men corrupted and tortured by Melkor. Evil influence transforms every creature into something entirely different: the Hobbit Gollum/Smeagol is an example of that. Tom Shippey notes that Sam is not disposed to any kindness towards Gollum, but, after experiencing the burden of carrying the Ring, spares his life on Mount Doom, despite being betrayed by him previously.[6] Even Sam's simple mind understands Gollum's pain.

There's racial hatred against the Orcs? As Yalçın observes, after the destruction of the Ring, most Orcs flee, but the Free Peoples don't pursue them. Only some of those in Sauron's service decide to stand their ground and face destruction. In conclusion, every race has different features, but there's not a real form of racism in Tolkien.

Races as Human Qualities and Aspects

American professor and writer Richard L. Purtill[7] thinks that races in Tolkien's work are like aspects of human beings. Elves and Men are similar, but Elves represent the love for arts, aesthetics, and knowledge.

The most distinctive trait of Elves is immortality. This is a privilege. But it also means that they are bound to the world and its destiny till the end. So, if Men envy the Elves their immortality, Elves, in turn, are tired of their endless lives and envy Men their mortality. Moreover, Elves can't accept time changing the world, and their grip on it slipping away. They cling to the past, but doing so they refuse God's design, the natural proceeding of the story. Sauron was able to exploit this weakness: Elves are greedy in a way; they have a will to power in their desire to keep things as they are. King Denethor, a nobleman with Elven blood, is similar to them in his resistance to change. Men are nobles, knights, heroes in a traditional sense, while Hobbits as a race don't frequently display courage, but they can be brave if the need arises. Hobbits' unforeseen bravery can change the world; this is what happens in The Lord of the Rings. In *The Hobbit*, Bilbo is seen as a useless little fellow by the Dwarves, who have difficulty believing what Gandalf said, enlisting him in the adventure as a "burglar." But as the group travels east, Bilbo manages to help the Dwarves many times. He's inventive, and he has a moral stature that compels him to come to aid his fellow adventurers in dangerous situations. He's successful, and because of this, grudgingly the Dwarves come to recognize his importance. As Bilbo tries to help Dwarves, Men, Elves to reach an agreement about the division of Smaug's treasure, Purtill notes, the Hobbit grows to almost heroic stature. Purtill notes that Dwarves are a race that shows its weakness in the most evident way because of their material greed: they desire treasure, gold, richness.

Cooperation and Change

As we have seen, races in Middle-earth have a mix of qualities and shortcomings. They also have a story of distrust or hostility to each other. British critic Cristina Scull talks about that in her essay with the fitting title "Open Minds, Closed Minds in The Lord of the Rings."[8] Open-mindedness seems to be a quality held in great respect by Tolkien. Prejudice and mistrust do exist in Middle-earth. But many of his characters struggle to evolve, expanding the boundaries of their experience. Scull states that a "plea for more tolerance" is implicit in Tolkien's narration.

Scull shows that there is mistrust not only between different races, but also within races. The Hobbits are divided into three branches: Fallohides, Stoor, and Harfoots.

They are wary of other Hobbits: not only those of a different breed but even those living in another part of the Shire. They see Bree's inhabitants as outsiders; Lobelia Sackville-Baggins uses the word "Brandybuck" as an insult against Frodo (it's a family name). Everyone is "queer" for everyone else. Scull notes that even when the War of the Ring came to Hobbit lands, they stuck to their own closed-mindedness. The Hobbit dictator, Lotho, was ignorant of the world. He used the aid of Men to gain control of the Shire, but later he was eliminated by them. The Hobbits were not able to rebel or regain freedom until Frodo and his three friends from the Fellowship return. The Shire is saved by the leadership of Hobbits who have seen the external world and learned, but this is a lesson that many will not remember. The Hobbits are just concerned about what happened to their land and hardly ask anything about Frodo, Sam, Merry, and Pippin's adventures. The Hobbits' case is not isolated. It's quite common, with the rivalry and mistrust between Elves and Dwarves as the case more obvious to Tolkien's readers. But, as Cristina Scull notes, while Tolkien shows many closed minds in his world, he immediately gives us examples of people who work to overcome these limitations. First, some characters change because of compassion. In the beginning, Frodo thinks Bilbo should have killed Gollum, so Gandalf has to intervene and tell him that he talks that way because he's never seen him. After having met Gollum, Frodo will show mercy several times (Sam is not as quick to change his mind). After returning to the Shire and fighting to free it from Saruman's influence, Frodo strives to win this struggle with the minimum bloodletting and avoid excessive vengeance.

Other characters overcome their differences, fighting together in the common struggle against Sauron. Legolas the elf and Gimli the Dwarf constitute the typical example. Scull notes that Tolkien is realistic in these developments: there's not a "miraculous rapprochement" of Elves and Dwarves, but an effort to understand each other.

Less remembered is the race of the Wild Men of the Woods, the Woses or Drúedain: the Men of Rohan treat them as barbarians and savages. But they give help to the Rohirrim anyway. Aragorn will compensate them with a land of their own, where other people will not enter if not invited.

Close-mindedness in Boromir and Denethor is not about races, even if they are prideful and, maybe, a bit self-important. It's about the city they represent, Minas Tirith, capital of the kingdom of Gondor. It's the most significant human domain involved in the war and the bulwark against Sauron's armies. Denethor, the king, and his firstborn, Boromir, approach all problems with the aim of defending their land. Denethor is also unwilling to abandon the stewardship of the kingdom. He's the Lord of Gondor; in his opinion, the allies are inferior in status. Every goal, even if fair and noble, takes second place behind Gondor's salvation. Scull suggests that his feeling for the city is motivated by self-love and the pride of his political position. So, when he thinks that he has no surviving heir, he loses interest and thinks about suicide. Denethor is not ready to perceive the greater good, and his son can't overcome his suspicions and lack of confidence in the allies (the Elves in particular). Boromir doesn't understand why everyone is so reluctant about the Ring, even if apparently he accepts the decisions at the Council of Elrond, where the allies formulate a strategy for the conflict. His distrust of the Elves and wizards remains, so he'll try to take the Ring by force after Frodo refuses to give it. Anyway, Boromir looks like a loyal member of the Fellowship until that moment, and he dies trying to save Merry and Pippin from the Orcs. He would have accepted Aragorn as a leader, a thing that we couldn't say about his father. But he puts his homeland first, in a moment that requires a more open mind. Ironically, the returning king Aragorn will allow the stewardship of Gondor to continue, with Faramir (Denethor's second son) as the leader.

The Orcs are the only race that never receives merciful treatment, Scull notes. In victory, the Rohirrim will spare the Wild Men of Dunland, employed by Saruman against Rohan. Likewise, Aragorn makes peace with the Men who fought in Sauron's service. He gives land to released slaves. The much-criticized exception is that of Orcs. While there's a moment of compassion for human enemies (we all remember Sam's thoughts about the dead Southron), to kill Orcs is a good thing. They are the enemy that the good guys may destroy without regret. Scull states that Tolkien was aware of that, but he didn't change the perspective that Orcs are irredeemably evil. Tolkien's opinion is a bit evasive in the *Letters*,[9] where he affirms he's not competent enough, as a theologian, to say if the nature of his Orcs is heretical or not, but they are not evil in origin, because they are not created as Orcs, because Morgoth has twisted and corrupted other creatures to make this race. Still, in the books, the Orcs do exist as such and they are, without exception, wicked and evil. In Scull's opinion, Orcs could be one negative aspect of human nature. This would give a more symbolic significance to their destruction. But she refrains from insisting on this hypothesis and admits that the Orcs are an exception to the tolerant nature shown in the books.

This essay is an appropriate response to the many critics who claim Tolkien wrote about an immutable world where everyone has to stay at the assigned place (for instance, Michael Moorcock). In fact, a mind that doesn't accept some kind of change is often defeated.

Orcs Don't Change, Orcs Are Real

Helen Armstrong[10] examined the nature of good and evil characters in Tolkien's works. Her essay, titled "Good Guys, Bad Guys, Fantasy and Reality," emphasizes their relationship with today's world. In *The Hobbit*, we encounter the Goblins (Orcs) as weapon-loving people: they can manufacture them, or they can force their prisoners to do the work, hinting that these unfortunate slaves are worked to death. It's plausible that Orcs are the creators of modern machines, especially those used to destroy and kill people en masse. The Orcs, as Armstrong notes, were in origin creatures of the god Melkor (in the *Lost Tales*), then Tolkien wrote (in *The Silmarillion*) that they are bred from corrupted Elves. In any case, they behave following predictable lines. They don't reform; not one of them switches sides or shows free will. They are not followers of their evil master. They act as cannon fodder or disposable tools.

While this is not what other critics say about Orcs, they definitely don't change sides, so we have not a single Orc who redeems himself in the whole of Tolkien's works. Still, if they are tools, they are intelligent ones. Tolkien surely has humans in mind when writing about them or defining their behavior because Men can commit the same kind of evil. In Tolkien's work, Armstrong states, the Orc is automatically an enemy. So characters that meet Orcs fight them, run, or hide. Whatever the choice, if they fail, they die unless the Orcs have a reason to postpone their killing. Armstrong notes that since Tolkien was a soldier in the First World War and lived through the Second World War, he knew about real evil.

Armstrong admits that the abuser himself may have been abused in the past, but she thinks that human behavior can reach a point where there's no common ground between perpetrator and victim. She gives the examples of soldiers raping and killing civilians, gangs killing their victims with kicks and knives, mass killings, and systematic rape and enslavement of women in conflicts like the wars in former Yugoslavia or Azerbaijan. It comes to a point where the victims can't see any common humanity with their tormentors.

Human beings can be something alien, cruel, terrifying. And they can enjoy it. To deny that such people really exist would be an illusion. So, in Tolkien's work, we have ugly personifications of our fears, like the Orcs, and there are real living people who receive better treatment. The Haradrim or Easterlings are allies of Sauron, but Armstrong notes an instance in which an Easterling tribe did not betray its loyalty to western people (in *The Silmarillion*). People like Wormtongue (King Théoden's treacherous counselor) turned bad, but they enjoyed free will. The Mouth of Sauron, one of the Black Númenóreans, is the worst because he was from an ancient and noble breed of Men, so his betrayal is due to greed, not to fear or ignorance.

Orcs Are Human Beings

About the Orcs, the aforementioned Guido Schwarz thinks[11] that Tolkien's vision is dangerous, so dangerous that it's the real reason he wrote his criticism about Tolkien's work. Orcs are mean, smelly, ugly, and want to kill us. They also have bad teeth. With his typical humor, Schwarz notes that maybe it's just because we have better dentists than they do; it doesn't prove we are better people. The problem with Tolkien is that if you kill an Orc you didn't do something evil, killing another living being. You are a hero because Orcs have to be killed.

Once the Orcs were Elves, Schwarz notes. Then Melkor captured them and mutated and tortured them until they became the opposite. Orcs embody the evil in us, the dark instincts or thoughts that make us imperfect. They are a split part of ourselves, not a race of their own because this would give them a right to live. Now they are so different that we don't recognize them as a part of us, so we can kill them without remorse.

But if we kill the "Orc" in reality we are killing another human being. Moreover, we are not getting rid of the evil part of ourselves: instead, we are making it grow. Orcs, on the other hand, hate everything and themselves; often they do that by hating other Orcs.

In Tolkien's works, every subtlety is made to lead us to hate them. They are evil, bred to be evil. They can generate, so Orc children must exist somewhere. Are they evil, and deserving to be killed too? We don't know because the author never shows very young Orcs, just Orcs of different sizes. The orcs destroy nature and fell trees (we see them in Peter Jackson's movies); they build machines and siege engines, everything Tolkien hated and would have liked to banish from the world. When they attack, they come in large numbers, so to defeat them is always a sign of bravery. The final defeat of the Orcs means that we can eliminate evil, but to destroy evil in ourselves we can't just chop off a limb. We need first to outsource this evil to someone else. This means that we'll feel justified in thinking others responsible for our shortcomings because in real life we have no Orcs to slaughter. So, Tolkien is leading us in a bad direction, telling us that we can destroy evil by killing other people. But this scheme exists in many fantasy novels.

Dwarves as Jews

The similarity between Dwarves and Jews is defined as obvious by Tolkien himself in an interview, as quoted by Rebecca Brackmann,[12] and in letter 176,[13] where Tolkien says that, like the Jews, the Dwarves are at once native and alien in their habitations. Brackmann states that the depiction of Dwarves changes after the publication of *The Hobbit*, and that several traits of their description come from anti-Semitic stereotypes. Dwarves are not included in the heroic ethics that we find in Tolkien's work, at first. Probably the author became aware of this and changed their presentation in The Lord of the Rings. In Tolkien's early work, the depiction of Dwarves followed Scandinavian legends. They could be evil and even ally themselves with Orcs. In *The Silmarillion*, the worst examples of their greed and violence begin to be expunged from Tolkien's work, but at the same time, as Brackmann notes, the author's perspective becomes ambiguous. Dwarves are a separate race; their creation is by the Vala Aulë, one of Ilúvatar's helpers. Aulë doesn't exactly remember the form of the "children" Ilúvatar wants to create, so the result is different from Elves and Men. This is equivalent to saying that Dwarves are not really children of God. Moreover, they lack individual will because Aulë is not able to give it to them. The Vala has crossed the limits he should have respected as a sub-creator, but (differently from Melkor, we note) he repents and offers to destroy his creatures. Ilúvatar, in his compassion, allows the Dwarves to have life and awareness, but he refuses them as his firstborn children. They will remain Aulë's sons and adopted sons for Ilúvatar, who forecasts future contrasts between them and the "real" children.

So Dwarves are the oldest race but not the chosen one. Brackmann finds a similarity with those Christian writers who thought Jews were replaced as the chosen people by Christians (supersession). The similarities do not end there. Dwarves are given Scandinavian names, but their language is different, so complicated and ill-sounding that they are not allowed to use it, except in their private conversations.[14] Later Tolkien created the Dwarves' language, using Semitic-sounding words.

Brackmann states that, in *The Hobbit*, written before the complete evolution of the author's Middle-earth, we can already see the use of "anti–Semitic tropes" to depict the Dwarves' difficult relationship with people they encounter. As for their looks, the Dwarves' beards are a typical characteristic of Jews in medieval depiction. In *The Hobbit*, we see the Dwarves as cowards and greedy. This is in line with stereotypes in use when Tolkien wrote the book. Brackmann also states that, like Jews, Dwarves are also continuously complaining and whining (about Beorn's house chosen as a refuge by Gandalf, or about being forced to travel inside barrels when escaping from the Elves). By contrast, the Hobbit Bilbo—who starts out as a complete novice—matures during his adventures, effectively becoming the company's leader. Moreover, the Dwarves are obsessed with the gold that belonged to them, even if they make clear that their present situation is not bad. They don't really need the gold, but they start a quest to get it back. Even if they fight to remove Smaug the dragon, a worthwhile enterprise, the main motive of the Dwarves' actions is the love for gold. When they savor the treasure and can touch it, they become even more avaricious. Their behavior is clearly wrong when they deny any reward for Bard, the hero who killed Smaug; they refuse any compensation for Lake-town's people, who lost everything when the dragon destroyed their city. The Dwarves' refusal is even more striking because the Men who are in need helped them win the treasure. Brackmann notes that the dragon could have put a curse on the gold, causing this behavior because it's what happens in *Beowulf*, a poem that could have been a direct inspiration for Tolkien. But the Hobbit Bilbo is not affected by anything similar, so what we see is the depiction of Dwarfish greed. This way, Dwarves are outsiders with respect to the heroic ethos of Tolkien's world. In Tolkien's words, they often are treacherous and tricky. Thorin and his group are decent people, but you must not expect too much from them.

It's a known fact that Tolkien, when asked about his "arisch" origin by a German publishing house in 1938, sent a very pugnacious answer[15] deploring any race doctrine. Brackmann notes that even an unfavorable critic like China Miéville defends Tolkien against charges of racism based on facts like this: in his opinion, it's true that Tolkien wrote of a world in which races do exist and define individuals, but he's not a racist. Brackmann thinks that active discrimination and persecution is not the only face of anti–Semitism: there's also the belief that racial Jewish identity does exist, complete with specific physical and psychological traits. So one can have Jewish friends and still be an anti–Semite, maybe being unaware of this. Brackmann speculates that Tolkien had understood what he did with the Dwarves' identity in *The Hobbit* and felt guilt or a need to rectify it. This feeling could have had a part in his answer to the German publisher quoted above. As a fact, she states, the author changed the Dwarves' depiction in The Lord of the Rings. Gimli, the Dwarf in the Fellowship, is different from the Dwarves in *The Hobbit*. He's not motivated by revenge or by financial gain, but he shows unwavering bravery. He's not "different"; he fully adheres to Tolkien's heroic values. He quotes proverbs in which these values are present, so the whole race is reflected in his spotless conduct. In *The Hobbit*, Thorin and his company are committed to the reconquest of the Lonely Mountain for vengeance and treasure. In The Lord of the Rings, when passing through the mines of Moria, Gimli doesn't mention the treasure that could be found there; he just desires to visit an ancient domain that was home to his people and is important to him for cultural reasons. When he knows Lady Galadriel's beauty, he says that it's above all the jewels beneath the earth. Talking with Legolas, the elf, he exalts the beauty of the Glittering Caves. When Legolas says, as a joke, that Gimli should not tell other Dwarves of the caves because they would destroy their beauty to extract minerals, the Dwarf answers that no one of his people would do anything like that. This is, obviously, in direct contrast with the way Dwarves are depicted in *The Hobbit*. Moreover, with Gimli's depiction, we know that Dwarves are a warrior race: their axes are feared, their battle cry is heard on many battlefields.

Brackmann states that in Appendix A of The Lord of the Rings, Dwarves are substantiated in their aversion to evil. The Rings can make them greedier, but nothing else. This way, the avarice of Dwarves could have an external source.

Tolkien couldn't rewrite *The Hobbit* extensively to conform to his newfound respect for the Dwarves' moral qualities. Brackmann states that, although he changed some scenes, Tolkien could not do more without altering the book's plot sensibly. Anyway, Gimli's heroic stature and a new appraisal of the Dwarves in The Lord of the Rings put the Dwarves back into Ilúvatar's design. As for the Dwarves' depictions in other works, Brackmann examines some of the *Unfinished Tales*. But we can't know in what form the author would have published this material, had he lived long enough to do it.

Now we need to ask ourselves if the difference in the Dwarves' depiction between *The Hobbit* and The Lord of the Rings is as intense as Brackmann thinks. Regarding Dwarves' bravery, we have Thorin coming out from his fortress with his followers and participating in the Battle of the Five Armies. In Brackmann's opinion, it's not clear if heroism is the reason, or they want to defend their treasure no matter the risk. Moreover, when fighting with Orcs and Wargs, we are told that the great Dwarf gleamed like gold in a dying fire. This description could be seen as undermining Thorin's valor, creating another reference to the Dwarves' love of gold. As for the cause for the Dwarves' heroism, even if they had decided to fight for self-interest, it's not relevant for two reasons. First, because in any case, they have left the relative security of their fortified position; second, because whatever their motive, they are fighting and dying. As for the gleaming like gold undermining the idea that a Dwarf can be a brave fighter, Brackmann's opinion is stretched and based on an arguable interpretation. So, while in *The Hobbit* the Dwarves are avaricious and ingrate, they are not cowards. Are they whiny? They indeed oppose every idea or solution that Bilbo proposes. We need, first of all, to note that this is part of the gradual growth of Bilbo in their eyes: at the beginning, they belittle everything about their Hobbit companion, then they learn to trust him, and at the end, they give a grudging acknowledgment of his qualities. The main Dwarfish moan is about being shut into barrels to escape the Elven prison. Now, we know that Bilbo's idea is going to succeed, but the perspective that Thorin and his companions are facing is not so appealing. They will float in the water with minimum access to air and a distinct chance of drowning without being able to do anything to save themselves. After that, they'll be totally reliant on being pulled out from the barrels by external aid. There's nothing to worry about, is there? In a fairy story world, they get a positive result: with some passengers a bit worse for wear, everyone is alive and reasonably well. It seems a quite desperate expedient in the real world, one that could easily result in several deaths. It's not difficult to understand if the Dwarves see Bilbo's proposal as a last-ditch solution, to be tried only when every other option is impossible. As for Gimli's generous courage in The Lord of the Rings, different from the shrewd behavior of Thorin and his company, the stakes in that story are very high, and Gimli is aware of that, so it's doubtful if the author has changed the whole race's behavior. Ultimately, while Brackmann is crafty in creating her argument, the only authentic, solid basis is Thorin's company's greed and pettiness.

There's a direct answer to this essay on Dwarves: Renée Vink, a Dutch author and translator, has done a thorough examination of Brackmann's evidence.[16] The first element she challenges is that a male beard is Jewish because Dwarves in Norse sources are depicted with beards. Tolkien was undoubtedly aware of this. Vink takes exception to the Dwarves' continuous complaining, noting that the author portrays them as individuals with different dispositions. Some are excessively whiny; some are moderate in their complaints (and the Hobbit Bilbo is not exempt from this weakness). Vink has no explanation for the supposed change of attitude by Tolkien regarding Jewish courage. Maybe the Dwarves in The Hobbit weren't imagined as Jews at the time. It's quite improbable that Tolkien didn't have present the biblical stories of warlike Jews, but it's possible that some facts in World War II, for example the Warsaw insurrection in 1943, changed the author's mind. Still, we have no evidence of a change of mind. Dwarfish names from the Poetic Edda don't give a definite answer. Some suggest fear, and others don't. Brackmann thinks that some (unpublished at the time) accounts in The Silmarillion about the Dwarves' creation already show the link with Jews existing. But there are two versions of the story. Vink states that the Dwarves, as we see them in The Hobbit, are more related to the Norse myth, and the creation account criticized by Brackamm was written after that book, so the comparison between Dwarves and Jews is a subsequent one. The racial language of the Dwarves as a secret speech is also from a later time.

Vink defines two hypotheses: Tolkien, influenced by anti–Semitic medieval sources, gave a negative view of the Dwarves, then rectified it after witnessing the tragic events of the Second World War. Or he took inspiration from the Nordic sources that gave a negative portrait as well, then gradually he took a more sympathetic outlook on the

Dwarves, first in *The Hobbit*, then in The Lord of the Rings. Greed and good craftsmanship could derive from the myth but also from a racial stereotype.

In a later rewriting of *The Hobbit*, Tolkien made Thorin's greediness not a racial trait but a personal flaw. So it's clear that the author revised his description here. Still, Vink notes that in the *Unfinished Tales*, the Dwarves' greediness appears again. To make it even more complicated, in *The Peoples of Middle-earth* we have members of a sub-race of Dwarves, the Petty-Dwarves, being mistreated by their brothers. Finrod the elf, indeed, willing to extend the fortress of Nargothrond, enlists the aid of the Great Dwarves that have no problem in expelling their smaller brethren. There's no doubt that Finrod and his Dwarf friends look very bad here.

Vink's conclusion about the Jews-Dwarves analogy is that an accurate analysis of the sources negates a complete correspondence, as Brackmann tries to demonstrate. The similarities exist, but they are partial, or in part, speculative.

An analysis about the Dwarves races by David A. Funk[17] gives us more points for consideration. Funk observes (quoting from *The Silmarillion*) that the Dwarves' creator, Aulë, had a perpetual enmity with Melkor, the rebel Ainur. Melkor was envious of Aulë's craftsmanship, because he desired to make things on his own, but was not able to. Melkor remained a destructor or a perverter of others' creations. Funk states that the creation of Dwarves by Aulë is caused by his foresight about the need for a sturdy, resistant race to help the First-born (Elves and Men) in the long fight against evil. While there are enmities between the Dwarves and the First-born, their biggest efforts are against Melkor's minions.

Moreover, Dwarves are simple, understandable characters; they provide a link between everyday life and dangerous adventure because you'll find them in both. For example, they help Gandalf with the fireworks in the Shire at the beginning of The Lord of the Rings. These silent workers and hardy warriors balance out the elegance and refinement of the Elves. They are not seduced by Saruman's rhetoric, and even Sauron can't tame them using the Rings. Tolkien noted in The Lord of the Rings that Dwarves can't be enslaved by them. As for lust for power, Dwarves are not susceptible to it. They want to stay on their own, so we don't have any "empire" built by them in Tolkien's legendarium.

Dwarves' qualities and shortcomings are based on human traits, as usual with Tolkien's storytelling. So this race can be noted for the pride in its craftiness, perseverance, secretiveness, avarice, and many other distinctive features, but they are not really alien in their thinking.

Dwarves are not famous for physical beauty, but they can create wonderful, durable objects and goods. So whatever the stereotypes Tolkien used imagining them, they are a positive force; after Sauron's defeat, they are destined to return peacefully to their work.

I believe that it is necessary, then, to frame the problem of racism in Tolkien: On the one hand, we remember that the author never declared himself a racist, nor did he attribute the mark of a higher origin to his people or to his beloved Nordic myths. On the other hand, the Orcs are presented to us as the main enemy, the same Orcs who are simply described as dirty and bad. However, if the racial division of the humanoids of Middle-earth is discrimination, it is based on objective differences, clearly perceptible and therefore not really closely related to the concept of real racism. The Orcs present us with another problem, in my opinion: more on that later. Races in the legendarium are, between other things, something like social classes in the real world: the Hobbits are the peasants, the Elves are the nobles, and so on. I recognize that classism may have been an aspect of Tolkien's personality and work, as well as that of a man of this time, and therefore do not necessarily rebuff the critics' ideas on this point. I do not think it possible to brand an author who loves his people a racist. The fact that the heroic members of the Fellowship of the Ring are all white is largely justified by the type of literary operation Tolkien performed, that is using Nordic myths and medieval sources to create his imaginary world (or "creating an epic for England").

4

Sex and Gender in
The Lord of the Rings Trilogy

Obviously the "anachronistic" nature of Tolkien's work, in addition to raising the accusation of political and economic conservatism, was bound to open another front for him: sexuality, women's rights and equality, and the very ability to relate to the female universe. In his review[1] of *The Return of the King* critic Edwin Muir launched an attack, starting with the fairytale atmosphere of The Lord of the Rings trilogy and the scarce importance of normal female relationships to many of the protagonists, giving the reader the image of a world full of children: the characters are like children, pretending to be adults and heroes. Hobbits are children who can never reach puberty whilst humans can be situated at the end of middle school. None of them know anything about women. Tolkien noted with annoyance[2] that he would have liked to hear what women thought about Muir's "knowledge of women." The criticism, strange but evocative, makes us think about the estrangement of a modern reader, struggling with this plot where relations between the two sexes do exist (for example: Éowyn, who falls in love with Aragorn before shifting her interest to Faramir; Aragorn's love for Arwen; Sam and his Rose Cotton) but do not really seem passionate or painful. They are treated as abstract or platonic. Such relationships seem relegated to the story's periphery, and there certainly are not moments of tension or betrayal, as in the legend of Lancelot and Guinevere, and no dramatic heroines, like Brunhilde in the Nordic sagas.

Certainly, armed conflict is the essential theme of The Lord of the Rings, and it is a story mainly involving men. However, the minor importance of women has been interpreted as misogyny on Tolkien's part. The aforementioned Catharine Stimpson, after accusing Tolkien of class snobbery, also moves on to the machismo accusation: "Behind the moral structure is a regressive emotional pattern. For Tolkien is irritatingly, blandly, traditionally masculine."

119

No Sex—We Are Hobbits

Feminist scholar Brenda Partridge wrote a controversial essay[3] about sexuality in The Lord of the Rings. This belongs to those criticisms addressed towards Tolkien's work, starting from an extremely modern and politically polarized sensitivity, and from a political point of view. The essayist states that Tolkien perceives women as only being fit for traditional roles, through an extremely conservative point of view: even though they may be beautiful and solemn, their characters are dull. For example, a woman who should be powerful, Goldberry (Tom Bombadil's wife), is shown as a housewife. Yes, she's beautiful, divine, enchanting: when Frodo and his fellow Hobbits visit Tom Bombadil's house her sight gives them joy. But when her husband and the Hobbits start a conversation between males, she disappears from the scene, maybe to sleep or to take care of some domestic chore.

Partridge admits that Galadriel is a more powerful character. The Elf Queen of Lothlórien is more influential than her husband, Celeborn, who is less accurately characterized. She is a combination of a fertility goddess, Venus (the classic goddess of love), and the Virgin Mary (as recognized by Tolkien himself in letter 142). Her power is even more remarkable because she can resist the lure of the Ring: when Frodo gives it to her, she gives it back. Her gifts will be indispensable to Sam and Frodo's survival in their quest to go to Mordor and destroy the Ring. But, in Partridge's opinion, Galadriel, with all her wisdom and power, is just a remote and idealized female divinity, standing on a pedestal and inspiring the knights: a glorified, stereotyped character, removed from the real world and transformed into a distant icon.

Éowyn, the Rohirrim princess, is not a goddess, and is thus not as powerful as Goldberry or Galadriel. A character with some complexity, she's unhappy about the limitations her female condition implies. She's wavering between obedience to her uncle (the king of Rohan, Théoden) and the desire to perform heroic deeds. Tolkien appears sympathetic to her feelings, and we'll see Éowyn riding into battle disguised as a warrior, and fighting the Nazgûl king. Doing this, she has abandoned the task she was conferred by King Théoden, to rule the kingdom while the men went to war.

She distinguished herself in the fighting, but Tolkien made her rebellion an effect of unrequited love for the hero Aragorn. The solution to every problem will be marriage with a suitable companion, Faramir of Gondor.

In regard to Tolkien's approach to sexuality, the essayist finds some interesting observations based on the character Shelob, the giant spider who manages to capture Frodo while he's marching through Cirith Ungol, on his fateful trip to the Crack of Doom: "Shelob's lair, reached by entering a hole and journeying along tunnels, may also be seen to represent the female sexual orifice. At the entrance Frodo and Sam have to force themselves through the bushy, clutching growths (the pubic hair)."

Frodo pierces the web with his sword (an obvious phallic symbol), and is then overwhelmed by Shelob, who paralyzes him with poison: he must be rescued by the loyal Sam. Therefore a battle begins, a life and death struggle with the monster. Shelob represents evil, but it's a female monster. Her soft, floppy body recalls the female sex.

Thus, amidst this struggle, similar to sexual intercourse, the Hobbit penetrates and defeats Shelob, but, even when Sam is victorious, he seems fragile and dominated by the dimensions of this hideous female-monster body. Partridge, in her examination of this sequence of events, finds a large amount of strong sexual symbols. Even the light-giving phial, Galadriel's gift to Frodo, suffers the fate of being interpreted as a phallic symbol.

This scene can be interpreted as Tolkien depicting his horror of female sexuality, which would also be well rooted in his religious beliefs. Is this a correct analysis, or does Partridge see sex everywhere, making a clumsy use of Freudian symbols? Did Tolkien intend to depict a horrible monster with no ulterior motives, or did he subconsciously end up representing one of the things that scared him the most: female sexuality? Apart from the right or wrong use of Freudian symbols, Partridge sees in this fierce battle Tolkien's mindset about women. Shelob, a female being with a sexual appetite, is a threat, like other classical prior examples: Pandora, opening the infamous box and letting loose all the evil contained therein, or the Sirens singing to entice men and lure them into catastrophe. While a male enemy is an obvious threat fueled by physical strength, Partridge states, women are seen as more astute and devious. Maybe this can't be taken at face value: while male evildoers in The Lord of the Rings use mainly brute force, Sauron, their leader and lord, is different. Although he's supposed to be male, he has no physical form and must rely on a mixture of coercion, seduction, and terror to subdue his enemies, in a trial of willpower that is completely immaterial.

If we are to accept what Partridge claims to be obvious, would this be a new discovery or simply confirmation of what we already know, namely that Tolkien was a conservative (and came from a rather puritan society)?

Examining the author's background, in particular Tolkien's group of male friends, the Inklings, Partridge analyzes their intense relationship. The Inklings met regularly to talk about various academic and artistic matters, including readings of their own prose and verses. The group is a typical example of middle-class British males of the times: educated in all-boys schools, they created in adult life similar brotherhoods. They were a group of somewhat different individuals regarding beliefs or cultural interests: their clannish bond was based on the personal friendship between men. Most of the "dons" (university tutors) were married, but the university environment was mainly male. Anyway, these men needed male friendships because they did not hold the female intellect in high regard (concerning Tolkien in particular, letter 43[4] is revealing).

Partridge wonders if an erotic element was present in the relationship between C.S. Lewis and Tolkien. She states that irrefutable evidence exists about Lewis's "sexual ambiguity," but this (be it true or false) doesn't necessarily involve Tolkien. It's relevant to note that, in Tolkien's biography, Humphrey Carpenter indicates that Lewis dismissed any suggestion of homosexuality in his male relationships. Moreover, Tolkien's and Lewis's preference for simple masculine clothes, Carpenter suggests,[5] was in contrast to the dandyism and "implied homosexuality" of another segment of the Oxford population.

Anyway, deep same-sex friendships were common at the time, and they do exist likewise today. In Partridge's opinion, in The Lord of the Rings, male relationships with females are distant and formal, while friendships between males are more relaxed and helpful.

What Tolkien experienced in real life was a strong influence on his representation of male and female characters in The Lord of the Rings. The exclusion of women in his social life reflects on the scarce participation of female characters in the plot, and on their sporadic presence as well. Tolkien had mythology and courtly romance as possible sources for the depiction of women, but what he could find there was probably a reinforcement of his own prejudices, and of his contradictory views on sexuality and gender roles. Similarly, in terms of the friendship and affection between Sam and Frodo, Partridge finds proof of the homosexual relationship (or tension) between the two, which may possibly be seen as a similar error to that of her interpretation of Shelob's lair. Here, the comment made by Marion Zimmer Bradley, regarding Edmund Wilson (as we mentioned above) and the existence of the idealized male relationship in ancient literature, may prove useful.

Joseph Pearce,[6] a right-wing Christian writer, states that Partridge, "having failed to fathom the philosophical depths," has fallen into "the sexual shallows of Freudian 'analysis.'" Obviously, the interpretation of the fight between Sam and Shelob is where her obsession becomes obvious, he states. Writing from a religious perspective, Pearce affirms that fantasy writers today, ironically, would be more vulnerable to Partridge's criticism. They have reduced the genre to beautiful, muscled males and scantily clad females, in a world where might makes right. In Tolkien's works religious symbolism is present; in the fantasy games, comics, and books of today it's totally lost. "Ultimately what both the sexist and the anti-sexist interpretations have in common, apart from the overemphasis on sex itself, is a spiritual blindness."

Michael D.C. Drout and Hilary Winne[7] note that Partridge in this essay "over-reads every possible sign of sexuality and becomes positively 'phallus-happy.' Partridge's article is nearly always mocked on those occasions when it is cited."

However, it's worth noting that Nick Otty, in his aforementioned essay, explains Shelob's scene much as Partridge does. The giant female spider is a peculiar character. She's the only female in the entire book who is interested in reproduction. Tolkien gives to Shelob, a monster, all the female sexuality excised from his purer characters (Galadriel, Arwen, Éowyn, Rose Cotton). A symbol of the predatory female, the spider eats her male companions. Therefore, her attempt to eat Sam and Frodo must be interpreted as an attempt to steal the Hobbits' virginities. Nick Otty states that Shelob's death is the result of her attempted rape of Sam, but in *The Lord of the Rings* Shelob's fate is not known. Anyway, the scene is, in this critic's opinion, quite explicit.

Consequently, if Partridge's "mocked" essay is over the top, we must know indeed that she was not alone in her opinion. The reader will decide about the nature of Shelob's sex fight with the Hobbits.

A Lack of (Sexual) Life

John Molyneux, the aforementioned Trotskyite critic, considers the sexual life of Tolkien's characters—or rather, the lack thereof. Bilbo and Frodo seem to live their whole lives in celibacy, without difficulty; Elrond gets married when he is 4,000 years old; at 2,500 years old, Arwen is still a virgin; Aragorn is married at 89; and so on. Many of these characters, indeed, have the possibility of enjoying a longer life than that of a normal man by virtue of rank or race, but Faramir and Boromir, vigorous men aged 30 and 40, respectively, are celibate. There are no scenes depicting any sexual desire. For Molyneux, this is part of the fantasy world of Middle-earth, imbued with a sexism that is archaic and chivalrous, that places women on a pedestal. Molyneux contrasts

Tolkien's treatment of women with "the active misogyny found in Ian Fleming or Norman Mailer.[8] There are no wicked women or femme fatales (unless you count Shelob, the female spider) and his very few key characters are certainly not weak or subservient."

Putting Them on a Pedestal

Tolkien did, as we've seen, respect women and put them on a pedestal. Critics acknowledge this, but not as a positive trait. Joseph Pearce thinks[9] the reason is that Tolkien gives women roles that are unquestionably feminine. Feminists obviously don't like that: as we have seen, Germaine Greer expressed her disappointment when Tolkien was chosen as the most influential writer of the century. In Pearce's opinion, Éowyn, the only successful warrior woman in The Lord of the Rings, finds her "ultimate fulfillment" in marriage (with Faramir, the successor in the role of Steward of Gondor after his father's death). Leaving the path of war and choosing to be a wife is a healing of her spirit. This outcome, Pearce states, is an outrage for the feminist reader. But Éowyn's choice is not going to diminish her status. Marriage will not negate her role in the killing of the Witch-king. Pearce compares Éowyn's victory to the Virgin Mary crushing the head of the serpent. But Tolkien's respect for his women characters only meets his detractors' efforts to depict him as a male chauvinist. In Pearce's opinion, Tolkien doesn't look down on women. His error was, maybe, to put his female characters on a pedestal, in a dignified position that is perhaps undeserved. For Pearce, "Germaine Greer's hostility to Tolkien can be likened to the ingratitude of a maiden who has no desire to be saved from the dragon."

But this strong counterattack conveys the impression of a show of political (or gender) antipathies on Pearce's part, rather than a defense of Tolkien's work.

Queens and Goddesses

Philosophy teacher Chiara Nejrotti[10] analyzes Tolkien's female characters, including The Silmarillion divinities (in fact helpers of the one God, not divine themselves). Some of these are powerful: Varda, ruler of stars, and nature goddess Yavanna, the queen of all growing things. Others are compassionate and are reminiscent of Christian values: for example Nienna, the mourner, teacher of hope and mercy. One figure common in pagan pantheons is not present: the Great Mother, in her dual role as a giver of life but also death. Also, there is not a goddess who incarnates fecundity and sensual love (like pagan goddesses Aphrodite, Freya, Frigg). While Tolkien took inspiration from Northern sagas and ancient mythology, his universe has foundation in the Bible, medieval tradition, and Christian values. Anyway, Nejrotti denies that Tolkien's female characters are inferior to men. Women act on a different plane, as counselors, guides, advisors—their roles are spiritual rather that physical and material. In Celtic and Germanic worlds women's status was equal to men's in many respects. Women could be powerful priestesses and warriors, and they could inherit land. The wife of a feudal lord could manage his fief while he was away and be a leader of troops if necessary. This condition endured in medieval times, slowly declining until Roman law prevailed. In Tolkien's world women are sometimes even more important than the men with whom they pair. Nejrotti gives us some examples: Arwen, Lúthien, and Idril, of Elven blood, are superior to their mortal spouses. Melian is superior to her husband Thingol: she is a Maia, less powerful than a Vala but still belonging to the Ainur, spiritual entities generated by Ilúvatar before the creation of the world. Powerful women like Galadriel and Lúthien are related to light. Evil female characters, conversely, bring darkness. These are the monstrous spiders Ungoliant and her daughter Shelob. The first, who was even a "destroyer" of light, helped Melkor in the destruction of the two Trees of Valinor, magical beings giving light to the world, priceless and irreplaceable. The second is able to capture Frodo, but Sam will save the hero. The two female spiders are aggressive and their hunger is insatiable. They fit with the negative aspects of the pagan Great Goddess, so it is possible that Tolkien utilized consciously this mythical detail. Nejrotti does not believe that the female spider monsters are born from sexual repression on the part of Tolkien, but she does not delve into the subject. She notes another feature of Tolkien's female characters: all of them are in a couple, or will be (Éowyn is not in the beginning, but she will marry Faramir). Does this come from a scarce consideration on the part of the author? Does this mean a lack of autonomy? Nejrotti does not think so. This critic thinks that man and woman are companions in the common destiny of their lives. This is the meaning of the great love stories in The Lord of the Rings and Tolkien's other writings. This aspect of Tolkien's narrative does in fact exist, and it reflects the real love the author and his wife, Edith, experienced. For example, Arwen rarely appears or acts, and her father initially does not consent to her marriage with Aragorn. Therefore, Arwen waits and endures, in obedience to her father's wish, and because of war. This is an example of courtly love: circumstances keep the lovers apart and the wait puts their bonding to the test, but it is also a cause of moral improvement and future joy. This is consistent with the source material Tolkien used in the creation of his world. It is at the same time quite similar to his own experience, because a person he loved and respected, Father Francis Xavier Morgan, imposed a three-year interruption to Tolkien's relationship with his future wife, Edith Bratt.

What about the lack of sexuality in The Lord of the Rings? Nejrotti thinks the topic is of little consequence. Critics who give importance to it judge Tolkien's work with the mentality of our deconsecrated, modern world. The duty of knights and warriors is a common trope: self-sacrifice and no time for pleasure. An example of this, quoted by Nejrotti, is Yvain, a character by French poet Chrétien de Troyes (twelfth century). Yvain leaves his lady to go on an adventure, and he stays away so long that when he returns, he has to conquer her love again.

Nejrotti states that in Tolkien's world male friendship was a kind of love more heightened and satisfying than sexual love (because it lacks carnality). Men and women during Tolkien's times did not like the same things; their lives and cultures were different. Because of this, a man had to look for other men to find those who shared the same values. In The Lord of the Rings, we have more friendship between men than love stories. This does not mean sexuality was taboo for the author. Nejrotti supposes that, in Tolkien's opinion, maybe spirituality did come first, but sexual love was also obvious and natural in a couple, so it needed no description.

Do We Need All of That Sex Anyway?

I asked[11] Italian critic and writer Giovanni Agnoloni for an opinion about the rare presence of sexuality in The Lord of the Rings. His opinion is not very different from Nejrotti's. "There may have been a sort of modesty in Tolkien, due (once more) to his Christian mindset, or simply to his mentality of a man raised first by his mother and then by his guardian, a priest. But—I might surprise you, I'm aware of this—I don't completely agree with the vision according to which Tolkien's works (anyway, mainly focused on the epical theme of the fight against the Evil) are devoid of sensuality (if not of sexuality). The point, in my own view, is: Tolkien places so much importance on Love as an expression of Light in one's life, and therefore on its capacity to drive one's choices and actions, that the intensity of such feeling and of one's devotion to it (that is, fidelity) can shake and inspire the entire course of a character's existence. Let us think of Beren and Lúthien, or of Aragorn and Arwen, whom I've extensively reflected on in my own contribution to *Tolkien: Light and Shadow* (the essay "Tolkien: The Shadow of Fear and the Light of Desire"). These stories of passion and fidelity are so intense that the very idea of sex, in them, is—so to say—obvious, or anyway naturally implied. Describing it expressly could only have trivialized it."

Daniel Timmons, writing in *Mythlore*,[12] notes that modernist critics criticizing Tolkien seem to forget that in the vast majority of literature there's no display of sex. Moreover, it is nonsense to judge a book for what is not mentioned in it. To depict Tolkien's female characters like Arwen or Galadriel or Éowyn in their sexual activity would be completely dissonant with the nature of his work. Speculations on the part of Otty and Partridge (as we have seen above, viewing the Shelob episode as a violent sex encounter) are, in Timmons's opinion, completely off the mark and show more about the mentality of these critics than about Tolkien's work. The readers, when reading Shelob's battle with Sam, never think of it as a sexual struggle. By the way, if they want to know about the author's attitude towards love, sex, and marriage, readers and critics can be easily satisfied, because in Tolkien's letters this subject is addressed. His views are not progressive, make no mistake about it, but he shows no timidity or revulsion about the matter of sex.

With regards to the Hobbits seen by Edwin Muir as boys who will never reach maturity, Timmons lists various instances in which the Hobbits show clearly that feminine attractiveness and glamour does affect them. While Partridge notes that the love between Sam and Rose Cotton will never be as intense as the relationship between Sam and Frodo, Timmons states that this criticism is "obtuse," because the experience the two Hobbits shared in the last leg of their journey with the Ring is something unique. In Timmons's opinion, Tolkien is not squeamish about love or sexuality. He's able, in contrast, to see them in an appropriate and right way.

A Not Unrealistic Perspective on Relationships

An essay[13] by Brazilian critic Cristina Casagrande debates the topic of difficult relationships in Tolkien's works. Casagrande examines the teachings life gave him, when he had some disagreements with his wife about several topics, religion among them. Tolkien wrote about impossible love stories, men and women overcoming all kind of obstacles to be together. But he also wrote about problems in relationships. In the posthumous (1980) *Unfinished Tales* we have the story of Aldarion and Erendis. He was a Númenórean king, an explorer who loved the sea. His voyages kept him far from home, so he neglected his wife, Erendis. She was embittered, because she could not enjoy such a long life, being of lesser status than her husband. Aldarion's absences weighed on her.

In *The Silmarillion* we have the unhappy story of the Elven princess Aredhel, wife of Eöl the Dark Elf, a skilled metallurgist. It was not a happy union. She was of the Noldor clan of Elves, which Eöl hated. Nevertheless, Eöl used magic to bind her to him and married her anyway. After some time Aredhel was homesick, so she went away with her son, but after Eöl found her, he tried to kill her son with a javelin. Instead, he killed her, because Aredhel stepped into the path of the javelin.

This demonstrates that Tolkien did not limit himself to the description of cold queens on a pedestal or perfect love stories, but wrote of unhappy and cursed unions as well.

A More Gentle Form of Power

In the essay by professor Nancy Enright, "Tolkien's Females and the Defining of Power,"[14] female power is examined from a different perspective. This critic looks at the traditional, muscular male power as expressed in The Lord of the Rings, finding that it gives way to a more tempered model, aware of its own limitation. King Aragorn, inspired by the wisdom of an alternative, spiritual power, is the model of this different kind of warrior. Boromir, the traditional male hero, is morally weaker and destined to fail. Female characters are not present in battle, with the notable exception of Éowyn. Their interaction with the battlefield is more complex and indirect: they personify Tolkien's criticism of traditional power, military and political. Enright notes that Tolkien criticism is often focused on the scarcity and lack of importance of female characters. But this doesn't take into account their importance from a religious perspective. You need to understand Tolkien's Christian perspective to realize their importance. In The Lord of the Rings, female characters show an "inversion of power" that will be necessary for the ultimate victory.

Arwen is a typical example of this kind of female power. She's described as beautiful, but her charm is not just physical. She's noble in appearance; her eyes show wisdom and her real age. Arwen doesn't leave Rivendell; she doesn't perform any mission. She's devoted to Aragorn, and she sends her banner to him, giving encouragement but also noting that the decisive moment has come: if he doesn't win, all hope will be lost. Arwen is also notable, obviously, for giving up her immortality out of love. This is a Christ-like choice, Enright notes; Arwen's power is shown through humility, in the sacrifice of her more-than-human nature. She will try also to help Frodo when the strain of his mission starts to show, giving him her necklace, and then her right to sail west to immortality.

At the end of Aragorn's life, Arwen will go to the woods of Loth-lórien, but the Elven lands are now deserted. There's no enchantment in those woods now. Tolkien doesn't soften the account of her solitary death in any way. But Arwen's sacrifice echoes the Elves' waiver of their presence in Middle-earth.

Galadriel, the bearer of one of the Elven Rings, is the more powerful character in The Lord of the Rings, in Enright's opinion. Galadriel's power is not bent on domination but healing and understanding, an alternative to male power. Galadriel greets the Fellowship's members offering hospitality and wisdom. She summons the White Council to resist the Dark Lord's aggression. But she knows that her power cannot be unlimited, and freely renounces the Ring when Frodo gives it to her. Although Galadriel is a penitent[15] because she didn't obey the will of the Valar, Galadriel in The Lord of the Rings shows the greatest spiritual power.

In Tolkien's work, this is the power that, ultimately, wins the battle. Arwen and Galadriel, Frodo and his Hobbit friends, are not in the men's field of action made of physical strength. This is, as the critic notes, a distinctly Christian feature because Jesus's story is a story of renunciation of power and a victory through love. Although none of them is comparable to Jesus, these characters in some aspects show the same renunciation of power.

The perspective changes with Éowyn, a more complex character in relation to power issues. She has the courage and the spirit of her brother, Éomer, but she's born "in the body of a maid," as Gandalf explains in The Lord of the Rings, so she's destined to care for her ailing uncle, a role she hated. Is Tolkien a feminist here? Not explicitly, but he perceives Éowyn's frustration at her own powerlessness. She knows she's able to fight, but she's kept from doing what she wants to do. Until she decides to disobey. She kills the Nazgûl in battle, proving her worth. But, in this critic's opinion, Éowyn's victory is not complete, because her understanding of power is the male one.

So, in Enright's opinion, Éowyn does not forfeit her newfound freedom when she leaves the warrior role. Her power will be deeper and stronger by renunciation. Her love with Faramir is the love between two people wounded by the same strength-dominated culture: Éowyn because she is a woman, Faramir because he is the weaker brother in comparison to the perfect hero Boromir. They have proved their worth on the battlefield, but war is not going to give them peace and health. In

Éowyn's case, she has to move on from her unrequited love for Aragorn. The painful rejection, Enright states, is in part the reason why she went into battle, and still a wound to be healed. Faramir's love is Éowyn's healing. For some critics, this is the renunciation of her attempt to override gender roles, a victory for the patriarchy. But, in Enright's opinion, this transformation is more than going back to traditional roles. Éowyn will leave any desire for power and domination, changing to healing, and the love for things that grow. She now loves the Elven kind of power, in the moment of the coming age of Men.

In conclusion, Enright states that The Lord of the Rings is a story of battle and adventure only on the surface. It's also more than a challenge between good and evil. The book is about the choice characters make in relationship to power, where the better choice is the Christian value of healing, love, and gentleness.

Tolkien gives success to humility, triumphs to the less powerful protagonists. This is why characters who make the right choice are females or Hobbits. But this kind of power doesn't belong to people who can't choose anything else: Tolkien's characters give up the other kind of power, based on dominance and strength, to favor the right one.

In Enright's opinion, if we connect the definition of power in The Lord of the Rings with the characters' gender, we understand that the book is not about male power and muscular heroism.

Taming the Wild Shieldmaiden

Éowyn is probably the most controversial character created by J.R.R. Tolkien. She rebels against the role her family has chosen and proves her worth on the battlefield. The only woman in The Lord of the Rings who actually takes up arms, she goes to the battlefield and defeats the Nazgûl king. Éowyn is a seemingly modern character, based on Nordic folklore and mythology, where they have female warriors (shieldmaidens) who may not necessarily be a fictional invention.[16]

After that, however, her subversion of traditional values ends, and she reverts to the role that could be expected from her. In so doing, she turns into a disappointment for those critics and readers who saw the behavior of a modern woman in her exploits.

Let's go over her history. Éowyn is the daughter of Théodwin (sister of the Rohan king, Théoden) and Eomund, a commander who fell at the hands of Orcs. Her brother, Éomer, is an important character in The Lord of the Rings, destined to succeed to the throne of Rohan. Initially, our heroine must take care of King Théoden, disabled by the sinister influence of Grima Wormtongue (the spy sent by Saruman). Éowyn then insists on taking up arms and fighting, despite being given the task of looking after the royal house whilst her uncle (King Théoden) is engaged in war. Determined to fight, and in love with Aragorn, Éowyn will not obey; in the end, she disguises herself and fights in the Battle of the Pelennor Fields secretly.

Some critics seem to think Éowyn is a marginal, accidental character in the story. Robert W. Butler and John Mark Eberhart argue in their piece[17] that Tolkien was not interested in females, so the female characters have little to do. Éowyn, a manifest exception to the rule, owes her existence to Priscilla Tolkien, the author's daughter, who arguably wanted a strong female character in the plot. Biographer Daniel Grotta supports this claim,[18] maintaining that Priscilla wanted more romance and women in the story. Even so, this doesn't necessarily mean Éowyn is a redundant character. Éowyn indeed has a heroic journey, a "heroine journey" that seemingly leads to the achievement of an important goal. She has her own plot and a quest within the larger story, for a while appropriating the male warrior role. For good or bad, she distances herself from the other females in The Lord of the Rings.

Critic Joseph Campbell, in his work on comparative mythology,[19] argues that Éowyn performs *separation* (going to war) and *initiation* (killing the Nazgûl). She seems to offer a new generation of readers a viable model, seeing as she intentionally rebels against the orders of the king, the same orders that reduced her to a stereotypical gender role (guarding the house). When Aragorn, the hero of The Lord of the Rings, sees Éowyn for the first time, he sees her as hard and cold, and thinks that her femininity has not yet blossomed, despite her being over 20 years of age: almost as if a strong and severe attitude implies a lack of maturity in a woman. However, when the intervention of the good wizard, Gandalf, frees the king from Grima's evil influence, Éowyn gets to govern the country, whilst the king, called to arms, goes to war. To recognize his niece's status, the king gives her a sword and a breastplate. Critic Kevin Maness in his essay[20] states that "this ceremonial arming of Éowyn is the first in a series of her costume changes, each of which indicates her current relationship to her gender."

Still, at this moment she is not expected to use the weapons she's given as a symbolic emblazonment. Whether this is relevant or not, we'll see a series of changes in Éowyn's apparel and weapons, following her next transformations. As a matter of fact, the heroine will soon realize that this new role has little real importance, so she expresses her dissatisfaction to Aragorn. In this circumstance, Aragorn can't give her any contentment, so she expresses her disappointment about having her place in the house with the famous words: "But when the men have died in battle and honour, you have leave to be burned in the house."

Éowyn does not want to wither over time in a cage of a house, she knows the limitations defined by male rules and decides to rebel. She wants more! The words said by Aragorn, who reminds her that her role is of considerable importance, are not enough because he does not understand her desire for more choice. So she decides to make her own choices.

She dresses as a knight, armed and ready to start her quest or adventure. She will ride on the battlefield, defend the dying king Théoden, challenge the Lord of the Nazgûl, and defeat him, being wounded in the fight. Probably everyone remembers her saying "No living man am I," warning the Ringwraith that his alleged invincibility is not going to be valid this time. According to Maness, the nature of Éowyn's wound, struck on the sword arm, the same arm that eliminated the king of the Nazgûl, becomes a symbolic castration, even in the moment of victory. In fact, it is the arm that wielded the sword, arguably a phallic symbol giving her male power. We should always be wary when a critic uses Freudian symbolism, but it could be accurate here. The sudden shift of the story, in fact, begins here: it's the second part of Éowyn's subplot, the one in which she abandons masculinity. Is this a regression or an evolution of her character? Is it convincing? Difficult to decide.

In her convalescence, Éowyn falls in love with Faramir, and, like any self-respecting princess, she will end up marrying one of the few noble characters who are equal to her, in this case, Faramir, Steward of Gondor, the most important human kingdom. Although the power will go to Aragorn, the rightful king, and rediscovered heir, Faramir will remain in office as head of state.

After discovering Éowyn's deeds, the men will ask themselves why she has chosen that path. According to Éomer, his sister's "illness" began when Éowyn laid eyes on Aragorn, so her behavior is built on unrequited love. So Éowyn may have sought death due to disappointment. Gandalf blames the evil influence of Grima Wormtongue, but he also notes that Éomer has his horses, freedom to travel, and the glory of heroic deeds. He seems to tell him that he's taking all of this too much for granted, inasmuch as he forgets that his sister, born into the body of a maid, has the same spirit as he does, but not the same freedom.

When Éowyn is convalescing she's restless and depressed. Probably she feels that her participation in the war didn't give her what she was looking for. Nevertheless, she seeks news of the war, complaining that women (those present in the Houses of Healing) cannot give her any information. Instead of finding opportunities to return to war, she meets Faramir, also wounded. This rebellious woman, under the male gaze, doubts herself for the first time. Faramir's courtship wins her heart, so Éowyn eventually chooses marriage and abandons rebellion.

In the *Letters*, we found some more words[21] by Tolkien about Éowyn: he doesn't think she's really an Amazon, although she certainly is not a wet nurse. Still, brave women are capable of great military deeds in a time of crisis. Tolkien was certainly aware of the supporting and fighting role that many women undertook during World War II: even British women, though not at the same level as the Russian female snipers or the Yugoslav partisans. Probably this is not enough for modern readers, who are baffled by the sudden renunciation of the warrior role on the part of the wounded Éowyn. Still, critic Mariah Huehner thinks[22] that the film version by Peter Jackson is even more unsatisfying. While the film has Éowyn "moon over Aragorn," in The Lord of the Rings she gives him a curt answer, as we have seen above, exposing how her role had a meaning just as an aid to the men. She calls him out; she is not deferent at all. Huehner argues that Tolkien wrote a valid proto-feminist character, while the movie ruined it.

In an essay by Ana María Mariño Arias,[23] Éowyn is seen as a woman who makes her own choices. Having demonstrated her worth on the battlefield, she has nothing more to prove; knowing Faramir she has realized that war is a means and not an end. Moreover, she's a prominent member of the royal family in Rohan, so nobody is going to reproach her for leaving her people without a guide when she abandoned her home to follow the army. After the war, she can leave behind the days when Grima's influence could doom her to a frightful destiny. She can forget Sauron's influence, get in contact with a court more civilized than that of the Rohirrim, enjoy her fame as a great heroine, and marry. In this critic's opinion, Éowyn is not "normalized" by "patriarchy," but simply evolves and chooses the more befitting way of life. This way, Éowyn gets the "happy ending" denied to Arwen.

Katherine Hesser's opinion is completely different. She notes[24] the struggle and contradiction of feminine and masculine elements in Éowyn's character. She remains in a nurturing role when taking care of Théoden in the king's court and even on the battlefield, when she will fight to defend his dying body. In the exchange she has with the Nazgûl, Éowyn stays on defense, exhorting the Witch-king to leave the dead in peace, then announcing that she will "hinder" the Nazgûl if she can. Rather than killing the powerful monster, she is extending on the battlefield her nurturing role. The first time Merry sees her, Éowyn is wearing an awkward combination of feminine clothes and a warrior's armor from the waist up, with a helmet over her flowing hair. Even the definition of "shieldmaiden" is not fully a recognition of her fighting role. Éowyn is not fully a Rider of Rohan indeed. She remains in a subservient role. After the battle, when she marries Faramir, Éowyn's successes are forgotten: she joins Arwen and Galadriel as another idealized female character. So Hesser argues that in Middle-earth we have "trophy wives" but not working mothers.

Some questions about the creation of female characters were also addressed by Jennifer Neville, a Canadian university professor, dealing with Éowyn's character in the chapter she wrote in *Reading The Lord of the Rings: New Writings on Tolkien's Classic*, edited by Robert Eaglestone.[25] For Neville, the women in Tolkien's works are disappointing. The misogynistic depiction of women comes from both the time when the books were written and the medieval period as understood by Tolkien, because it was the basis for his fiction. Tolkien would have interpreted women as powerless in his reading of the epic *Beowulf*, and so would have consequently described those of Rohan as directly related to the ancient Anglo-Saxon world. According to Neville this interpretation is wrong from the beginning, but this is not simply the author's fault: the responsibility lies with previous scholars (such as Frederick Klaeber, a German authority in the interpretation of the text), influenced, just as Tolkien himself was, by the prevailing worldview of the period in which they carried out their studies.

First of all, the scholar is certain that, although Tolkien denied an overly direct correlation, the Rohirrim (the people to whom Éowyn belongs) are equivalent to the Anglo-Saxons, in both their customs and the phonetics of their names. For example, the personal and direct relationship of King Théoden with his men and the exaltation of glory in battle, to be achieved before dying, are common to both cultures. The king's house in Rohan is similar in appearance and ceremonial function to that which appears (bearing practically the same name) in *Beowulf*. These are just some of the obvious similarities. The character of Éowyn, who offers a cup to the nobles in the royal house, is intended to be feminine and passive, initially. When she dares to rebel, Tolkien writes a seemingly modern transformation: Éowyn challenges the Rohirrim culture. That is, the culture upon which the Rohirrim are based in The Lord of the Rings. But, as Neville states, this female passivity is not really present in Old English poetry.

This passive role, according to Neville, is Victorian; it is an old-fashioned interpretation, accepted by Tolkien but not supported by the texts. If one reads the poem carefully, they will notice that Wealhtheow, King Hrothgar's wife, is not simply a wife, guest, and mother. The role of this powerful woman is evident when the hero, Beowulf, goes to

King Hrothgar to offer him help against the monster Grendel. At the time when the story within the poem is set, the Angles and Saxons were beginning to migrate to England, but their cultural homelands included northern Germany and parts of Holland and the Scandinavian countries, in particular, Denmark. Hrothgar is a Danish king, whose power was strongly undermined by Grendel, because the troll has been devouring his men for years. Grendel's acts are demonstrating that the king cannot protect his subordinates or bring order to his own kingdom. The Danes have lost both honor and reputation. At the same time, Beowulf puts Hrothgar in a difficult position, because the hero offers to do what the Danes could not. So Beowulf comes to Hrothgar as a respectful suppliant; he asks for permission to fight Grendel. The king would be happy to see the troll defeated, but in public he doesn't welcome Beowulf as a savior. He maintains that Beowulf is coming to repay some old obligation. Although Beowulf came to gain glory by destroying the monster that persecutes the Danes, and therefore promises Hrotgar a big favor, the king wants to keep him at bay so as not to make a figure too poor in front of his people: if the foreign hero comes to help Hrothgar, he must do so from a somewhat subordinate position. At this point Queen Wealhtheow offers Beowulf a drink from the cup used by the king, and states that his arrival is the realization of one of her wishes. However, the queen does not simply offer mead to the hero to quench his thirst. According to Neville, previous scholars did not fully grasp that, in making him drink from the king's cup once the drinks have already been served, Beowulf is somehow made to accept a vote in favor of Hrothgar, and that this faith that the queen puts in the hero also becomes a commitment: Beowulf is called to fulfill his promises. The queen offers to place the newcomer in a subordinate position in the Danish court, at the same time asserting her own control over him. Beowulf accepts, agreeing to defeat the monster, or die trying. Wealhtheow therefore cannot be mistaken for a waitress: she has her own political power, complementary to that of her husband. Later, after the victory, she also opposes her husband's desire to make Beowulf his heir at the expense of the royal couple's children. Wealhtheow gives gifts to the hero but reminds him, with a veiled threat, that there are men who obey her. Neville points out that in the past, the queen was considered pathetic and also an instigator of arguments, but she is in fact a woman who wields her own power, and exercises it consciously. The hero, Beowulf, is rewarded, but he will not be adopted by the king; therefore it is the queen who will have the final word on the succession. There are many things that this woman cannot influence, but Hrothgar and Beowulf will also have their share of failures in the story.

Tolkien does not create any woman of comparable power in the palace of Rohan, which is seemingly inspired by the ancient Anglo-Saxons of the poem (though this is not confirmed by the author). Éowyn is a figure lacking any political power, and King Théoden has no strong woman by his side, no queen who would certainly have prevented Grima Wormtongue from carrying out his schemes. When Théoden has recovered and goes to war, the kingdom is entrusted to her, but she doesn't care about this delicate office. Her interactions with Aragorn are personal, not political as they could be.

So it's Tolkien's responsibility to have interpreted Beowulf in a patriarchal and traditional way, according to Neville. But it is important for the story that Éowyn starts as a seemingly marginal and powerless character. In The Lord of the Rings the small, weak, forgotten people must do the heroic deed. Frodo and Sam must bear the Ring, because the more powerful characters can't control it. The powerful Aragorn and Gandalf struggle to face the Witch-king of Angmar, because heroic men can't kill him. But someone who is not a man can. With her skill and bravery, and with the help of a Hobbit (another "small" character), Éowyn can do that.

Éowyn becomes a renowned queen for her actions but is not on the same level as a male hero: and if she were not marginalized at the beginning of the adventure, her actions would not harmonize with those of the other "humble" protagonists of the plot.

According to Neville, Tolkien therefore follows the ideas of other scholars, and does not understand that Beowulf's legend offers a valid example of a powerful woman, thus reinforcing the archaic patriarchal trend, whereby women must have a non-leading role in society, and returning Éowyn to the typically female role of wife and healer. However, it is also true that in Tolkien, the traditional masculine power is not capable of winning the most important challenges on its own. Neville remembers a detail already highlighted by others: single men (or more generally male figures without women by their sides) often do not succeed in the stories told by Tolkien, while the greatest success lies with those who form a harmonious couple (Aragorn-Arwen, Galadriel-Celeborn, Sam-Rosie etc...). In the Tolkienian message of the "sanctification of the humble" it is often the small and the weak who achieve the greatest victories; therefore Éowyn will enjoy a moment of triumph, because she does *not* have a heroic stature. Neville criticizes Tolkien's understanding of old Anglo-Saxon culture: The author in her opinion did not fully understand the texts underlying his fantastic creation. He didn't see that the women of the ancient Anglo-Saxon world could have effective power. But the conclusion is not hostile towards

Tolkien or the meaning of his creation: "As we live our modern lives, we may choose to feel patronized by Tolkien's women, but, unless we can claim to be a Beowulf or Aragorn (a route not open to normal men, either), Tolkien's message may not be so disempowering as has been thought."

The aforementioned Chiara Nejrotti states[26] that Éowyn is one of the more interesting characters in Tolkien's Middle-earth. She refuses to be left behind when the men go to war; still her state of mind is born from desperation more than a real warrior spirit. Beautiful but cold, unhappy, in Aragorn's description, Éowyn is a witness of the court's decay, because Théoden was under Wormtongue's evil spell. She has lived in sorrow and disgust, and then unrequited love for Aragorn will cause more sufferance for her. Still, the role of a warrior woman (a theme present in chivalrous epic) is not her destiny. Meeting Faramir, she will find a new love born of peace and joy, and not of desperation. Éowyn giving up the warrior role is not going back to submission, but finding her real nature. This way, Nejrotti denies that Éowyn gave up her own emancipation.

Homosexuality in The Lord of the Rings

The British university lecturer Esther Saxey raises a point regarding the theme of sexuality in the works of Tolkien[27]: it is assumed that, in The Lord of the Rings, there are more or less covertly homosexual couples. Is this a legitimate assumption? We note in passing that, for another critic, the aforementioned John Molyneux, the question of homosexuality and homophobia in Tolkien's world is very easily resolved: in the fantasy world of Middle-earth, homosexuality does not exist. Nonetheless, Saxey is suspicious of this: it comes from the book's homosocial world. She wonders if this results from a modern interpretation, perhaps fuelled by the movies. The reference to the films (by Peter Jackson) is a must, seeing as they include many intimate scenes between the characters. In order to make the story more pleasing to the general public, the production included romantic moments that were not present in the book (and these, in turn, trigger the imagination of the authors of fan fiction). This amplifies the above-mentioned stories (though they do remain important, an example being the relationship between Arwen and Aragorn) and generally adds importance (and minutes of on-screen action) to sentimental relationships and female presence. This means that there's a shift in the perspective between the film and the novel, where male hierarchical relationships are the norm. In the books, we were already on "difficult, intensely homosocial ground," so the films "destabilized that precarious homosociality." We care little here about Peter Jackson's films per se: however, if we are to believe Saxey, the films have made the fabric from which the masculine relations in Middle-earth are woven very clear, evident, and unambiguous. Saxey goes on the offensive against Tolkien's oblique manner: she quotes Edwin Muir and Catharine Stimpson to say that Tolkien's life and fiction are both lacking when compared to an ideal of heterosexual maturity. So here we go again with the "childish characters who know nothing about sex," but also considering the author's sexuality. His relationship with the Inklings, his intense intellectual life in circles of all-male friends, is juvenile in this critic's opinion.

Tolkien's attitude towards sex is evasive and even hostile, especially in the famous fight scene between Sam and Shelob. The relationship between Frodo and Sam is the one that is most intensely targeted, an opportunity for Saxey to enter directly into the topic: can we say that Sam and Frodo are lovers? And we can't limit our search for an answer to textual evidence; we should listen to the audience reaction. The moments in which it seems that Frodo and Sam are in a homosexual relationship can be justified by the fact that, in the family of Bilbo and Frodo, there are no women or children, and this leaves room for the other Hobbits who will take part in the adventure. Bilbo's life is altered by the presence of the Ring; all the others are too young to be married. But Sam's faithful love for Frodo, the way he looks at him while he sleeps, touches him, etc., could lead to the presumption that this is more than a simple, affectionate friendship. There is a lot of physical contact between the two, which is motivated by the plot. When Frodo is convalescing at Rivendell in Elrond's house, after being struck by the Nazgûl king, Sam timidly touches his hand, and whilst blushing, exclaims that it finally feels warm, explaining that it had been so cold whilst Frodo was seriously ill. Saxey wonders why Sam blushes: contact between the two is probably inappropriate in a situation where there is no war to justify it. In the appendices of The Lord of the Rings, many characters get married and have children, and Sam is one of them, yet he is reunited with Frodo after the death of his wife, Rosie, when he is permitted to sail to the islands of the West. Gimli is also allowed to undertake the journey, perhaps because of his friendship with Legolas, perhaps because of his devotion to Galadriel: even for Tolkien nothing more can be said on the matter.

The essayist wonders what these elements prove: sexual contact, romantic devotion, non-heterosexual identity? In Tolkien's sub-creation of Middle-earth same-sex relationships are not mentioned; therefore many fans think that they can't be perceived there, because they are missing.

But, in Saxey's opinion, we cannot ignore the strong similarities between their world and ours. Heterosexual relationships, which are the norm, are organized in the same way. So it's logical to assume that same-sex relationships do exist, as in our world. Their lack in the stories is just a pretext to avoid talking about them. Saxey finds a parallel of Sam and Frodo's "story" in *Maurice*, a novel by E.M. Forster, which tells the story of the gay relationship between a middle-class homosexual man and a working-class bisexual: with this precedent, she shows that the homosexual relationship can therefore take place in the context of a homosocial hierarchical relationship.

However, it is difficult to prove the homosexual relationship between Sam and Frodo in The Lord of the Rings, as there are few explicit examples of heterosexuality to use as a comparison. Rose Cotton, Sam's future wife, appears to be a character in name only. According to Saxey, the fans resistance to believing this heterosexual story is a good reason to insist on a same-sex relationship between Frodo and Sam. Disgust expressed by online fans at the idea of these Hobbits as lovers is arguably just homophobia. The innocent, childlike Hobbit having a same-sex relationship generates even stronger protest indeed. The essayist comes to the conclusion that she will not outrightly say that Sam and Frodo are lovers but will certainly not dispute it either and says that many characters and situations in The Lord of the Rings are ambiguous.

Having said all of this, however, my conclusion is that Saxey in the end did not prove anything of what she affirmed or hypothesized. The fact that certain situations in movies can be more easily interpreted to be a certain way, or that fan fiction has insisted on certain misunderstandings, says nothing about books. It is true that the relations between Frodo and Sam have often been seen with some embarrassment among modern readers, precisely because of its extremely different context. When Tolkien wrote the affectionate words they say to one another, it was unthinkable to put them in a homosexual context. Was he a man who lived in a homosocial environment? Tolkien's working environment was certainly a "masculine" one, but this was true for the majority of the men of his time. The idea that he was "intensely" homosocial and tried to live in an eternally immature world could be more apt when thinking of a man who spends time on hobbies or expensive sports, maybe even dangerous ones, in order to affirm his masculinity, at the expense of the family budget or the care of his children, rather than a man like Tolkien. Nonetheless, he kept his intellectual life separated from family life, and maybe liked the first one a bit more. As

Nancy Martsch reports,[28] at a certain point the Inklings were meeting three times a week, so we can assume Tolkien was very often with them, leaving his wife home with the children. John Garth, in his work titled *Tolkien and the Great War: The Threshold of Middle-earth*,[29] notes that in the T.C.B.S. (short for "Tea Club, Barrovian Society," formed in the King Edward's school at Birmingham) Tolkien and his friends didn't spread gossip about their sentimental liaisons. Still, he couldn't stand to compartmentalize his life, so that the T.C.B.S. knew nothing of Edith, his future wife. He introduced her to the group. She was well received, but a female relationship could be felt as a destabilizing component in the all-male T.C.B.S., as noted by essayist Nicole duPlessis.[30] Moreover, the same thing didn't happen during Tolkien's years as a teacher in Oxford: Edith was excluded from Tolkien's relationships with the Inklings and other male friends. Why? In the essay by duPlessis we have the hypothesis of the exclusion of his wife as a ruthless act on Tolkien's part, the man taking his sexist privilege with the inevitable exclusion of his wife from any chance of intellectual growth. DuPlessis, who argues that Edith's and J.R.R. Tolkien's marriage was possibly a non-perfect match, still acknowledges that it lasted for over 50 years, and that Tolkien loved his wife. In the biography by Daniel Grotta we have a lively description[31] of Tolkien's years as a teacher in Leeds, before his move to Oxford as a professor of Anglo-Saxon in 1925. In this time Tolkien and his wife were happy, in Grotta's narrative. They were both involved in the university social life. Tolkien was also active in sports, and seen as a friendly and informal teacher. After the move to Oxford, it seems that something had changed. Edith "declined to become socially involved with her husband's colleagues." Grotta states that she was aware of her cultural inferiority and did not share Tolkien's interests. In Oxford, he became more distant from anything unrelated to the academic world.

As usual, it is not easy to draw a definite conclusion. Tolkien's involvement with his intellectual world may have been an exclusion "de facto" of his wife. Certainly, multiple pregnancies were also a burden for Edith. Anyway, although some of Tolkien's traits as a man could be seen as peculiar (an uncommonly deep faith, for example), his marriage and its problems seem rather ordinary.

Regarding the relationship between Sam and Frodo (which, in my opinion, is the only one to really present embarrassing moments for the reader), Tolkien explains[32] that Sam's character is inspired by the British infantry soldiers—in particular the orderlies, or "batmen"—who took care of the officers. The "batman" (the origin of the word has nothing to do with the superhero or with bats) was a figure capable of impressing the officers since, in the English class society, contact with this guy was one of the rare moments when a man of the ruling classes had a relationship with someone from the working class. Moreover, this relationship, even with all the hierarchical subordination, was made very "real" by the war's harsh circumstances. Tolkien, a reluctant officer, a man who had ill adapted to the life of the barracks and would have done without the war, considered the "batmen" far superior to himself. He was probably impressed by these men, who were used to fatigue and able to make do, whose duty was to make the difficult living conditions of the trenches less burdensome for the officers, and who, at the same time, were obedient and respectful. So, once again, let us recall Marion Zimmer Bradley's words (in response to Edmund Wilson) about the heroic and idealized male friendships. Saxey, in conclusion, neither manages to bring out this (hypothetical) gay potential in Sam's character, nor is she successful in going beyond the giggle and gossip that some scenes from The Lord of the Rings can inspire. When sensitive themes are touched upon, if someone has a strong reaction (for example, someone who cannot tolerate the idea of Sam and Frodo being gay), it is immediately interpreted as an indication of homophobia or repressed homosexuality. However, a real basis beyond this search for the guilty conscience or the Freudian slip is missing. It is just a case of having a lot of argumentative and polemical attitudes, alongside arguments that could be a waste of time outside the psychoanalyst's studio.

Let us move on to another critical opinion, this time not a hostile one, which better explains the question of male friendships in Tolkien's work. In her essay, titled "Oh ... oh.... Frodo!: Readings of Male Intimacy in The Lord of the Rings,"[33] Anna Smol takes up the theme of suspicious intimacy between males that arises from watching Peter Jackson's films, noting how Tolkien's work arouses strong reactions based on sex, despite being a book devoid of adult sexuality.

Smol notes that medieval-style literature in Victorian and Edwardian times—roughly from the first half of the nineteenth century until the beginning of the twentieth century, almost until the First World War—was connected to children, so Tolkien's work could be seen as a revival of that genre. In the modern period, says Smol, medieval literature, which was not at the high level of elegance or class required of the era, was considered suitable for boys, who read it in a very abbreviated and simplified form. Children's books often included the legends of King Arthur, various chivalrous adventures and historical novels about heroes of the Middle Ages, material that was considered educational, but in reality, the medieval literature had to be censored, in order to be suitable for children, according to the nineteenth-century conception of wanting children to be as ignorant as possible regarding sex.

In fact, Tolkien criticized the fact that the fairy tale was not considered suitable for adults, as if there was an exclusive relationship between fairy tales and children, and the fairy tale was better suited for the latter: "Fairy-stories have in the modern, lettered world been relegated to the 'nursery,' as shabby or old-fashioned furniture is relegated to the play-room, primarily because the adults do not want it, and do not mind if it is misused."[34]

Tolkien, notes Anna Smol, certainly had read medieval children's literature, but he also knew the reality, thanks to his studies, and it was to this that he referred when writing his books. It is obvious that many critics have not understood this, and as a consequence (and it would be the case, as we have already seen with Edwin Muir), his heroes are assimilated to the pre-pubescent characters of children's literature, and his work judged as immature. In the same way, the representation of the war in The Lord of the Rings was seen as a childlike and naive representation of heroism that, in light of the events of the First World War, was false and inadequate. According to Smol, all of this was a source of irritation for Tolkien, who stated, not without reason, that his work was misrepresented. The essayist believes that many critics failed to perceive a complex twentieth-century writer beyond the medieval setting of Middle-earth and the adventures of Tolkien's characters. Tolkien participated in one war and sent his sons to fight another. The setting of male friendships in his stories, with females being absent or quite far away, and a lack of heterosexual relationships, needs to be put in the context of the author's war experience in the First World War. According to Smol, Tolkien had experienced these feelings during and after the First World War, when others had talked about it openly, but The Lord of the Rings was published after the Second World War, when a new way of understanding and treating sexual arguments had made it uncomfortable to refer to these themes of male friendship. Therefore Tolkien has been attacked and sometimes ridiculed, and the relationship between Sam and Frodo became uncomfortable for the public (and even more so when it was made into a film), since the reader or viewer wants to clearly understand if these characters are homosexual or not, regardless of whether their stance on sexuality is positive or negative.

The essay by Anna Smol is certainly useful to understand these aspects (and the misunderstandings that derive from them); as for the analysis of the "slash fiction" about the male characters of The Lord of the Rings, I believe that there is no need to comment, as this is alien to the purpose of these pages.

Female Power in Tolkien

Edith L. Crowe gave an unexpectedly positive evaluation of Tolkien's work in her essay "Power in Arda: Sources, Uses and Misuses."[35] The essay starts with the rhetorical question: "Can I be a feminist and still like Tolkien?" Crowe's answer is positive because, for one thing, anyone in her generation sticking strictly to books advancing feminist values would have had precious little to read. While this is not an enthusiastic appreciation of Tolkien's perspective on women, Crowe provides some recognition of his books. Tolkien's work is not, in her opinion, completely averse to feminism. To think that, one must have a very narrow opinion about his writings, and also about feminism. While female characters are scarce, they often enjoy a positive attitude from the author. In Crowe's opinion, the fundamental issue is power and its uses. In Middle-earth, the ultimate source of power is a male god (Eru or Ilúvatar), but he's better at delegating power than the traditional Yahweh of Judeo-Christian heritage. He leaves the creation of Arda to his helpers, without continuous interference. With the sub-creation by the Valar, Tolkien includes female power at a very high level of his universe, excluding the very top. The Valar are in fact embodied as females or males following their own nature and disposition. So we have powerful female "goddesses" (or beings similar to divinities), among them Varda, who is the most feared by Melkor. In the political and social world, power may be associated with physical skill, strength, or resources, but also with charisma, access to information, personal magnetism. In the opinion of this critic, it's true that Tolkien rarely gives the first kind of power to women, but they often get some strong power of the second kind. This kind of power is held in great importance: for instance, Galadriel wields it, and she's clearly a very influential character in the legendarium. Moreover, females don't lack courage or political skill: Tolkien gives several examples of this. Because of the patriarchal structure of Middle-earth societies, women may exert these qualities rarely. But there's also a very reasonable justification: constant military engagements in Tolkien's world generate the need for leaders with both political and military abilities and the necessity of leaving their own territory to wage war in other countries. Women are capable of last-resort home defense, but it's obviously more appropriate that they are not in the front line, because they give birth and care for children. Crowe quotes *Female Power and Male Dominance*, Peggy Sanday's cross-cultural research on several societies, including some in which females are in power: the mechanism of society is determined by environment, conflicts, and culture. Anyway, the difficulty of waging war and being a mother can easily be seen by common sense.

Éowyn is an example of a powerful female in Tolkien's works. We have no details, but she is trained in the use of weapons, and she is a skilled rider, because she can follow the army in war. In the Battle of the Pelennor Fields, she has great success. Had she chosen to stay home, she could have been the legitimate leader of the Eorlingas while Théoden and Éomer were away. Crowe observes that being a member of the reigning house is, in this case, more important than sex.

Similarly, the sovereign of the Númenóreans is the eldest child, not the eldest son. Lúthien is another example of a female showing physical courage.

Crowe's conclusion is that while men hold the majority of power positions in politics, war, and the economy, Middle-earth has a good share of powerful females as well. Societies are more based on links of hierarchy and relationships than on raw domination. The power of the blade is more often associated with evil, while the nurturing power is good. Male and female qualities are seen as different but complementary. Last but not least, in Tolkien's universe violence against women does exist, but it's not against women as women. Marauders and destructors like the Orcs are violent against everybody. In conclusion, Tolkien's work, after a close analysis, is more related to female power than we might think.

About Psychoanalytic Approaches

Can we really trust criticism conceived through psychoanalysis of the author through his text? Thomas Honegger thinks[36] that this kind of approach is problematic. The use of Freudian symbols in its more crude and simplistic ways, for example the sword as a phallus, is useless and misleading, and it's not how Freud would have used his own concepts. Freud's methods are intended to treat patients the therapist meets in person, but they are used by critics to understand literary texts instead, and, in this manner, to develop conjectures about the authors. Another error is, in the case of Tolkien's works, to analyze characters that often are lacking in realism or do not evolve during the story. The Jungian approach is more akin to Tolkien's use of symbols, images, and characters, because it privileges the archetypal relevance. Still, aesthetic (artistic) imagery is a conscious literary development; it doesn't come from the unconscious. So it's wrong to interpret it that way. Honegger is a bit skeptical, but he seems to find Jungian interpretation useful (sometimes). The only advice we can give is to be wary of psychoanalytical studies of literary texts.

What Do You Expect from Tolkien?

Tolkien was a man of his time who wanted to explore a mythological past in his writing, so he could not deliver the Middle-earth that feminists (or gay activists) wanted. The reasons are to be found in his conservatism, and in the epic literary subject he was dealing with, which gave scarce opportunities for romance and was inappropriate for sex scenes. Some critics have asked: did Tolkien's characters live their long lives without sex? We could ask instead: are these considerations about sex lives reasonable in the context of a story about a pressing conflict that leaves no space for other activities or distractions? Let's consider Aragorn's case. Born in 2931, he married in 3019, after a long life of monitoring Eriador and other places of Middle-earth. He is descended from the chieftains of the Dúnedain, so he's a very special human; he enjoys a very long life, but it's a lot of time anyway without a woman. Did he remain absolutely celibate before wedding Arwen? Did he come into marriage a virgin? Tolkien doesn't tell, but we can assume talented Aragorn had his experiences, by similarity with our world. We can also assume that Arwen remained a virgin, under the care of her father Elrond, for the same reason. We can "almost" be sure of that, although in the magic world of Middle-earth things could be different, and people are very different (Elves, for example). But do these details really matter? No, they are not relevant to the story being told; moreover they can't find space in the spirit Tolkien gave to his legendarium.

About gender issues, let us not forget that Tolkien created female characters of undoubted power (such as Galadriel) and one heroine who breaks male dominance in military affairs. The "shieldmaiden" of Germanic and Scandinavian lore is Éowyn, who, after proving her worth, forfeits the arms and gets married. Certainly, Tolkien sees the woman as a Catholic, which means he attaches great importance to her, but only in traditional roles. When writing to his son Michael (letter 43, already mentioned), Tolkien focuses on issues related to love and sex, talking about it with both reserve and realism. Surely, there is nothing that is contrary to or deviates from the Catholic doctrine, nothing strange or unexpected. Relationships between men and women may have changed since Tolkien wrote the letter, although the fundamentals are more or less the same, but it is interesting to find out, for example, how he was perfectly aware of the fact that man is not monogamous by nature but must be, if he wants a stable relationship. Among the warnings addressed to his son was a reflection on fidelity in marriage: Tolkien admitted that fidelity is often a mortification (and that it is not achieved without a conscious effort), but wrote that, although marriage is an error, as there always comes a time in which you think you could have found someone more suitable, the search for self-realization in a new relationship is only an escape. I can imagine that Tolkien gave these moral lessons to his son as a wise instruction, but although sexual relations are viewed from the angle of Catholic orthodoxy (whose toughness Tolkien acknowledges) the author does not seem to lack reflection, concreteness, and even realism in what he writes. Catholic yes. Bigoted, ignorant of sex and women, no. In his work, Tolkien steers away from explicit sex and from any situation that could be seen as inappropriate: we could not expect anything else (and certainly not homosexuality, explicit or not). The customs, we must note, evolved quickly in the twentieth century, and Tolkien, despite being a "modern" writer, from this point of view, is now a man of two or three generations ago. Let us keep this in mind. A reader may find more exciting sexual situations in most fantasy books, but they will not find them from this writer, and if they already know a little about Tolkien before taking his books in hand, then they should not even expect these kinds of situations. Indeed, they should be aware, from the outset, that they will not find anything particularly bubbly, and that even the crudest scenes of death and battle will not be shown with bloody complacency. However, it is important to remember that the meanings are there, and they are powerfully expressed. If, in some respects, Tolkien may be out of date or removed from current thinking, let us remember that millions of people have read his books and not all were Catholic. There are feminists, gays, and practitioners of free love who enjoyed the work of the Oxford professor all the same. And we can see why.

Obviously, the letters left by Tolkien can provide us with a snapshot of his life as it really was, but for those who want to believe that Tolkien was a repressed homosexual or a misogynist there's always the way of psychoanalyzing the author through the text, or using structuralist analysis to find a different meaning. The reader will have to create his/her own opinion.

5

Religion and Tolkien

If you write fiction and strive to include Christian values in it (as Tolkien did), sure you're going to meet some criticism. If the writer finds inspiration in pre–Christian legends and myths, all the more reason to find himself in trouble. To understand the difficulty of being in harmony with the Catholic Church when writing about fantasy and magic, it is enough to look at the troubled relationship between the Harry Potter saga and the religious hierarchies. In 2003 Joseph Ratzinger, the future Pope Benedict XVI (2005–2013), wrote a scathing letter to a German scholar, Gabriele Kuby. He invited[1] the writer to expose the dangers caused by these books: insidious seductions, corrupting and distorting souls that still aren't formed. Moreover, Ratzinger desired to deny any rumor about a supposed Vatican approval of the young magician's adventures.

The Church changed its approach some years later, with a piece on the daily newspaper *L'Osservatore Romano*,[2] a review of the movie *Harry Potter and the Half-Blood Prince*. In the opinion of journalist Gaetano Vallini, the author J.K. Rowling writes about magic in a way that makes it impossible to see the work of Providence. Still, the distinction between good and evil is clear, and the audience is encouraged to identify with the forces of good. Also, Rowling's story unmasks the myth of the human reason that tries to give an answer to everything.

So, even in a good-natured story like Harry Potter, the favor of the Catholic Church must not be taken for granted. Tolkien was able to dodge any condemnation on the part of the Church, but his work drew criticism nonetheless.

Tolkien, Christian or Pagan?

Ronald Hutton, professor of history at the University of Bristol, in his essay "The Pagan Tolkien,"[3] tries to examine Tolkien's religious views and his sub-created world, stating that Tolkien's explanations about it don't match with his writings. This is a difficult approach, as Hutton clarifies, because Tolkien didn't want a biography created about him. The author's written records do not explain much about the creation of its setting, except for the letters, but these don't cover the first seminal years of Tolkien's worldbuilding. Letters that were written after the publication of The Lord of the Rings, in this critic's opinion, are sent to specific people for specific purposes, so we can't really take them at face value. Moreover, these documents can't enlighten us about the earlier periods of Tolkien's life and work. Hutton notes that many of the letters dedicated to the religious perspective never reached their recipients because they were discarded and kept as drafts in Tolkien's home.

This critic has broached two relevant topics. First, the information reservoir about Tolkien's thoughts and opinions is rather limited; a selected collection of letters is the main source. Second, how he had decided to cover the religious perspective was a source of doubts for him. Tolkien stated that The Lord of the Rings was a Christian work, but admitted that this characteristic was "unconscious" at first.

Hutton also raises some doubts about the commonly accepted story of Tolkien's lifelong commitment to Catholicism, based on the memory of his mother's sacrifice and the paternal figure of Francis Xavier Morgan. This sounds true in hindsight, but we know that Tolkien's faith wavered, and he almost ceased to practice during his time at Leeds University. In this essayist's opinion, when Tolkien helped C.S. Lewis (his friend of the Inklings group) to convert to Christianity, maybe he was reconnecting himself with the faith.

Last but not least, Tolkien stated that he didn't want his world to be explicitly involved in the Christian religion and that he didn't feel obligated to be coherent with Christian theology. This last claim comes from letter 269.[4] W.H. Auden, Tolkien's friend, had asked if the irredeemable nature of the race of Orcs was heretical. Tolkien answered that he had no sufficient knowledge of theology to answer that question, and he didn't think he should commit himself to fit with Christian theology anyway. But, he "supposed," Orcs were not evil in origin. Another element of Tolkien's Middle-earth that does not coincide with Christian doctrine is reincarnation, a privilege of Elves. Hutton quotes a letter[5] to be sent to a bookshop manager, in which Tolkien defends his work, claiming that what is wrong for theology could exist in his legends and that the possibility of reincarnation can't be denied as a potentiality. Tolkien wanted his world to be a fruit of his imagination, not an allegory of Christianity or anything else. In the critic's opinion, it's "significant" that Tolkien never sent the letter.

Evaluating drafts of unpublished stories written during Tolkien's youth, Hutton concentrates on Middle-earth's religious elements. The first one is Ilúvatar, the divinity of Tolkien's world. He's quite similar to the Christian God and is helped by other heavenly beings, the Ainur. One of these is the rebel, Morgoth, a Satan-like figure who goes into the material world and spreads evil there. Others have power over the elements. This system is Neoplatonic, in Hutton's opinion. Neoplatonism is an interpretation of Platonic philosophy having a supreme being creating lesser divine entities that take care of the world's various aspects. In Tolkien's world, Ilúvatar "sings" to make the Ainur, and their songs, in turn, create the world. The presence of various gods, or divine entities, reminds us of the Greek and Latin mythologies Tolkien confessed to loving very much. These divinities were prone to fight among themselves, another fact that shows a pagan origin. Having faerie creatures superior to humans (Elves, for example) is another determining factor in Hutton's judgment because this would be impossible in Christian stories.

Tolkien made several adjustments to his mythology to underline the Christian element. The proofs are in several letters. *The Silmarillion*, published posthumously by his son Christopher, is the final result.

Hutton criticizes several elements in The Lord of the Rings as examples of a Christian attitude. The hand of Providence is one of the most evident. But, in the critic's opinion, what we see as Providence could be the impersonal force of fate. Another aspect of Providence that is missing is the ending of events giving salvation infallibly to those who believed.

Another feature Hutton notes is the "celebration of the underdog," which is the sanctification of humble Hobbits as the tale's heroes. Hutton states that this element is lacking in pagan mythology but also in medieval Christian romance, so this feature has nothing to do with Christian theology. It's more probably love for the Hobbits on the part of the author.

In Hutton's opinion, another seemingly Christian element is the reward for those merciful characters who show pity for the enemy. But in Middle-earth, being compassionate is never the best strategy for the good guys. Sauron, Melkor, and Saruman receive a second chance and use it to create more calamities. Another character, Gollum, fails to be redeemed and commits treason. In this case, Gollum's action is guided by Providence to give a desirable outcome, the Ring's destruction. But this is just one of several endings Tolkien considered before deciding which one he wanted to use. Hutton presumes Tolkien chose a conclusion for the Ring scene that would satisfy those wishing for a Christian meaning. Still, it was not his primary purpose (Frodo being unable to conclude the quest with his sole willpower being the more critical element).

Hutton concludes his essay by stating that Tolkien belongs to a group of authors who "mixed together Pagan and Christian themes to produce a blend of both."

Ronald Hutton is smart in his rereading of Tolkien's work, presenting it from an unusual perspective. Suddenly, it appears that Tolkien was not so interested in creating a world inspired by Christianity. Still, Hutton bases some of his conclusions on guesswork about the various versions of the author's manuscripts.

With reference to Gollum's role in the Ring's destruction, we have a remark[6] from critic Farid Mohammadi of Azad University (Iran). He restates the Christian meaning of Frodo's failure and Gollum's intervention. Bilbo first, then Frodo, showed "mercy and compassion towards that pathetic creature, doomed to die anyway, in that most tragic way." This way, Christian values of pity and mercy had the power to accomplish the mission of destroying the Ring and redeem the world, more than weapons and magic. The more utilitarian, pitiless opinion in this quandary is Sam's inclination to kill Gollum and be done with him. If Gollum had been eliminated, the Ring couldn't have been destroyed by his intervention. He had to play his part with his treason, in the same way as Judas Iscariot caused Jesus's crucifixion and the accomplishment of God's will.

"The Christian Tolkien: A Response to Ronald Hutton" is an essay[7] by professor and theologian Nils Ivar Agøy, directly responding to the essay by Hutton we've just commented on. Agøy starts by calling into question that Tolkien almost ceased to practice his religion during his youth. The relative affirmations are found in a letter[8] written in 1963, so it's part of that same late source material Hutton thinks one has to treat with caution. Tolkien was writing to his son Michael during a time in which the latter lamented a sagging faith. So this could have been a show of solidarity to his son, having experienced the same difficulties. However, Tolkien was immediately identified as a Catholic by his friend C.S. Lewis when they met in the 1920s. Agøy doubts the Neoplatonism element being present in Ilúvatar and his Valar helpers, because there's no source stating this.

There's no demonstration about another of Hutton's theories, that it's unchristian to portray some nonhuman creatures as more gifted than Men. Also, the Elves may have better knowledge about the Valar and Ilúvatar, but this doesn't put them in more eminent status with respect to Men.

As for the gods quarreling, Agøy states that Tolkien described them this way in *The Book of Lost Tales*, a work clearly inspired by northern mythology, coherently with Tolkien's attempt to create a mythology for England at the time (the 1920s). For the author, religion and mythology are different concepts; the latter is not relevant to religious meaning. In fact, in *The Silmarillion* (a late work, published posthumously), the Valar are still called gods and the Elves still reincarnate. This contradicts Hutton's theory of a gradual transformation of Tolkien's legendarium into a shape agreeable to Christian consciences. Agøy admits that Tolkien experimented with several solutions and concepts in his worldbuilding, but, in his opinion, Hutton bases his conclusions on invalid premises.

Other topics were touched by Agøy. The creation from nothing by Ilúvatar is coherent with Christian themes, whereas pagan gods give a new form to chaos or shapeless matter. The world is destined to end (as in Christian beliefs) so it's not cyclical (pagan systems). Providence may be divine or coming from fate, but the characters' actions in The Lord of the Rings are based on moral norms and not on Providence. The celebration of the weak may be lacking in Christian romance of the Middle Ages, but it's present in the New Testament. The forgiveness and pity towards Gollum are important because in all solutions Tolkien imagined for the Ring's final scene, Gollum is there, and his presence leads to the Ring's destruction. Regarding Elven reincarnation, present in Tolkien's legendarium but not accepted by Christianity, Agøy states that this prohibition doesn't apply because Elves are a nonhuman species with a soul, so Agøy thinks Hutton's thesis is contradicted and fallacious.

We need to ask ourselves a question: Does the fact that Elves are "nonhuman" really validate their reincarnation? And if so, why?

Ronald Hutton replied to Agøy in another essay[9] admitting that it's not easy to find a definite truth about a matter so controversial. While it is not necessary to dwell on the minutiae of this exchange, an important topic is analyzed. Hutton analyzes the perspective on magic during ancient, medieval, and early modern times. Christianity could accept such a force only if its source is the Christian God. If we have the handling of natural forces unknown to the majority of people, the source of magic is the world God created, so it's legitimate. The second source of magic could be directly God, using an angel or a human as the instrument, and suspending natural laws. In this case, we have a miracle. Other sources of magic are demonic. Demons do not have the divine ability to create, but they can manipulate nature's powers or illusions.

Folklore and tradition have the use of magic judged by its results, so magic is just a tool and not good or evil by itself. In Tolkien's work,

Hutton states, magic follows this latter principle. Elves and wizards have inherent or learned knowledge of magic; evil forces behave in a very similar way. Magic is used to create illusions and to a physical effect. Tolkien makes a distinction between two kinds of magic—*Magia* and *Goeteia*, the first considered good, the other bad—but states that in his tale that neither is to be held as good or bad per se.[10] The distinction is on the purpose of the use of magic. Elven queen Galadriel is loved by Christians and compared to the Virgin Mary, but, in Hutton's opinion, Tolkien modeled Galadriel's character on medieval enchantresses or pagan sorceresses (Circe, Medea). In Christian fiction, these kinds of characters are usually distrusted, if not even seen as enemies to be defeated (C.S. Lewis's Narnia is an example of this attitude). Still, Galadriel is a gentle and good fairy in Tolkien's Middle-earth. This is but one example of the pagan aspects of the story. Trees inhabited by spirits are another example of pagan elements included in the story. The essay on *Beowulf* shows, again, the author's admiration for the pagan legendary world: in this aspect, he's similar to the author of *Beowulf*, a Christian who sets his story in a pre–Christian world with biblical undertones. Even Tolkien's general approach to fiction, as expressed in the essay "On Fairy-Stories," is a defense of fantasy literature, but the parallelisms between fantasy fiction and Christian message are just in the epilogue. By that, Tolkien didn't mean that all fantasy should be Christian. Hutton adds that Tolkien's fiction didn't lead to religious conversions but helped fantasy to become a favorite genre.

History professor and writer Stephen Morillo is another supporter of the thesis that Tolkien's work is pagan. In his opinion,[11] the author was influenced by Nordic paganism and the Middle Ages, with a personal inclination towards sadness, fate, and loss, where redemption is not relevant.

Morillo says that we have to analyze Tolkien's spirituality and sensibility because in The Lord of the Rings there's no religion.

He starts by stating that there's no divinity present in the book. *The Silmarillion* (published posthumously) gives us something of a pantheon for Tolkien's world, but we don't see these deities in action in The Lord of the Rings. Even the evil Melkor/Morgoth, the only one to intervene in Middle-earth's affairs, has been defeated, so the evil leader is now Sauron, who is not a real deity. Lacking any direct reference to religion, Morillo states that the reader has to consider his own subjective response to Tolkien's work. The author claimed that his work is profoundly Christian, but it's not a simple allegory. Because of this, its meaning is open to interpretation.

The world of the third era of Middle-earth is in decline, sad and sorrowful. The Elves are leaving, and the Ringbearers, Frodo and Bilbo, will be forced to follow them. The Entwives are lost; the Ents can't find them. The victory against Sauron will not change this sadness. Everyone will accept their fate, will fight, will accept the loss of their place in this world. In Morillo's opinion, Middle-earth has a definite spirituality that could seem related to various religions, not just Christianity. Frodo's sufferings and struggle to destroy the Ring could be a Christian hero whose self-sacrifice saves the world, but the image is not perfect. He doesn't voluntarily cede the Ring, while Bilbo did; he needs the help of Sam and, incredibly, Gollum to complete his mission. Morillo thinks Frodo could be like a bodhisattva (a Buddhist figure helping others to reach Nirvana). Moreover, Frodo doesn't save the world through his self-sacrifice. Going down a path opposite to Christ's, Frodo goes out of the world and brings the third era with him. Frodo is in fact the herald of the fourth age, the age of Men. Therefore, there's no Christ figure in The Lord of the Rings. Tolkien, in this critic's opinion, didn't want to create a Christian world; he just worried about making it compatible at an abstract level. The world he imagined was born from different myths, populated by different creatures, speaking in tongues created by him, shaped by his fantasy. Pagan, mainly Norse, mythology influenced Tolkien's work and the author's relationship with the medieval world as he knew it after his studies. His knowledge of the medieval world—a lost place he could only visit in fantasy—could have sparked Tolkien's melancholy. His war experiences could have shaped his mindset as well. Even the characters behave not as medieval people but as scholars: Gandalf searches for clues about the Ring in the library of Gondor, characters are aware of the coming end of the Third Age, the whole story is supposed to be written in just one manuscript that we can read by pure chance. Morillo sees a similar feeling in the Norse myth, with the end of one age, the Ragnarök, the melancholy of the disappearing world.

In conclusion, Morillo doesn't deny that Tolkien was Christian, but he argues that this doesn't imply that Tolkien's work is.

Ralph C. Wood, professor of theology and literature, seeks an interpretation[12] that can reconcile the Christian vision of Tolkien with his interest in Nordic myths. Wood states that Tolkien was very impressed with the Nordic concept of fate or doom, the *wyrd*. This inconsistent, unpredictable force of the Germanic and Norse sagas doesn't find an equivalent in the Mediterranean world's mythology. The final battle of Ragnarök is a catastrophe in which even the gods themselves are destined to be defeated and made to disappear in darkness and chaos with all the world. All of this without the comforting truths of Christianity. Contrary to the repetition of these themes, made by C.S. Lewis in his works, Tolkien created his massive legendarium. In this mythological narration, the Christian values are present without being in the foreground. Wood argues that while The Lord of the Rings narrates a pagan age preceding the coming of Christ, even so Tolkien gives us the feeling of something strong and powerful intent on fighting evil. Even if Sauron manipulates his earthly adversaries through the Ring's deceitful power, the reader can perceive a divine ruler guiding his humble opponents.

In *The Children of Húrin*, Tolkien returned to the wyrd concept, telling of a powerful curse by Morgoth against the hero and his family. Húrin is a tragic hero. He fights heroically against Melkor/Morgoth but fails and is captured. Tragic, unfortunate events occur again and again in his life, and his progeny is not spared. Ilúvatar (God) controls the world of Middle-earth, but an unpredictable fate still can rule our lives. With the Húrin legends, Tolkien creates a world not directly controlled by God's will, but in which our decisions still have their importance, when we can accept our destiny with humility.

Húrin's son Túrin Turambar feels stronger than the wyrd (his name means Túrin Master of Fate), and this will be his ruin when he refuses the precautionary advice from an ally (Beleg the Elf) to avoid a direct assault against Morgoth's forces. Even in his virtue and valor, Túrin is not stronger than fate. Tolkien feels compassion for this character, a victim of destiny and chance. In Wood's opinion, the author simply thought life is this way; not everything is to be attributed to God and his decisions.

Author Catherine Madsen approaches the apparent lack of a religion in Tolkien's work in her essay "Eru Erased: The Minimalist Cosmology of *The Lord of the Rings*."[13]

It's true that, in *The Silmarillion*, the author gave us a cosmology as a base of his world, but it's a posthumous publication. Tolkien created this material with many revisions and changes, so he never completed it as a book fit for publication. Moreover, he didn't use it as a basis for The Lord of the Rings. In Madsen's opinion, the new story developed in an unpredictable way leaving its origin as a book for people who wanted "more Hobbits" and turning into a complex moral narrative. Consequently, *The Silmarillion* was revised and modified many times and never came to a satisfying conclusion. This book's publication was possible thanks to Christopher Tolkien's effort to sort and select material to give the public a coherent work. During his time, Tolkien could not fully reconcile *The Silmarillion* with The Lord of the Rings. In the book's monotheistic world, God is remote; there are no temples or religious rites. The extensive cosmology of *The Silmarillion* is just not there. Madsen explains several reasons why an explicit reference to religion would have been problematic. One, for example, is the Hobbits' Shire. A religious hierarchy would imply the presence of clergy made by Hobbits, which would conflict with the state of ignorance and isolation they experience in the books. Another is referring to *The Silmarillion*'s deities as "gods": the author didn't want any false deities in his work. Tolkien wanted a story built on religious values but not an allegory; he didn't want to preach or mention them openly. He wanted the reader to be free, so he was reticent about Christianity. We know from Tolkien's correspondence that The Lord of the Rings is meant as a religious and Catholic work, but any reference to this is in the symbolism and the story's meaning.

Madsen presents the religious problem of The Lord of the Rings as a series of necessary choices on the part of the author to reconcile the meaning of a moral and ultimately Christian "fairy story" and the pre–Christian world where it takes place.

Journalist and author Chris Mooney wrote an article titled "How J.R.R. Tolkien Became a Christian Writer,"[14] in which he maintains a point of view not unlike that of Madsen regarding the nature of The Lord of the Rings. Tolkien "breathed" his sensibility and faith into pagan myths and archetypes, creating Christian mythology despite the Middle-earth setting. One of the book's strengths is the pity and forgiveness: Gollum being spared by Bilbo in *The Hobbit* and by Frodo in The Lord of the Rings is the cause of the world's salvation. This is a much-debated theme. Mooney himself seems to admit that pity is not exclusively Christian. The critic notes three Christ-like figures: Aragorn, Gandalf, and Frodo, because they are willing to sacrifice their own lives and each experiences in a different way some kind of death and resurrection. Mooney quotes an interview with David Mills, editor of a conservative magazine, calling Tolkien's narrative "stealth evangelization." Christian values are not emphasized, but they are there. Tolkien differs from his friend C.S. Lewis, another Christian fantasy writer, because he's not overtly Christian and proselytizing, whereas Lewis was openly a Christian apologist.

Professor Carson L. Holloway tries to answer one question in his essay titled "Redeeming Sub-Creation."[15] The question is: Can Tolkien be serious about his sub-creation and at the same time in harmony with the Catholic faith? The critic states that Tolkien expressed worry about his own bond to Middle-earth, confessing to his future wife that it seemed a mad hobby.[16] Maybe he feared that it was frivolous to create a fantastic world and explore it mentally? Holloway thinks this was not Tolkien's opinion. But he worried about the opinion of others. Tolkien resolved these doubts staking his claim on fantasy and sub-creation.

Man does not have the ability to create new things from nothing, but he can change creatively God's own creation, without disrespect. Fantasy is both a manifestation of reality and an ability to imagine something new. Through sub-creation, the author captures the reader's attention, making him accept the reality of the story. Internal coherence is necessary for a story to be believable. Humility, Holloway adds, is necessary to understand that artistic sub-creation is "a gift." The author can't be possessive when creating or when enjoying his creation. This is because he'd make the same mistake as Melkor, the disloyal Vala who wanted his own music of creation in contrast with Ilúvatar. So, using a non-possessive, non-greedy process of sub-creation, Tolkien was able to create his fantasy world in perfect harmony with Christianity.

We have a problem similar to that discussed in Holloway's essay in this one, by Nils Ivar Agøy: "Quid Hinieldus cum Christo?—New Perspectives on Tolkien's Theological Dilemma and his Sub-Creation Theory."[17] The Latin phrase, written by a medieval clergyman in a letter to a bishop, refers to Ingeld, a warrior of English legends. The meaning is: "What has Ingeld to do with Christ?" Well, the question can be rephrased for Tolkien's work: How can a pagan world be reconciled with Christianity?

There is no doubt that the author was working with pagan material. His desire to write a "mythology for England" forced him to augment the scarce mythological material from tradition with his own creation. In the first version of his legendarium, Tolkien had several gods, similar to the ones in Norse mythology. Two of them were war gods. Then the author had to deal with the problem of giving this pagan mythology to the readers. How could a Christian write of similar things?

Tolkien altered and edited his legendarium to remove any excessive pagan element. In successive publications, he defended his work stating that it's not contrary to Christianity; in fact, it helps the reader to see and understand our world, sometimes offering visions beyond this world (the Eucatastrophe). The works where Tolkien defends his own perspective are "Mythopoeia," "On Fairy-Stories," and "Leaf by Niggle." In Agøy's opinion, the sub-creation theory was, in part, created to be the solution to Tolkien's quandary: the ability of Man to create, being made in God's image.

Tolkien's beliefs in this case are not wholly original; they come from philosophy and theology. Agøy cites writers George MacDonald, G.K. Chesterton, and Owen Barfield as some of the influences closer to Tolkien's times. But he thinks an important influence came from Nikolaj Frederik Severin Grundtvig (1782–1872), Danish theologian, historian, and poet. Scandinavian mythology was Grundtvig's lifelong interest: he united the fragments of Norse mythology to create a coherent story. He did this in a time in which mythology was a cornerstone of national consciousness: his work is comparable to Elias Lönnrot's gathering and writing down the old Finnish legends in the *Kalevala*. In Grundtvig's thought, myth was compatible with Christian faith, but also a basis for national identity. This affinity between the Lutheran faith and the mythological past broke down, in the Danish theologian's mind, in 1810, when he had a "conversion" to pure, unadulterated Lutheranism. Grundtvig didn't destroy his manuscripts (as he was initially resolved to do), but he added parts that connected his work to Christianity again. He struggled to validate the myths he loved with the religion he followed, so he imagined a continuing process of creation on the part of God so that Christianity was the truest and perfect myth, but pagan mythology was a light in the dark, giving glimpses of the Truth. Good pagans in a sinful world could exist. Their only shortcoming was not being Christians yet. In Grundtvig's opinion, the Scalds of the North created mythology complimentary to Christianity: they narrate human life and adventures in the world, while Christianity tells the truth about eternal matters. Obviously, Grundtvig didn't condone any pagan worship, while he appreciated the Northern natural philosophy. The sub-creation theory as invented by Grundtvig starts from the poetic ability and its function: to uncover, not to invent. Creating is the process that Man can use to achieve the image of God he carries with him (as God's creature). Man is a creator because he's both the image and creation of God. Poetic ability permits Man to glimpse the higher truth, but this ability can lead to bad results if misused because Man needs God's help to distinguish between truth and lies. The word is the instrument of the poetic ability, given to Man as the lord of other creatures. Word contains an image of God's word of creation indeed.

By this point, we have to ask ourselves: Did Tolkien know about Grundtvig? Was he influenced by his theories, so similar to Tolkien's own? As a pioneer in Anglo-Saxon studies, Grundtvig was certainly known to Tolkien. The Danish philologist in his time worked on the epic poem *Beowulf*, as Tolkien did during the following century, possibly finding Grundtvig's work as one of the main references available. The critical assessment of *Beowulf* is similar in both scholars' work. Love for Anglo-Saxon and Scandinavian culture, the need to reconcile it with Catholic faith, and a theory to create the needed justification: these are common factors in Tolkien and Grundtvig. Still, Agøy has no conclusive evidence of Tolkien being inspired by the Danish theologian.

The Valar as Inefficient Deities

Burt Randolph wrote[18] about the role fulfilled by the Valar as the guardians of the world. A badly managed role, in his opinion. Since Tolkien paid attention to every detail, it would be strange if he didn't notice this. Being the angelic powers watching over the world, the Valar were custodians of Middle-earth. They were responsible not only for the Undying Lands of Valinor but for the rest as well: at least they had to care for Elves and Men, probably for Dwarves and Hobbits too. Sure the Valar were capable of powerful acts; in fact, they destroyed Elenna by a deluge to punish the arrogance of the Númenóreans, a strong human kingdom of the Second Age of Middle-earth. By this statement, Randolph shows how the Valar lack neither power nor the ability to use it. Furthermore, it's clear that Morgoth and Sauron are dangerous threats to the world and all the people living in it. So, the Valar had the power. But how did they use it? Randolph, whose knowledge of Tolkien's worldbuilding in 1968 was, of course, limited by the fact that he was writing before *The Silmarillion* was published, lists several events in which evil was spreading, and some of the Valar come to Middle-earth for various reasons. When Morgoth stole the Silmarilli, Fëanor's attempt to recover them by force did not receive the endorsement of the Valar. Consequently, Fëanor's desperate struggle against Morgoth failed, and he died as a result. Then we had the fall of Gondolin and the destruction of Beleriand; then Eärendil the half-Elf finally obtained help from the Valar. Morgoth was defeated, but Sauron managed to hide and waited for the chance of a comeback.

Afterward, Sauron forged the Rings and caused another war, being defeated by the Númenóreans. But Sauron created trouble again, in a new way. He managed to corrupt the Númenóreans, so they attacked the Land of Valinor (the sacred land of the west). They hoped to win immortality, but all they got for their arrogance was utter destruction. Randolph notes that the Valar caused the death of many of the people of Númenór, but were more lenient with the forces of evil.

Morgoth established his kingdom, stole the Silmarils (jewels), killed the Two Trees that gave light to Valinor. His armies massacred Elves and Men. Whole regions were devastated. When Sauron was defeated, he was allowed to come back again. It seems that fighting evil is done at a terrible cost to the people of Middle-earth.

The Valar may be limited in what they can do by the will of "the One," that is, God (Ilúvatar). But their performance as Guardians of the World is quite poor, Randolph argues. He still thinks that Tolkien produced a fantastic work, but he wonders why Tolkien chose this kind of performance for the Valar.

This essay touches a sore point, a possible plot hole, a frustrating aspect of Tolkien's work. The Valar decide, for their own reasons, to stay in their western heavenly lands after the first battles against evil. Tolkien here was in a dilemma. He liked his mythology, born from his love for Nordic legends. But he didn't want to overplay this aspect because he wanted to create, with The Lord of the Rings, a book supporting Christian values. So the almost divine Valar can't appear too often, else the narration could sound too pagan in nature. This is a valid reason, but how does it work in the book?

The pains and tribulations of Elves, Men, and all the Free Peoples of Middle-earth are linked to a more fundamental question: Why is evil (the absence of good) allowed to exist? Why doesn't God Almighty crush it as soon as it manifests itself? In the real world, the answer is that people have free will. They can decide to create evil or to fight against it. In Middle-earth, maybe the problem is different: Morgoth, an entity that we could call the devil himself, roams the lands of Tolkien's world; he calls to his help devilish and powerful beings, like the balrogs and dragons. He perverts living creatures to create the Orcs, fanatical warriors devoted to his cause. In front of these powerful enemies, the Free Peoples suffer terrible defeats, with the Valar's help arriving when their situation is desperate.

John Garth, quoting *The Book of Lost Tales*, notes[19] that Tolkien himself argued that the Valar should have moved war against Melko (Melkor/Morgoth) after the destruction of the Trees. But they didn't, so Middle-earth has become a tormented world. Garth finds a reason for this in Tolkien's life experience. His image as a respected teacher and author, living a well-ordered life fully involved in work and family, pertains to his later years, when he was professionally settled. However, Tolkien never had any serenity or a stable situation in his younger years. His life was studded with tragedy and loss. After some happy years in the village of Sarehole, he was forced to move in precarious city accommodations; he witnessed the struggles and the death of his mother. Then he had to go to war. There was no paradise or security for him.

Tolkien the Myth Maker?

Richard L. Purtill, an American professor and fantasy writer, examined Tolkien's myth-making in *J.R.R. Tolkien: Myth, Morality, and Religion*.[20] Purtill argues that while Tolkien's books can't claim actual myth status, somehow they are more than just stories. Myths are stories of gods or heroes with a religious or moral significance, believed to be true by the people who tell them. In contrast, the myth creator doesn't necessarily think every detail of the story is authentic. He uses imagination, traditions, and legends to create a narration about the deeds of mythical characters. Gospel resembles original myths in many ways and is considered authentic by believers. In contrast, original myth can be used for literary purposes by writers and audiences who don't believe in its religious meaning. Even humor can exist in myth (it does exist in Homer), but it must be presented in a particular way, maintaining seriousness when the scene is about the solemn or the magic. Purtill states that Tolkien tries to create a literary myth "as close as possible in our day to original myth. Tolkien was, of course, not foolish enough to think of himself as creating gospel (though a few of his madder readers may make this error)." In Purtill's opinion, there's a need for myths that is not satisfied these days. Tolkien couldn't create new myths but linked his works to the gospel's truth, the "primary belief" Christians accept. So readers enjoy Tolkien's literary myth because of their beliefs supporting it. There's no way to create an original (new) myth today, but it's possible to incorporate the truth people believe into a literary myth. This is what Tolkien did, Purtill argues. The famous passage in which Tolkien talked of creating a mythology for England[21] is not to be interpreted as Tolkien viewing himself as a creator of an original myth. He was speaking of writing stories. He specifies that a fairy story (or myth) must include "elements of moral and religious truth," although not in an explicit form. The Lord of the Rings is undoubtedly a Christian book. But the author understood that it would be absurd to try and create an original myth in modern times. Tolkien knows his work is an artistic expression, a literary myth. In the *Letters*[22] Tolkien reveals that the book's real theme is not the struggle for power and domination. The war is just the setting in which the characters operate and have to make their choices.

The Sub-Creation and Its Critics

In Tolkien's opinion fantasy is not entirely made up, as Tom Shippey notes.[23] Still, Shippey argues that maybe he was not entirely sure about this. Tolkien remained equivocal when talking about the possible reality of fantasy, which could be something like "making or glimpsing of Otherworlds."[24] Tolkien thought that creating fairy stories was something between a rational and a mystic activity. The artist could create fantasy by sub-creative Art. Still, the wonder of the fantastic world derives from the Image: this Image exists independently of the writer, is something magic, a spell, essentially true but so difficult, or impossible, to prove. Yet existing, in Tolkien's opinion. His vision of fantasy litera-ture was quite ambitious.

In Dal Lago's opinion,[25] Tolkien and the Inklings, his group of fellow writers, were embarked on something like an anti-modernist crusade (in this context, Dal Lago cites mainly C.S. Lewis, Owen Barfield, and Charles Williams). They did not belong to the same religious denomina-tion because while Tolkien was Catholic the others were Anglican. But all of them were deeply religious, and their cultural environment was strongly conservative and hostile to modernism. They shared a pater-nalistic outlook on women (moreover, their group admitted no women); this point of view reflects the marginal role women assume in Tolkien's and Lewis's narrative works. They wrote essays on medieval literature, literary and theological criticism. Medieval myths were an inspiration for the Inklings for they longed to create literature both mythological and moral, as opposed to modernity with its uncertainties and skep-ticism. C.S. Lewis made a vast literary output about Nordic antiquity and its moral values. The medieval era inspired the Inklings because it was a world ordered according to principles of faith. It was compatible with their ideas, even when it was a pre–Christian world. In their opin-ion, the sub-creator, the writer, continues the creation (sub-creation) with his words, inspired by God. In this way, the Inklings created new, alternative mythologies. Their mythopoiesis (creation of myths) should be seen as an instrument to access another spiritual reality. In Dal Lago's words, sub-created worlds are "more real than the one we live in" because the faculty of language connects both of them to reality, and the truth in the sub-created world is not empiric but divine. So, Tolkien and Lewis "really thought that their right as sub-creators came directly from God." The fantasy writer would be a kind of prophet. In a more direct way, Lewis writes about a struggle between Satan and Christ on several planets or in a parallel world; Tolkien created his fantasy world with no allegory, religion, or politics. Dal Lago concludes: "Inklings mythologies became familiar to our world, even if their readers are not always aware of their nature or pastoral function."

Mark J.P. Wolf argues[26] that a sub-creator belongs to a particu-lar group of authors who create an imaginary world for reasons that go beyond the need to have a setting for their narrations. The cre-ation of a secondary world uses concepts from the primary world (the world created by God), creating new combinations and possibilities. Humans have this skill because they are created by God, who made the primary world from nothing, a possibility the sub-creator doesn't have. A sub-creator writes with some moral or religious purpose.

Therefore, Wolf explains why Tolkien presents himself as a sub-creator, and you may or may not give a meaning to this. It's obvious that other writers are not interested in a similar claim (we can seriously doubt that Michael Moorcock, China Miéville, George Martin, or Joe Abercrombie want to be called sub-creators).

In Daniel Grotta's biography, there's another speculation about Tolkien as a creator of myth.[27] As a given fact, Grotta states, Tolkien believed that language, words need stories and myths, so he may have written The Lord of the Rings as an attempt to better comprehend the link between language and mythology. Following Tolkien's theory of sub-creation, we could also suppose that he was trying to see if a credible myth could become "a point of reference for the real world." The only way to verify this was to see what the readers could discover in the book. Grotta thinks that this could be why Tolkien never talked about the meaning of his work or, when asked, answered that there is no meaning. If a reader could find meaning in the book, he wouldn't need to be told about it. Tolkien wanted the reader to suspend disbelief and enter Middle-earth just like it was part of the real world. A theme that he admitted was central in his writing was death, and the inevitability of it, and what death means for the single man.

If Grotta's hypothesis is true, we'll never know, because Tolkien would have observed the outcome of his efforts without revealing anything about it.

But It's a Manichean Battle

Jason Boffetti argues[28] that evidence for Tolkien's astonishing theological consistency and thoughtfulness can be found simply by reading his published letters. There Tolkien admits that in creating Middle-earth he carefully constructed a world with the same moral contours as our world. Throughout the novels, Middle-earth's ethics and metaphysics are consistent with the moral world we know: corruption of the will, not a magical power, or just fate, lies at the heart of evil acts. "Magical" objects—like technology in our own world—are good insofar as they are used for good ends. A willingness to share in suffering is a necessary part of taking up our moral duties. He carefully avoids painting the struggle between the Free Peoples of Middle-earth and the minions of the archvillain Sauron as a strictly Manichean battle of "good versus evil." Tolkien's approach is more Augustinian: The characters of Middle-earth are distinguished above all by what they love. Among the Free Peoples, one finds both the noble and the corrupt. Every character can be ruined by the sin of pride, and the wicked have the capacity for moments of good action (such as Gollum) and even moral redemption (such as Boromir).

In The Lord of the Rings we certainly have good versus evil, but individual characters make different decisions. What Boffetti says is critical because the two powers in the struggle are obviously good and evil, for most of the readers. As we have seen, Tolkien thought the struggle was not important; the individual choices were.

Eru as a Distant God

Polish critic Tadeusz Andrzej Olszański analyzes[29] the problem of evil taking into account Tolkien's legendarium. The existence of evil is a philosophical problem in concurrence with a God that is benevolent. European religion is based on an Indo-European dualistic tradition, with a good entity struggling against an evil one, while in Semitic tradition God can act in favor of good or evil, but evil is the result of resistance to God. Christianity emerged from Semitic tradition but developed in the Indo-European world, so we have a benevolent God but also a Satan, an adversary of lesser but not insignificant power. In Tolkien's theodicy, before creation, we had Eru (God) and the void. The void is nothing, but it exists as space where a different thought can be formulated: an objection to God. Olszański quotes the Bible (Book of Genesis) where God saw the light, and it was good; he kept it separated from darkness. Darkness obviously was different (not good); but God contains all the different meanings, so an initial seed of evil can emerge. It appears with the Ainur, because they are God's helpers, and they have all the different aspects of divinity. Among them is Melkor: he's not evil at the beginning, but he becomes independent and proud. He's not the only one to go beyond the limits set for the creators, but he doesn't repent like Aulë or Ossë.

Eru doesn't destroy evil but incorporates it into his plan to create good and beauty from evil itself. The good deeds and sacrifice of those who fight evil could not, in fact, exist without Melkor's rebellion. It could look as if Providence, or the will of God, has predestined the triumph of the good side, but it must be earned. There's not a certainty of victory in the struggle, no fixed destiny. Ilúvatar's sons can't depend on fate or a divine hope for salvation. They have to fight for self-salvation. The "final victory" after the many defeats will come only at the end, in the Dagor Dagorath, the Last Battle, when Melkor/Morgoth will be slain, following the prophecy of Mandos. After this battle, the world will be renewed. In Olszański's opinion, Tolkien's legendarium gives us evil born from the desire for independence, the resistance against Eru the creator, following the Semitic concept of evil. But Eru is a distant god: he permits that his helpers manage the creation of reality, and when they rebel, he accepts the contraposition of good and evil, a Manichean view more similar to the Indo-European tradition. After the Third Age and the Númenórean rebellion, things change. Eru is forced to intervene and to change the nature of the world; the world becomes spherical and Valinor (the blessed land in the West) is separated. Eru's intervention also means that the role of the Valar is diminished. Providence will guide Men's action, preparing the world for the Christian revelation.

In conclusion: several critics debated about the religious nature of Tolkien's work. He himself defined it as Christian, but this doesn't stop some scholars from calling it pagan. It's clear that Christian messages and morality are present in The Lord of the Rings, as it is clear that Nordic pagan legends have influence in Tolkien's work, an influence mitigated by the author. We have several examples of this "Christianization" of themes: think about the "social responsibility" of heroes, or the necessity of relinquishing and destroying the Ring, the symbol of power. Tolkien walked a tightrope between the mythology he loved and his own Christian faith, creating an acceptable compromise (acceptable for anyone except some very dedicated and severe Christians). The material left unpublished after the author's death is to be read with caution: we don't know if he was going to publish it, or in what form. Anyway, there's no pagan comeback in the material you can find in The Silmarillion and other posthumous works.[30]

Conclusion

I read The Lord of the Rings trilogy for the first time around the age of 18, solely for the pleasure of fantasy reading, like many did. Then, having then re-read the main works a few times over the years, I gradually began to appreciate the less obvious aspects, but always sought, first and foremost, the pleasure of a good read. In this Tolkien's masterpiece, there are actually parts that I find slow, even quite boring; the work as a whole, however, is fascinating, even re-reading it after so many years. I am not a Tolkien "fan," to put it briefly, even though I do recognize his greatness. I am not even aligned with his worldview, neither in terms of religious faith nor with respect to his anti-modernism, but on this second point I do not consider Tolkien a ridiculous reactionary. I must admit that his words sound an alarm bell that rings even louder today, almost half a century after his death. Not even Tolkien's passion for preserving the countryside and its pretty landscapes sees me one hundred percent in agreement, because I personally prefer the concept of sustainable development (and the hope that it can be put into practice).

Simply put, I am not "on Tolkien's side" even though, by presenting some of his critics in these pages, I rarely felt aligned with their points of view. Obviously, I do not share the snobbish views about this author with those who did not even consider him worthy of any consideration. Even if there is some truth in the criticisms, I do still appreciate his work. An author's ideology should not be a reason for not liking his writings, especially when the main purpose of the narrative is not overtly political. Two things really make me cringe at Tolkien criticism: when there's exaggerated intrusion into the author's private life, and when criticism borders on open slander and insult, sometimes under the guise of elegant humor. The former can be a necessity to understand his way of thinking, however, and critics are certainly free to engage in the latter.

In my opinion, many arguable aspects of Tolkien's world, such as the social or political, should be evaluated without forgetting that it is a fairy tale world, referring to a mythological past. Of course, the author lived in modern times.

Therefore, one can criticize this author and his choices from a current point of view. Still, I find certain ferocious accusations that presume malicious and reactionary ideological operations in Tolkien's work to be excessive, and I believe that caution should be exercised in drawing "morals" from every aspect of his work. Being as it is a fairy tale, it is normal to talk about a distant land, knights and kings, and a fight against evil.

The Enemy Is a Human Being

Talking about the Orcs, here is my greatest problem with Tolkien's work. It's not that I believe the way Orcs are treated means Tolkien is a racist. As Patrick Curry wrote,[1] it's an insult to readers' intelligence to think that they transfer their feeling about Orcs to the swarthy or slant-eyed people (as by Tolkien's description) they encounter on the street. The problem is different, a problem that was noted by some[2] of the critics.

I know fairy stories present us terrible feats: Hansel and Gretel burning the witch in the oven is just an example. In Tolkien's work, the Orcs are treated as cannon fodder; they are hateful and hated. Still, Tolkien wrote The Lord of the Rings, fairy story or not, in a time when he should have known better. Moreover, he admitted[3] that Orcs have a soul and in theory could find redemption. But it never happens. He wrote that Orcs are not really another race, but they are treated as if they were, giving the good guys the certainty that they are evil. Easterlings and Southrons are probably forced to fight; the Orcs are always Sauron's willing minions. When Tolkien states that his work is not about a fight of good against evil, but it's about the individual choices, this means the choices of those on the good side. The others are not important. He creates a setting where the Orc as an enemy is irremediably "other." The humanity of this enemy is denied, the possibility of communication is not there. Tom Shippey wrote that Beowulf could never reason with the troll Grendel, but Grendel is something of a mythological enemy, one of a kind. Supernatural beings like the Balrogs are the embodiment of spirits; they are not persons. The Orcs are people, though, though apparently a category of people who can be killed without remorse; two heroes in the book engage in a friendly competition to see who can score the greater body count. I'm not a bleeding heart, but this is a bit much. The Orcs as conceived in The Lord of the Rings are targets for blood sports and justification for a merry and self-righteous sadism. Worst of all, it's not difficult to take the "evil" label and apply to someone: this is an operation you see every day in politics and war. Whatever justification I tried to find, I couldn't avoid an unpleasant feeling when confronted with Tolkien's Orcs, even if, obviously, they are depicted as universally bad. The fact that Tolkien is a Christian writer makes me even more puzzled. Besides that, in today's world, where hate is fuelled and channeled by social media under the guise of righteous motives, we don't need the hunt for easy targets as Tolkien's "Orcs."

My Criticism about the Story

To criticize the worldbuilding of the most successful fantasy author can hardly give good results. Still, I have something to say about it. The peoples of Middle-earth have no religion, no churches, no worship. God, "the One," is immensely remote. We know why Tolkien did it, obviously: he didn't want a pagan world. But the situation these people live in, generation after generation, makes no sense. Maybe not everyone needs to pray, to worship. But for the majority, organized religion is a must. With rites, a clergy, temples, and so on. In fact, in the real world some kind of religion is found everywhere, in several forms, in all historical times. Tolkien went against the rule and got away with it.

I also have an issue with his characters. As we've seen, Tolkien denied the plot had real importance. The Lord of the Rings is not about a fight for freedom, it's not about good guys fighting against evil, it's not about absolute evil. The story is about characters' choices. As we've seen, whoever makes the wrong choices is lost. He dies. Some good characters die also, but yielding to evil leads to sure death. The only ostensible exception is Frodo, but he's overpowered by his impossible task; he doesn't make a conscious, free decision when he decides to keep the Ring. Even Frodo is unable to live in peace after the conflict. Anyway, I would have liked to see someone spared from Tolkien's rule. For example, a heroic Boromir who makes up for the bad decision to attack Frodo and comes back into grace, instead of being killed so early. Also, I'd like a bad guy who is not a monster so terrible that is impossible to talk to him. A leader of the Southrons or Easterlings who rebels against the Dark Lord and fights for Gondor. A patrol of Orcs that deserts and asks for quarter. I think these details would make a more realistic world and a better book. Probably many readers would disagree with me (and, obviously: do we really desire Middle-earth as a realistic world?), but not everyone. To tell the truth, a nuanced bad guy does exist. The hateful Saruman, good with words but disloyal, has a character arc in Tolkien's legendarium. As one of five wizards sent to Middle-earth to control Sauron's moves, Saruman was in fact an angelic creature. As a leader of the White Council, he directed the Free Peoples' resistance against Sauron's rise. Having decided that the Ring is an interesting artifact, Saruman acts in a self-serving way, limiting the actions against Sauron, telling lies, and acting to maximize his own chances to recover the Ring. For a time, he's still an independent leader and one of the "good guys." About two of the other wizards we know nothing certain. Another one is Radagast, maybe a bit naïve, too much interested in beasts and nature; he will help Saruman in good faith luring Gandalf into a trap. Gandalf, the only other successful wizard, is the one who will manage to save the situation and defeat Sauron, after dealing with Saruman. So, traitor Saruman fails to recover the Ring, fails to neutralize Gandalf after capturing him, and is then crushed in battle by the Ents. His plans to be Sauron's equal or rival misfire; he could be pardoned by Gandalf, but out of pride he refuses. As a consequence, Gandalf strips him of any power, so he's utterly defeated, but still alive. As a last bad deed, he will defile the Hobbits' Shire. His adversaries don't kill him, but this time he finally dies, killed by his own accomplice, Grima. His story is long and complex; he's not a likable character, but he enjoys a long, interesting plot, even if it ends in shame and ridicule. The problem is that these facts take place over a very long time. Tolkien narrates them in The Lord of the Rings and in its appendices, and in notes that were published after his death as *The Silmarillion* and *Unfinished Tales*. This means that when we see Saruman in The Lord of the Rings, he has already deserted the good fight and is allied to Sauron. He talks to Gandalf, tells some lies, reveals some of his goals trying unsuccessfully to convert Gandalf to his plans, then captures him. We don't see the evolution of his motives and decision-making, because he's already corrupted when we meet him. Of the other characters who make bad choices and die, Gollum doesn't offer real complexity, being torn between the need to recover the Ring and a failed attempt at redemption. Boromir is quickly eliminated when he tries to take the Ring; Denethor just descends into madness when he thinks all is lost. Saruman is the nuanced, sophisticated bad guy some critics think Tolkien could not create. There are a couple of problems with him, though. First, we just see the last phase of his long story arc. Second, he's an insufferable, arrogant scumbag from the start.

Women, Tradition, Utopia

Tolkien's stories are full of danger and battles. It's no wonder if we don't find many women there. If women have a traditional role in Tolkien's work, we must ask ourselves whether this really detracts from its value and how surprised and disappointed we really are. If Tolkien describes an ancient and traditional world, pervaded with values that are not incompatible with the Catholic religion, does this really disturb us, considering it does not even appear? As there are those who have judged these elements as real reactionary propaganda, I can assure you that I have read and appreciated Tolkien's work without being saddled in any way with his worldview, and I am sure that the same can be said for the vast majority of readers. The nostalgia that the author arouses in the reader has a complex meaning. It implies a radical critique of the modern world (and here, at least in part, I agree with Patrick Curry's interpretation), and not only in a reactionary sense. Tolkien's words should be considered as an artistic expression of the sorrow for environment's destruction. The reader can be encouraged to translate those feelings into political action, but he will not find any working ideology in Tolkien's work. The author had no formula to change things, and he realized that. He acknowledged that the need to build more houses could mean uglier cities or the destruction of the countryside.[4] Not a real choice. Tolkien understood this, yet he persisted with his utopia, his impossible desire, which inspired the actions of others.

Has the legendarium become a new myth? In the days of internet memes, we need to be cautious when dealing with this. It's difficult for a new mythology, in the sense of religious truth, to be universally shared in today's world. But if you hear in office gossip that a certain boss has been compared to Sauron, you immediately understand what they are talking about. Tolkien is commonplace, proverbial. From his stories we can extract bits of common wisdom. Maybe he is even a bit of a moral authority.

A "Popular" Writer

Finally, I propose my personal point of view on the author. As for Tolkien's style, we have seen that some critics have judged him as not being expressive enough, or bland and decidedly cloying, or unable to provide the reader with real information about what they are seeing. I, on the other hand, think his way of writing is generally valid and suitable for the purpose he wants to achieve. It is certainly not the only style

I appreciate, and I do not only read Tolkien or his imitators. Today, readers have broad alternatives. Writers who are very realistic in style and raw in language have taken the limelight of fantasy, putting an end to the prevalence of the Tolkien-inspired line, and in my opinion, this is not a bad thing. However, it is unlikely that The Lord of the Rings will be forgotten, like other books that have had their day, as its success has embraced several decades. Any thesis on Tolkien's literary limits, or his style as a writer, must be filtered with a very positive judgment from the public, enduring and not fortuitous: while the success of its most fortunate imitators is destined to fade, Tolkien's is constant, as far as we can tell. Tolkien, a writer of undoubted genius, bearer of ideas but certainly not inclined to throw himself into fights, had his say, and said it with incomparable grace and class. What he wrote also pleased readers who Tolkien presumably did not address, and whom he did not think about pleasing. He was able to stand in opposition to contemporary ideologies and ways of thinking, focusing on people's hearts and giving the reader, in stark contrast with the broken promises of the twentieth century (and presumably of the present century), the vision of a world rich in values and timeless beauty, much more attractive than our uncertain present. If it is disputed that his work is escapism, Tolkien's famous reply regarding the prisoner's escape, not to be confused with the deserter's escape, indicates self-awareness as well as slightly inviting us, the reader, to open our eyes, without imposing this idea onto us. This goes beyond the philological and academic studies that were the basis of his interest in telling stories. Tolkien was certainly not a politician, and what he had to say, he said as an artist, therefore with a rigorous coherence in his nostalgic dreams of a mythical past, or in his criticism of the present, a criticism that is generally only implicit anyway.

Tolkien attributes characteristics he considered to be negative in the contemporary world to the villains of his story: the will to commit heinous crimes, the use of an out-of-control science and industry to destroy what the natural and beautiful world has to offer. Contrary to what some of his critics believe, Tolkien was not on the side of any government and there was no nationalist sentiment in him: if he was anti-modernist, to simply call him a conservative is to misunderstand a large part of his thinking.

Tolkien wrote from a point of view that, in their opinion, was not palatable, but this does not mean that he wrote a political pamphlet, or a suggestive work of propaganda. Of course, there are those who take The Lord of the Rings as sacred text, but only because they read it from an established point of view (religious, socio-political) akin to that of the author.

You can be sure that millions of readers have enjoyed the quality of these books and appreciated its generic message of freedom and courage without reactionary ideologies surreptitiously entering their minds. The love for nature and a simple living is another aspect everyone can share. As noted by Patrick Curry when talking to readers from different nations,[5] every people has its "Hobbits," simple rural folks, and related traditions (and inevitable nostalgia, I could add, although I prefer big cities for myself). When

J.R.R. Tolkien

I began to look into the deeper meanings within Tolkien, rather than reading him simply as a fantasy author, I became reflective; sometimes I found myself in agreement, sometimes it led me to think about points of view I did not share, but I did not feel coerced to accept them. Should the "progressive" reader keep away from him, out of fear of becoming reactionary, homophobic, anti-feminist if they read it? If this was the correct perspective, then the progressive critics would be treating the reader as disabled, and they would be behaving in the same way as the clergy of other eras, creating lists of forbidden books so as to prevent them from falling into the hands of the God-fearing child. In short, aside from the all-too-easy accusation of envy that could be addressed to those writers who joined Tolkien's lynching, the vehemence of certain attacks is ridiculous and the hatred that shines through is not very uplifting.

Above everything, as much as one can look for limits in Tolkien's work, it cannot be denied, given his enduring popularity, that Tolkien succeeded in writing a popular novel, capable of reaching consciences through the genre of fantasy. Despite the opinion of the critics and the intellectuals, the readers themselves bestowed a great success on

Tolkien, certainly beyond the premise of his work. The author's political ideas seemed to have been ignored by most readers and certainly by those of the youth movements who made up the first great wave of The Lord of the Rings admirers: they had no trouble loving his stories despite the fact that they probably would not get along with Tolkien if they ever happened to discuss society and politics with him. What about the problems about the linguistic rendering of his words, which aroused a great deal of concern in the Oxford professor, including disagreements with the translators? They were completely bypassed by dozens of beautiful or ugly translations, in languages that could preserve nothing of the philological research or the original sonorities (and yet Tolkien's names sound so good). Was mythology the inspiration? That may well have helped, providing the author with excellent inspiration, but how many of the readers have a more than marginal knowledge of this?

With Tolkien, the fantasy had neither a new ideologue nor a guerrilla warrior; his detractors can rest easy. Most likely, without even wanting it, Tolkien has become (with all the limitations that the comparisons always have) like the despised popular writers of the feuilleton era. These were supplements of newspapers, serial stories you could cut out and collect at every issue. The feuilleton writers wrote cheesy or trashy stories to please an audience of unsophisticated tastes. Stories for simple people, for housemaids and seamstresses, and yet such celebrated authors as Alexandre Dumas (famous for *The Count of Monte Cristo*, *The Three Musketeers*, *Twenty Years After*, and other masterpieces) came from this unappreciated literary milieu. Victor Hugo's masterworks (*Les Misérables, Notre Dame de Paris*) were deemed worthy of a youthful or girlish audience, bad literature, offending morals and good taste; *Les Misérables* was banned by the Church. But these writers are popular still today. Like them, Tolkien will continue to please generations of readers.

Chapter Notes

Introduction

1. Germaine Greer, "Book of the Century, Germaine Greer on Our Readers' Poll," *Waterstone*, Winter/Spring 1997.

Chapter 1

1. Edmund Wilson, "Oo, those awful orcs!" *The Nation*, April 14, 1956.
2. Tom Shippey, *J.R.R. Tolkien: Author of the Century* (New York: HarperCollins, 2000), 66.
3. Letter 165, in *The Letters of J.R.R. Tolkien*, ed. Christopher Tolkien and Humphrey Carpenter (New York: HarperCollins, 2006), 219.
4. *The Letters of J.R.R. Tolkien*, ed. Christopher Tolkien and Humphrey Carpenter (New York: HarperCollins, 2006).
5. Maurice Richardson, "New Novels: Review of *The Two Towers*," *The New Statesman*, December 18, 1954.
6. Tom Shippey, *J.R.R. Tolkien: Author of the Century*, 306.
7. Quoted by Edmund Fuller, "The Lord of the Hobbits: J.R.R. Tolkien," in *Tolkien and the Critics: Essays on J.R.R. Tolkien's The Lord of the Rings*, ed. Neil D. Isaacs and Rose A. Zimbardo (Notre Dame: University of Notre Dame Press, 1968).
8. Quoted by Patrick Curry, "Tolkien and His Critics: A Critique," in *Root and Branch: Approaches to Understanding Tolkien*, ed. Thomas Honegger (Zurich: Walking Tree Publishers, 2005).
9. Ibid.
10. In *The Times*, December 18, 2002.
11. Marion Zimmer Bradley, "Men, Halflings, and Hero Worship," in *Tolkien and the Critics: Essays on J.R.R. Tolkien's The Lord of the Rings*.
12. Quoted by Patrick Curry, "Tolkien and His Critics: A Critique," in *Root and Branch: Approaches to Understanding Tolkien*.
13. Michael Moorcock, "Epic Pooh," in *J.R.R. Tolkien*, Bloom's Modern Critical Views, ed. Harold Bloom (New York: Infobase Publishing, 2008).
14. J.R.R. Tolkien, *Tree and Leaf* (New York: HarperCollins, 1964).
15. Burton Raffel, "*The Lord of the Rings* as Literature," in *Tolkien and the Critics: Essays on J.R.R. Tolkien's The Lord of the Rings*.
16. An archetype is a psychic image that is common to everyone. In the theory by the psychoanalyst Carl Jung (1875–1961), the human psyche possesses this innate experience, just like an instinct. For example, in Jungian theory everyone knows what a "hero" is, not because they learn it, but because this archetype is in the collective unconscious.
17. Catharine Stimpson, "J.R.R. Tolkien," in *Columbia Essays on Modern Writers, No. 41* (New York: Columbia University Press, 1969).
18. Thomas L. Gasque, "Tolkien: The Monsters and the Critters," in *Tolkien and the Critics: Essays on J.R.R. Tolkien's The Lord of the Rings*.
19. Richard L. Purtill, *J.R.R. Tolkien: Myth, Morality, and Religion* (New York: Harper & Row, 1984).
20. Christina Scull, "Open Minds, Closed Minds," in *Proceedings of the J.R.R. Tolkien Centenary Conference*, ed.

Patricia Reynolds and Glen H. Good-knight (Mythopoeic Press and The Tolkien Society, 1995).

21. Richard Morgan, "The Real Fantastic Stuff," suvudu.com, February 18, 2009, http://suvudu.com/2009/02/the-real-fantastic-stuff-an-essay-by-richard-k-morgan.html.

22. China Miéville, "Middle Earth meets Middle England," *Socialist Review* no. 259 (January 2002), https://socialistworker.co.uk/socialist-review-archive/tolkien-middle-earth-meets-middle-england/.

23. Edwin Muir, "Strange Epic," *Observer*, August 22, 1954, quoted by Humphrey Carpenter, *J.R.R. Tolkien: A Biography* (New York: HarperCollins, 1995), 222.

24. Tom Shippey, "Tolkien as a Post-War Writer," in *Proceedings of the J.R.R. Tolkien Centenary Conference*.

25. In *Beowulf*, Grendel is one of the hero's antagonists.

26. Tom Shippey, *J.R.R. Tolkien: Author of the Century*.

27. Fred Inglis, *The Promise of Happiness: Value and Meaning in Children's Fiction* (Cambridge: Cambridge University Press, 1981).

28. Kenneth McLeish, "The Rippingest Yarn of All," in *J.R.R. Tolkien: This Far Land*, ed. Robert Giddings (New York: Barnes and Noble, 1983).

29. Alan Bold, "Hobbit Verse Versus Tolkien's Poem," in *J.R.R. Tolkien: This Far Land*.

30. Janet Menzies, "Middle-earth and the Adolescent," in *J.R.R. Tolkien: This Far Land*.

31. Jane Chance, "Power and Knowledge in Tolkien: The Problem of Difference in The Birthday Party," in *Proceedings of the J.R.R. Tolkien Centenary Conference*.

32. Wayne G. Hammond, "The Critical Response to Tolkien's Fiction," in *Proceedings of the J.R.R. Tolkien Centenary Conference*.

33. Tolkien's legendarium is the body of work in which his myths are developed.

34. Charles Kane Douglas, *Arda Reconstructed: The Creation of the Published Silmarillion* (Bethlehem, PA: Lehigh University Press, 2009).

35. Thomas Honegger, "'We Don't Need Another Hero'—Problematic Heroes and Their Function in Some of Tolkien's Works," *Journal of Tolkien Research* 9, no. 2 (2020), https://scholar.valpo.edu/journaloftolkienresearch/vol9/iss2/8/.

36. Tom Shippey, *J.R.R. Tolkien: Author of the Century*, 213.

37. Jack Zipes, *Breaking the Magic Spell*, Lexington: University Press of Kentucky, 2002.

38. Roger King, "Recovery, Escape, Consolation: Middle-earth and the English Fairy Tale," in *J.R.R. Tolkien: This Far Land*.

39. Alessandro Dal Lago, *Eroi e Mostri: Il Fantasy Come Macchina Mitologica* [Heroes and monsters: Fantasy as a mythological machine] (Bologna: Il Mulino, 2017), 201.

40. Mark J.P. Wolf, *Building Imaginary Worlds* (New York: Routledge, 2012), 48.

41. Charlotte Haunhorst, "What Is the Hype about *The Lord of the Rings*?" *Süddeutsche Zeitung*, October 26, 2016.

42. Harold Bloom, ed., *J.R.R. Tolkien*, Bloom's Modern Critical Views (New York: Infobase, 2008).

Chapter 2

1. Professor Tom Shippey, author of one of the most important critical assessments of Tolkien's work (Tom Shippey, *J.R.R. Tolkien: Author of the Century* [New York: HarperCollins, 2000]) places him fully among twentieth-century writers, even for the topics covered.

2. Damien Walter, "Tolkien's myths are a political fantasy," *The Guardian*, December 12, 2014.

3. John Garth, *Tolkien and the Great War: The Threshold of Middle-earth* (London: HarperCollins, 2003).

4. Tom Shippey, "Tolkien as a Post-War Writer," in *Proceedings of the J.R.R. Tolkien Centenary Conference*, ed. Patricia Reynolds and Glen H. Good-knight (Mythopoeic Press and The Tolkien Society, 1995).

5. Letter 52, in *The Letters of J.R.R. Tolkien*, ed. Christopher Tolkien and Humphrey Carpenter (New York: HarperCollins, 2006), 63.

6. Andrew Harrison, "Michael

Moorcock: 'I think Tolkien was a crypto-fascist,'" *The New Statesman*, July 24, 2015.

7. Federico Guglielmi, *Difendere la Terra di Mezzo* [Defending Middle-earth] (Bologna: Odoya, 2013).

8. Nick Otty, "The Structuralist's Guide to Middle-earth," in *J.R.R. Tolkien: This Far Land*, ed. Robert Giddings (New York: Barnes and Noble, 1983).

9. Raymond Williams, *The Country and the City* (London: Chatto & Windus, 1973).

10. Patrick Curry, *Defending Middle-earth: Tolkien: Myth and Modernity* (New York: HarperCollins, 1997).

11. John Molyneux, "Tolkien's World—A Marxist Analysis," http://johnmolyneux.blogspot.it/2011/09/tolkiens-world-marxist-analysis.html.

12. Colonel Blimp is a British cartoon character, a reactionary, pompous, nationalistic, old military man.

13. Letter 153, in *The Letters of J.R.R. Tolkien*, 195.

14. The religious and philosophical conception of evil in Tolkien is the Augustinian or Boethian one (the evil seen as the absence of good, so having no reality in itself) and not the Manichean one (according to which good and evil are two opposing principles fighting each other). When I speak about Manichaeism in Tolkien's work in this book, I always intend it in the most common use of the word, referring to rigid and schematic division into two opposing sides characters, races, etc.

15. C.S. Lewis, "The Dethronement of Power," in *Tolkien and the Critics: Essays on J.R.R. Tolkien's The Lord of the Rings*, ed. Neil D. Isaacs and Rose A. Zimbardo (Notre Dame: University of Notre Dame Press, 1968).

16. Peter Kreeft, *The Philosophy of Tolkien: The Worldview Behind The Lord of the Rings* (San Francisco: Ignatius Press, 2005).

17. Nigel Walmsley, "Tolkien and the '60s," in *J.R.R. Tolkien: This Far Land*, ed. Robert Giddings (New York: Barnes and Noble, 1983).

18. "J.R.R. Tolkien," Special Issue, *MFS Modern Fiction Studies* 50, no. 4 (2004), https://www.jstor.org/stable/i26286376.

19. Tom Shippey, *J.R.R. Tolkien: Author of the Century*, 312.

20. From the contemporary report in the "Gesta Francorum" by an anonymous writer (https://sourcebooks.fordham.edu/source/gesta-cde.asp#jerusalem2): "Our men followed, killing and slaying even to the Temple of Solomon, where the slaughter was so great that our men waded in blood up to their ankles.... When the pagans had been overcome, our men seized great numbers, both men and women, either killing them or keeping them captive, as they wished."

21. Lucio del Corso and Paolo Pecere, *L'anello che non Tiene* [The ring that doesn't hold] (Rome: Minimum Fax, 2003).

22. John Garth, *Tolkien and the Great War: The Threshold of Middle-earth*.

23. Alexander M. Bruce, "Maldon and Moria: On Byrhtnoth, Gandalf, and Heroism in *The Lord of the Rings*," *Mythlore: A Journal of J.R.R. Tolkien, C.S. Lewis, Charles Williams, and Mythopoeic Literature* 26, no. 1 (Fall/Winter 2007): 149-59, https://dc.swosu.edu/mythlore/vol26/iss1/11/.

24. Letter 226, in *The Letters of J.R.R. Tolkien*, 303.

25. Tom Shippey, *J.R.R. Tolkien: Author of the Century*, 165+.

26. Letter 183, in *The Letters of J.R.R. Tolkien*, 243.

27. Andrew Lynch, "Archaism, Nostalgia, and Tennysonian War in *The Lord of the Rings*," in *Tolkien's Modern Middle Ages*, ed. Jane Chance and Alfred Siewers (London: Palgrave Macmillan, 2005), 77–92.

28. Letter 71, in *The Letters of J.R.R. Tolkien*, 82.

29. John Goldthwaite, *A Natural History of Make-Believe: A Guide to the Principal Works of Britain, Europe, and America* (New York: Oxford University Press, 1996).

30. Patrick Curry, "Tolkien and His Critics: A Critique," in *Root and Branch: Approaches towards Understanding Tolkien*, 2nd Edition, ed. Thomas Honegger (Zurich: Walking Tree Publishers, 2005).

31. Although this is motivated mainly by the fact that Tolkien places his stories in the distant past and, not being able to

introduce Catholicism there, he certainly does not want to introduce paganism into Middle-earth.

32. In his book *Difendere la Terra di Mezzo*, whose title is deliberately the same as that of Patrick Curry's book "Defending Middle-earth," Italian author Federico Guglielmi argues that the Anglo-Canadian writer tries to infer from Tolkien's work a sort of New Age philosophical manifesto.

33. Here and in the next paragraphs refer to *The Letters of J.R.R. Tolkien*, ed. Christopher Tolkien and Humphrey Carpenter (New York: HarperCollins, 2006).

34. George Orwell, "What is fascism?" *Tribune*, March 24, 1944.

35. Umberto Eco, "Ur Fascism," *The New York Review of Books*, June 22, 1995.

36. Fred Inglis, *The Promise of Happiness: Value and Meaning in Children's Fiction* (Cambridge: Cambridge University Press, 1981). Later, Inglis corrected this judgment in the essay "Gentility and Powerlessness"; see also Michael D.C. Drout, *J.R.R. Tolkien Encyclopedia: Scholarship and Critical Assessment* (New York: Routledge, 2007), 410.

37. Fred Inglis, "Gentility and Powerlessness: Tolkien and the new class," in *J.R.R. Tolkien: This Far Land*, ed. Robert Giddings (New York: Barnes and Noble, 1983).

38. Joseph Pearce, *Tolkien: Man and Myth* (New York: HarperCollins, 1998).

39. Lucio del Corso and Paolo Pecere, *L'Anello che non Tiene* [The ring that doesn't hold]. Translation by the author.

40. Gianfranco de Turris, ed., *Albero di Tolkien* [Tolkien's tree] (Milan: Bompiani, 2007). De Turris wrote the foreword and an essay, "Tolkien fra Tradizione e Modernità" [Tolkien between tradition and modernity].

41. Daniel Grotta, *J.R.R. Tolkien: Architect of Middle-earth* (Philadelphia: Running Press, 1992).

42. Lucio del Corso and Paolo Pecere, *L'anello che non Tiene*.

43. Jorge Luis Borges (1899–1986), Argentinian writer and essayist, was interested in philosophy and mythology; politically he was a conservative, anti-communist, and opposed to the Nazis. Ezra Pound (1885–1972) was a poet from the United States, modernist

in style; politically he was anti-capitalist and a fascist collaborator during the Second World War. Thomas Stearns Eliot (1888–1965) was a poet and literary critic who moved from the United States to England. Credited for shaping the British poetry of his time, he was a conservative accused of being an anti-Semite. Louis-Ferdinand Céline (1894–1961) was a French writer noted for his pessimism. An anti-Semite and accused of collaboration with Germany during the Second World War, he was pardoned. Yukio Mishima (1925–1970) was a Japanese writer. Traditionalist but decadent at the same time, he was a right-wing activist. After the failure of a botched military coup he died by ritual suicide. Gabriele D'Annunzio (1863–1938) was an Italian poet and journalist, and a fighter pilot during the First World War. Although he didn't claim to be a Fascist, he was considered a key figure at the start of the movement. In 1919, he led a militia to take the city of Fiume (now Rijeka), forcing Yugoslavia to cede it.

44. Gianfranco de Turris, "Tolkien fra Tradizione e Modernità" [Tolkien between tradition and modernity], in *Albero di Tolkien* [Tolkien's tree] (Milan: Bompiani, 2007).

45. Stefano Giuliano, "La tripartizione funzionale nella Terra di Mezzo" [Trifunctionalism in the Middle Earth], in *Albero di Tolkien*.

46. For example, in the notes of this 2011 post, Federico Guglielmi (writing under the pseudonym Wu Ming 4) is against the supposed link between Tolkien and Dumézil: https://www.wumingfoundation.com/giap/2011/12/il-professore-il-barone-e-i-bari-il-caso-tolkien-e-le-strategie-interpretative-della-destra/.

47. Sebastiano Fusco, "L'Uso del Simbolo Tradizionale in J.R.R. Tolkien" [The use of traditional symbol in J.R.R. Tolkien], in *Albero di Tolkien*.

48. Federico Guglielmi, *Difendere la Terra di Mezzo* [Defending Middle-earth] (Bologna: Odoya, 2013).

49. Lucio del Corso and Paolo Pecere, *L'anello che non Tiene*.

50. Julis Evola (1898–1974) was an Italian philosopher, intellectual, occultist, and radical traditionalist. His beliefs

can't be easily categorized, but he's generally associated with fascism and neo-fascist movements. Mircea Eliade (1907–1986), Romanian writer and historian, expressed fascist leanings in his youth. He's known for the theory of "eternal return," the connection through ritual to a mythical age.

51. The "Ur-Fascism" definition by Umberto Eco apparently neglects this fact.

52. A "squadrista" is a member of an action squad of the fascist militia.

53. Guido Schwarz, *Jungfrauen im Nachthemd—Blonde Krieger aus dem Westen* [Virgins in Nightgowns—Blonde Warriors from the West] (Würzburg: Könighausen & Neumann, 2003).

54. For information about Klaus Theweleit's theories, I've read: Kevin S. Amidon and Daniel A. Krier, "On Rereading Klaus Theweleit's Male Fantasies," *Men and Masculinities* 11, no. 4 (2009): 488-496.

55. Thomas Honegger, "More Light Than Shadow? Jungian Approaches to Tolkien and the Archetypal Image of the Shadow," published 2011 online at Scholars' Forum at The Lord of the Rings Plaza, https://www.academia.edu/12415836/_More_Light_Than_Shadow_Jungian_Approaches_to_Tolkien_and_the_Archetypal_Image_of_the_Shadow_.

56. Gloria Comandini, "Guerra e querela alla traduzione di Tolkien: facciamo chiarezza" [War and lawsuit against Tolkien's translation: Let's clarify], Seekers of Atlantis, January 15, 2019, https://www.cercatoridiatlantide.it/en/war-and-lawsuit-to-the-translation-of-tolkien-let%27s-clarify/.

57. Vanni Santoni, "Il Signore degli Anelli ha una nuova Voce," *Corriere della Sera*, December 22, 2019.

58. See for example: Oronzo Cilli, "Giù le mani da Tolkien, sì alla poesia, no all'ideologia" [Hands off Tolkien, yes to poetry, no to ideology], *Il Giornale*, January 13, 2019, and Gloria Comandini, "Guerra e querela alla traduzione di Tolkien: facciamo chiarezza," January 15, 2019.

59. https://www.wumingfoundation.com/giap/2018/06/tolkien-la-strada-prosegue-ancora/

60. Cesare Catà, "Perché non amo la nuova traduzione de Il Signore degli Anelli" [Why I don't love *The Lord of the Rings'* new translation], Huffingtonpost.it, November 14, 2019, https://www.huffingtonpost.it/entry/perche-non-amo-la-nuova-traduzione-de-il-signore-degli-anelli_it_5dcd0da9e4b03a7e0295233d.

61. Peter Kreeft, *The Philosophy of Tolkien: The Worldview Behind The Lord of the Rings*.

62. Joseph Pearce, "The Lord of the Rings and the Catholic Understanding of Community," in *The Ring and the Cross*, ed. Paul E. Kerry (Madison, NJ: Fairleigh Dickinson University Press, 2011).

63. Letter 186, in *The Letters of J.R.R. Tolkien*, 246.

64. Daniel Grotta, *J.R.R: Tolkien: Architect of Middle-earth*, 13.

65. Stephen Goodson claimed to be in possession of Tolkien's copies of a magazine, *Candour*, published by a cousin of G.K. Chesterton. On the webpage http://www.spearhead.co.uk/0208-sg.html he quoted some paragraphs that, allegedly, had been underlined by Tolkien himself. According to Wikipedia, Goodson, a Holocaust denier who died in 2018, has been a banker and the leader of the defunct "Abolition of Income Tax and Usury" Party in South Africa. It would be interesting to know where these magazines are now and, obviously, if Tolkien really had anything to do with them.

66. Letter 52, in *The Letters of J.R.R. Tolkien*, 63.

67. Ibid.

68. Nick Otty, "The Structuralist Guide to Middle-earth," in *J.R.R. Tolkien: This Far Land*.

69. Patrick Curry, "Tolkien and his Critics: A Critique," in *Root and Branch: Approaches towards understanding Tolkien*, ed. Thomas Honegger (Zurich: Walking Tree Publishers, 2005).

70. Vladimir Grushetskiy, "How the Russians See Tolkien," in *Proceedings of the J.R.R. Tolkien Centenary Conference*.

71. Sergey Kuriy, "Есть ли во «Властелине Колец» политические аллегории?" [Are there political allegories in *The Lord of the Rings*?], Школа Жизни—познавательный журнал [School of Life], November 10, 2008, https://shkolazhizni.ru/culture/articles/20146/.

72. Kirill Yeskov, Последний кольценосец [The Last Ringbearer]. For further information, see https://lotr.fandom.com/wiki/Kirill_Yeskov.

73. About this book, see, for example, https://sites.google.com/site/theblackbookofarda/.

74. About this author see for example https://www.goodreads.com/author/show/711906.Nick_Perumov.

75. Jessica Yates, "Tolkien the Anti-totalitarian," in *Proceedings of the J.R.R. Tolkien Centenary Conference.*

76. Alessandro Dal Lago, *Eroi e Mostri: Il Fantasy come Macchina Mitologica* [Heroes and Monsters—Fantasy as a Mythological Machine] (Bologna: Il Mulino, 2017).

77. Letter 92, in *The Letters of J.R.R. Tolkien*, 105.

Chapter 3

1. Letter 92, in *The Letters of J.R.R. Tolkien*, 105.

2. John Yatt, "Wraiths and Race," *The Guardian*, December 2, 2002, https://www.theguardian.com/books/2002/dec/02/jrrtolkien.lordoftherings.

3. From my interview with the author. Giovanni Agnoloni is editor and co-author of *Tolkien: Light and Shadow* (Torriglia: Kipple Officina Libraria, 2019).

4. Colin Duriez, *Tolkien and The Lord of the Rings: A Guide to Middle-earth* (Cheltenham, UK: History Press, 2013).

5. Oğuzhan Yalçın, "Racism has no place in the Middle-earth and in The Lord of the Rings," Karabük University, 2015, https://archive.org/details/RacismHasNoPlaceInTheLordOfTheRingsAndMiddleEarthOuzhanYalln.

6. Tom Shippey, *J.R.R. Tolkien: Author of the Century* (New York: HarperCollins, 2000), 143.

7. Richard L. Purtill, *J.R.R. Tolkien: Myth, Morality, and Religion* (New York: Harper & Row, 1984).

8. Christina Scull, "Open Minds, Closed Minds in *The Lord of the Rings*," in *Proceedings of the J.R.R. Tolkien Centenary Conference*, ed. Patricia Reynolds and Glen H. Goodknight (Mythopoeic Press and The Tolkien Society, 1995).

9. Letter 269, in *The Letters of J.R.R. Tolkien*, 355.

10. Helen Armstrong, "Good Guys, Bad Guys, Fantasy and Reality," in *Proceedings of the J.R.R. Tolkien Centenary Conference.*

11. Guido Schwarz, *Jungfrauen im Nachthemd: Blonde Krieger aus dem Westen* [Virgins in nightgowns: Blonde warriors from the West] (Würzburg: Königshausen & Neumann, 2003).

12. Rebecca Brackmann, "Dwarves are Not Heroes: Antisemitism and the Dwarves in J.R.R. Tolkien's Writing," *Mythlore: A Journal of J.R.R. Tolkien, C.S. Lewis, Charles Williams, and Mythopoeic Literature* 28, no. 3 (Spring/Summer 2010): 85–106, https://dc.swosu.edu/mythlore/vol28/iss3/7/.

13. Letter 176, in *The Letters of J.R.R. Tolkien*, 229.

14. Letter 25, in *The Letters of J.R.R. Tolkien*, 31.

15. Letter 29, in *The Letters of J.R.R. Tolkien*, 37.

16. Renée Vink, "'Jewish' Dwarves: Tolkien and Anti-Semitic Stereotyping," *Tolkien Studies* 10 (2013): 123–145, https://www.academia.edu/4638819/_Jewish_Dwarves_Tolkien_and_Anti_Semitic_Stereotyping.

17. David A. Funk, "Exploration into the Psyche of Dwarves," in *Proceedings of the J.R.R. Tolkien Centenary Conference.*

Chapter 4

1. Edwin Muir, "A Boy's World," *The Observer*, November 27, 1955.

2. Letter 177, in *The Letters of J.R.R. Tolkien*, ed. Christopher Tolkien and Humphrey Carpenter (New York: HarperCollins, 2006), 229.

3. Brenda Partridge, "No Sex Please—We're Hobbits: The Construction of Female Sexuality in *The Lord of the Rings*," in *J.R.R. Tolkien: This Far Land*, ed. Robert Giddings (New York: Barnes and Noble, 1983), 179–197.

4. Letter 43, in *The Letters of J.R.R. Tolkien*, 48.

5. Humphrey Carpenter, *J.R.R. Tolkien: A Biography* (New York: HarperCollins, 1995). Lewis dismisses being gay on page 148, style in clothes on page 125.

6. Joseph Pearce, *Tolkien, Man and Myth: A Literary Life* (San Francisco: Ignatius Press, 2001).

7. Michael D. C. Drout and Hilary Wynne, "Tom Shippey's *J.R.R. Tolkien: Author of the Century* and a Look Back at Tolkien Criticism since 1982," *Envoi* 9, no. 2 (Fall 2000), https://www.academia.edu/9116653/_Tom_Shippeys_J_R_R_Tolkien_Author_of_the_Century_and_a_look_back_at_Tolkien_criticism_since_1982_Envoi_9_2_2000_101_34_with_Michael_Drout.

8. Fleming is the creator of James Bond, Mailer a leading exponent of the beat generation.

9. Joseph Pearce, "Hobbits and Heroines," *The Imaginative Conservative*, January 6, 2016, https://the imaginativeconservative.org/2016/01/hobbits-and-heroines.html.

10. Nejrotti Chiara, "Dee e Regine—Il mondo femminile nell'opera di J.R.R. Tolkien" [Goddesses and queens—Feminine world in the works of J.R.R. Tolkien], in *Albero di Tolkien* [Tolkien's tree], ed. Gianfranco de Turris (Milan: Bompiani, 2007).

11. From my interview with Giovanni Agnoloni.

12. Daniel Timmons, "Hobbit Sex and Sensuality in *The Lord of the Rings*," *Mythlore: A Journal of J.R.R. Tolkien, C.S. Lewis, Charles Williams, and Mythopoeic Literature* 23, no. 3 (Summer 2001): 70-79, https://dc.swosu.edu/cgi/viewcontent.cgi?article=1319&context=mythlore.

13. Cristina Casagrande, "O feminino em Tolkien" [The feminine in Tolkien], in *A Subcriação de Mundos [recurso Eletrônico]: Estudos Sobre a Literatura de J.R.R. Tolkien* [The sub-creation of worlds: Essays on J.R.R. Tolkien's literature], ed. Cristina Casagrande, Diego Genu Klautau, and Maria Zilda da Cunha (São Paulo: University of São Paulo, 2019), https://www.academia.edu/41339100/O_feminino_em_Tolkien_The_female_in_Tolkien.

14. Nancy Enright, "Tolkien's Females and the Defining of Power," in *J.R.R. Tolkien*, Bloom's Modern Critical Views, ed. Harold Bloom (New York: Infobase, 2008).

15. Tolkien modified his view about this character: in later versions of Galadriel's story she is "unstained" by rebellion. See for example Michael D.C. Drout, *J.R.R. Tolkien Encyclopedia: Scholarship and Critical Assessment* (New York: Routledge, 2007), 227.

16. David Day, "Whether shield-maidens existed in reality is much debated," in *An Encyclopedia of Tolkien: The History and Mythology That Inspired Tolkien's World* (Riverside, NJ: Canterbury Classics, 2019).

17. Robert W. Butler and John Mark Eberhart, "In Tolkien, it's a man's world, and with good reason," *Chicago Tribune*, January 1, 2002, https://www.chicagotribune.com/news/ct-xpm-2002-01-01-0201010249-story.html.

18. Daniel Grotta, *J.R.R: Tolkien: Architect of Middle-earth* (Philadelphia: Running Press, 1992), 107.

19. Campbell, Joseph. *The Hero with a Thousand Faces* (Princeton: Bollingen Foundation, 1949).

20. Kevin Maness, "Taming the Wild Shieldmaiden: A Feminist Analysis of Tolkien's 'Heroinism' in *The Lord of the Rings*," University of Pennsylvania, 1995, https://www.jstor.org/stable/i26286376.

21. Letter 244, in *The Letters of J.R.R. Tolkien*, 323.

22. Mariah Huehner, "'I am No Man' Doesn't Cut It: The Story of Éowyn," *The Mary Sue*, January 27, 2015, https://www.themarysue.com/the-story-of-eowyn/.

23. Ana María Mariño Arias, "Women of Middle-earth: An approach to the role of women in *The Lord of the Rings*," University of Léon, https://www.academia.edu/23418731/Women_of_Middle_Earth_An_approach_to_the_role_of_women_in_The_Lord_of_the_Rings.

24. Michael D.C. Drout, *J.R.R. Tolkien Encyclopedia: Scholarship and Critical Assessment* (New York: Routledge, 2007), 168.

25. Jennifer Neville, "Women," in *Reading the Lord of the Rings: New Writings on Tolkien's Classic*, ed. Robert Eaglestone (London: Continuum, 2005).

26. Nejrotti Chiara, "Dee e Regine—Il mondo femminile nell'opera di J.R.R. Tolkien" [Goddess and Queens, feminine world in J.R.R. Tolkien's works], in *Albero di Tolkien* [Tolkien's tree], ed. Gianfranco de Turris (Milan: Bompiani, 2007).

27. Esther Saxey, "Homoeroticism," in *Reading The Lord of the Rings: New Writings on Tolkien's Classic*, ed. Robert Eaglestone (London: Continuum, 2005).

28. Nancy Martsch, "A Tolkien Chronology," in *Proceedings of the J.R.R. Tolkien Centenary Conference*, ed. Patricia Reynolds and Glen H. Goodknight (Mythopoeic Press and The Tolkien Society, 1995).

29. John Garth, *Tolkien and the Great War: The Threshold of Middle-earth* (London: HarperCollins, 2003).

30. Nicole M. duPlessis, "On the Shoulders of Humphrey Carpenter: Reconsidering Biographical Representation and Scholarly Perception of Edith Tolkien," *Mythlore: A Journal of J.R.R. Tolkien, C.S. Lewis, Charles Williams, and Mythopoeic Literature* 37, no. 2 (Spring/Summer 2019): 39-74, https://dc.swosu.edu/mythlore/vol37/iss2/4/.

31. Daniel Grotta, *J.R.R. Tolkien: Architect of Middle-earth*, 67.

32. Humphrey Carpenter, *J.R.R. Tolkien: A Biography* (New York: HarperCollins, 1995).

33. Anna Smol, "'Oh... Oh...Frodo!': Readings of Male Intimacy in *The Lord Of The Rings*," *Modern Fiction Studies* 50, no. 4 (Winter 2004): 949-979.

34. J.R.R. Tolkien, "On Fairy-Stories," in *Tree and Leaf* (Crows Nest, Australia: Allen & Unwin, 1964).

35. Edith L. Crowe, "Power in Arda: Sources, Uses and Misuses," in *Proceedings of the J.R.R. Tolkien Centenary Conference*, ed. Patricia Reynolds and Glen H. Goodknight (Mythopoeic Press and The Tolkien Society, 1995).

36. Thomas Honegger, "More Light Than Shadow? Jungian Approaches to Tolkien and the Archetypal Image of the Shadow," published 2011 online at Scholars' Forum at The Lord of the Rings Plaza, https://www.academia.edu/12415836/_More_Light_Than_Shadow_Jungian_Approaches_to_Tolkien_and_the_Archetypal_Image_of_the_Shadow_.

Chapter 5

1. Marco Politi, "Ratzinger contro Harry Potter: 'una saga che corrompe i giovani'" [Ratzinger against Harry Potter: "A saga that corrupts young people"], *Repubblica*, July 14, 2005, https://www.repubblica.it/2005/g/sezioni/spettacoli_e_cultura/harrypotter/harrypotter.html.

2. Gaetano Vallini, "La magia non è più un gioco sorprendente" [Magic is no more a surprising game], *L'Osservatore Romano*, July 13–14, 2009, https://www.vatican.va/news_services/or/or_quo/cultura/159q05b1.html.

3. Ronald Hutton, "The Pagan Tolkien," in *The Ring and the Cross: Christianity and The Lord of the Rings*, ed. Paul E. Kerry (Madison, NJ: Fairleigh Dickinson University Press, 2011).

4. Letter 269, in *The Letters of J.R.R. Tolkien*, ed. Christopher Tolkien and Humphrey Carpenter (New York: HarperCollins, 2006), 355.

5. Letter 153, in *The Letters of J.R.R. Tolkien*, 187.

6. Farid Mohammadi, "Mythic Frodo and his Predestinate Call to Adventure," *International Journal of Applied Linguistics and English Literature* 2, no. 5 (September 2013), http://www.journals.aiac.org.au/index.php/IJALEL/article/view/960.

7. Nils Ivar Agøy, "The Christian Tolkien: A Response to Ronald Hutton," in *The Ring and the Cross: Christianity and The Lord of the Rings*.

8. Letter 250, in *The Letters of J.R.R. Tolkien*, 336.

9. Ronald Hutton, "Can We Still Have a Pagan Tolkien?" in *The Ring and the Cross: Christianity and The Lord of the Rings*.

10. Letter 155, in *The Letters of J.R.R. Tolkien*, 199.

11. Stephen Morillo, "The Entwives: Investigating the Spiritual Core of *The Lord of the Rings*," in *The Ring and the Cross: Christianity and the Lord of the Rings*.

12. Ralph C. Wood, "Confronting the World's Weirdness: J.R.R. Tolkien's *The Children of Húrin*," in *The Ring and the Cross: Christianity and The Lord of the Rings*.

13. Catherine Madsen, "Eru Erased: The Minimalist Cosmology of *The Lord of the Rings*," in *The Ring and the Cross: Christianity and The Lord of the Rings*.

14. Chris Mooney, "How J.R.R.

Tolkien Became a Christian Writer," in *The Ring and the Cross: Christianity and The Lord of the Rings.*

15. Carson L. Holloway, "Redeeming Sub-creation," in *The Ring and the Cross: Christianity and The Lord of the Rings.*

16. Letter 4, in *The Letters of J.R.R. Tolkien,* 8.

17. Nils Ivar Agøy, "Quid Hinieldus cum Christo?: New Perspectives on Tolkien's Theological Dilemma and his Sub-Creation Theory," in *Proceedings of the J.R.R. Tolkien Centenary Conference,* ed. Patricia Reynolds and Glen H. Goodknight (Mythopoeic Press and The Tolkien Society, 1995).

18. Burt Randolph, "The Singular Incompetence of the Valar," *Tolkien Journal* 3, no. 3 (1968), https://dc.swosu.edu/tolkien_journal/vol3/iss3/2/.

19. John Garth, *Tolkien and the Great War: The Threshold of Middle-earth* (London: HarperCollins, 2003).

20. Richard L. Purtill, *J.R.R. Tolkien: Myth, Morality, and Religion* (New York: Harper & Row, 1984).

21. Letter 131, in *The Letters of J.R.R. Tolkien,* 144.

22. Letters 203 and 186, in *The Letters of J.R.R. Tolkien,* 262 and 246.

23. Tom Shippey, *The Road to Middle-earth* (New York: HarperCollins, 1993).

24. J.R.R. Tolkien, "On Fairy-Stories," in *Tree and Leaf* (Crows Nest, Australia: Allen & Unwin, 1964).

25. Alessandro Dal Lago, *Eroi e Mostri: Il Fantasy come Macchina Mitologica* [Heroes and monsters—Fantasy as a mythological machine] (Bologna: Il Mulino, 2017).

26. Mark J.P. Wolf, *Building Imaginary Worlds: The Theory and History of Subcreation* (New York: Routledge, 2012), 23.

27. Daniel Grotta, *J.R.R. Tolkien: Architect of Middle-earth* (Philadelphia: Running Press, 1992), 104.

28. Jason Boffetti, "Catholic Scholar, Catholic Sub-Creator," in *The Ring and the Cross: Christianity and The Lord of the Rings.*

29. Tadeusz Andrzej Olszański, "Evil and the Evil One in Tolkien's Theology," in *Proceedings of the J.R.R. Tolkien Centenary Conference.*

30. Biographer Daniel Grotta maintains that Tolkien was not even working on *The Silmarillion* anymore during his last years, maybe because the task of completing it was too heavy. See Daniel Grotta, *J.R.R. Tolkien: Architect of Middle-earth,* 154.

Conclusion

1. Patrick Curry, "Less Noise and More Green: Tolkien's Ideology for England," in *Proceedings of the J.R.R. Tolkien Centenary Conference,* ed. Patricia Reynolds and Glen H. Goodknight (Mythopoeic Press and The Tolkien Society, 1995).

2. I think Guido Schwarz, whose opinions generally do not convince me, is right about the Orcs' problem; likewise, I agree with Robert Westall (quoted by Jessica Yates) about the dangers of stereotyping the enemy. Moreover, John Molyneux notes how the reader is led to overlook the Orcs' treatment: this is an interesting consideration of how easy it is to stick a damning label on someone.

3. Letter 153, in *The Letters of J.R.R. Tolkien,* ed. Christopher Tolkien and Humphrey Carpenter (New York: HarperCollins, 2006), 195. This draft letter was never sent; still, Tolkien's ideas about the Orcs in the 1950s are clearly expressed.

4. Daniel Grotta, *J.R.R. Tolkien: Architect of Middle-earth* (Philadelphia: Running Press, 1992), 146.

5. Patrick Curry, *Defending Middle-earth: Tolkien: Myth and Modernity* (New York: HarperCollins, 1997), 31.

Bibliography

Works by J.R.R. Tolkien

The Book of Lost Tales. Parts 1 and 2. Crows Nest, Australia: Allen & Unwin, 1984.

The Hobbit. Crows Nest, Australia: Allen & Unwin, 1937.

The Letters of J.R.R. Tolkien. Edited by Christopher Tolkien and Humphrey Carpenter. Crows Nest, Australia: Allen & Unwin, 1981 (first edition). Page references are based on the HarperCollins, 2006 edition.

The Lord of the Rings. 3 vols. Crows Nest, Australia: Allen & Unwin, 1954 and 1955.

"On Fairy-Stories." In *Tree and Leaf*. Crows Nest, Australia: Allen & Unwin, 1964.

The Silmarillion. Edited by Christopher Tolkien. Crows Nest, Australia: Allen & Unwin, 1977.

Unfinished Tales of Númenor and Middle-earth. Edited by Christopher Tolkien. Crows Nest, Australia: Allen & Unwin, 1980.

Works by Others

Agnoloni, Giovanni, ed. *Tolkien: Light and Shadow*. Torriglia: Kipple Officina Libraria, 2019.

Bloom, Harold, ed. *J.R.R. Tolkien*. Bloom's Modern Critical Views. New York: Infobase, 2008.

Brackmann, Rebecca. "Dwarves Are Not Heroes: Antisemitism and the Dwarves in J.R.R. Tolkien's Writing." *Mythlore: A Journal of J.R.R. Tolkien, C.S. Lewis, Charles Williams, and Mythopoeic Literature* 28, no. 3 (Spring/Summer 2010): 85–106. https://dc.swosu.edu/mythlore/vol28/iss3/7/.

Butler, Robert W., and John Mark Eberhart. "In Tolkien, It's a Man's World, and with Good Reason." *Chicago Tribune*, January 1, 2002. https://www.chicagotribune.com/news/ct-xpm-2002-01-01-0201010249-story.html.

Campbell, Joseph. *The Hero with a Thousand Faces*. Princeton: Bollingen Foundation, 1949.

Carpenter, Humphrey. *J.R.R. Tolkien: A Biography*. New York: HarperCollins, 1995.

Casagrande, Cristina. "O Feminino Em Tolkien" [The feminine in Tolkien]. In *A Subcriação De Mundos [recurso Eletrônico]: Estudos Sobre a Literatura De J.R.R. Tolkien* [The sub-creation of worlds: Essays on J.R.R. Tolkien's literature], edited by Cristina Casagrande, Diego Genu Klautau, and Maria Zilda da Cunha. São Paulo: University of São Paulo, 2019. https://www.academia.edu/41339100/O_feminino_em_Tolkien_The_female_in_Tolkien.

Catà, Cesare. "Perché Non Amo La Nuova Traduzione De Il Signore Degli Anelli" [Why I don't like the *Lord of the Rings'* new translation]. Huffingtonpost.it, November 14, 2019. https://www.huffingtonpost.it/entry/perche-non-amo-la-nuova-traduzione-de-il-signore-degli-anelli_it_5dcd0da9e4b03a7e0295233d.

Chance, Jane, and Alfred Siewers, eds. *Tolkien's Modern Middle Ages*. London: Palgrave Macmillan, 2005.

Cilli, Oronzo. "Giù Le Mani Da Tolkien, Sì Alla Poesia, No All'ideologia"

183

[Hands off Tolkien, yes to poetry, no to ideology]. *Il Giornale*, January 13, 2019. https://www.ilgiornale.it/news/gi-mani-tolkien-s-poesia-no-allideologia-1628045.html.

Comandini, Gloria. "Guerra E Querela Alla Traduzione Di Tolkien: Facciamo Chiarezza" [War and lawsuit against Tolkien's translation: Let's clarify]. Seekers of Atlantis, January 15, 2019. https://www.cercatoridiatlantide.it/guerra-e-querela-alla-traduzione-di-tolkien-facciamo-chiarezza/.

Curry, Patrick. *Defending Middle-earth: Tolkien: Myth and Modernity*. New York: HarperCollins, 1997.

Dal Lago, Alessandro. *Eroi e Mostri—Il Fantasy Come Macchina Mitologica* [Heroes and monsters: Fantasy as a mythological machine]. Bologna: Il Mulino, 2017.

Day, David. *An Encyclopedia of Tolkien: The History and Mythology That Inspired Tolkien's World*. Riverside, NJ: Canterbury Classics, 2019.

Del Corso, Lucio, and Paolo Pecere. *L'anello Che Non Tiene* [The ring that doesn't hold]. Rome: Minimum Fax, 2003.

De Turris, Gianfranco, ed. *Albero Di Tolkien* [Tolkien's tree]. Milan: Bompiani, 2007.

Drout, Michael D.C., and Hilary Wynne. "Tom Shippey's *J.R.R. Tolkien: Author of the Century* and a Look Back at Tolkien Criticism Since 1982." *Envoi* 9, no. 2 (Fall 2000): 101–134. https://www.academia.edu/9116653/_Tom_Shippeys_J_R_R_Tolkien_Author_of_the_Century_and_a_look_back_at_Tolkien_criticism_since_1982_Envoi_9_2_2000_101_34_with_Michael_Drout.

Drout, Michael D.C., ed. *J.R.R. Tolkien Encyclopedia: Scholarship and Critical Assessment*. New York: Routledge, 2007.

duPlessis, Nicole M. "On the Shoulders of Humphrey Carpenter: Reconsidering Biographical Representation and Scholarly Perception of Edith Tolkien." *Mythlore: A Journal of J.R.R. Tolkien, C.S. Lewis, Charles Williams, and Mythopoeic Literature* 37, no. 2 (Spring/Summer 2019): 39–74. https://dc.swosu.edu/mythlore/vol37/iss2/4/.

Duriez, Colin. *Tolkien and The Lord of the Rings: A Guide to Middle-earth*. Cheltenham, UK: History Press, 2013.

Eaglestone, Robert, ed. *Reading the Lord of the Rings: New Writings on Tolkien's Classic*. London: Continuum, 2005.

Garth, John. *Tolkien and the Great War: The Threshold of Middle-earth*. London: HarperCollins, 2003.

Giddings, Robert, ed. *J.R.R. Tolkien: This Far Land*. New York: Barnes and Noble, 1983.

Goldthwaite, John. *A Natural History of Make-Believe: A Guide to the Principal Works of Britain, Europe, and America*. New York: Oxford University Press, 1996.

Greer, Germaine. "Book of the Century, Germaine Greer on Our Readers' Poll." *Waterstone*, Winter/Spring 1997.

Grotta, Daniel. *J.R.R. Tolkien: Architect of Middle-earth*. Philadelphia: Running Press, 1992.

Guglielmi, Federico. *Difendere La Terra Di Mezzo* [Defending Middle-earth]. Bologna: Odoya, 2013.

———. "Tolkien in Italia: La Strada Prosegue Ancora." Wu Ming Foundation. https://www.wumingfoundation.com/giap/2018/06/tolkien-la-strada-prosegue-ancora/.

Harrison, Andrew. "Michael Moorcock: 'I think Tolkien was a crypto-fascist.'" *The New Statesman*, July 24, 2015. http://www.newstatesman.com/culture/2015/07/michael-moorcock-i-think-tolkien-was-crypto-fascist.

Haunhorst, Charlotte. "Was soll der Hype um Herr der Ringe?" [What is the hype about *The Lord of the Rings*?]. *Süddeutsche Zeitung*, October 26, 2016. https://www.sueddeutsche.de/kultur/serie-hass-auf-kunst-was-soll-der-hype-um-herr-der-ringe-1.3215404.

Honegger, Thomas. "More Light Than Shadow? Jungian Approaches to Tolkien and the Archetypal Image of the Shadow." Published online, 2011, at Scholars' Forum at The Lord of the Rings Plaza. https://www.academia.edu/12415836/_More_Light_Than_Shadow_Jungian_Approaches_to_Tolkien_and_the_Archetypal_Image_of_the_Shadow_.

———. "'We Don't Need Another

Hero'—Problematic Heroes and Their Function in Some of Tolkien's Works." *Journal of Tolkien Research* 9, no. 2 (2020). https://scholar.valpo.edu/journaloftolkienresearch/vol9/iss2/8.

Honegger, Thomas, ed. *Root and Branch: Approaches towards Understanding Tolkien.* Zurich: Walking Tree Publishers, 2005.

Huehner, Mariah. "'I Am No Man' Doesn't Cut It: The Story of Éowyn." *The Mary Sue*, January 27, 2015. https://www.themarysue.com/the-story-of-eowyn/.

Inglis, Fred. *The Promise of Happiness: Value and Meaning in Children's Fiction.* Cambridge: Cambridge University Press, 1981.

Isaacs, Neil D., and Rose A. Zimbardo, eds. *Tolkien and the Critics: Essays on J.R.R. Tolkien's The Lord of the Rings.* Notre Dame: University of Notre Dame Press, 1968.

"J.R.R. Tolkien." Special Issue, *MFS Modern Fiction Studies* 50, no. 4 (2004). https://www.jstor.org/stable/i26286376.

Kane, Douglas Charles. *Arda Reconstructed: The Creation of the Published Silmarillion.* Bethlehem, PA: Lehigh University Press, 2009.

Kerry, Paul E., ed. *The Ring and the Cross: Christianity and The Lord of the Rings.* Madison, NJ: Fairleigh Dickinson University Press, 2011.

Kreeft, Peter. *The Philosophy of Tolkien: The Worldview Behind The Lord of the Rings.* San Francisco: Ignatius Press, 2005.

Kuriy, Sergey. "Есть ли во «Властелине Колец» политические аллегории?" [Are there political allegories in *The Lord of the Rings*?]. Школа Жизни - познавательный журнал [School of Life—Educational Magazine], November 10, 2008. https://shkolazhizni.ru/culture/articles/20146/.

Maness, Kevin. "Taming the Wild Shieldmaiden: A Feminist Analysis of Tolkien's 'Heroinism' in *The Lord of the Rings.*" University of Pennsylvania, 1995.

Mariño Arias, Ana María. "Women of Middle-Earth: An Approach to the Role of Women in *The Lord of the Rings.*" University of Léon. https://www.academia.edu/23418731/Women_of_Middle_Earth_An_approach_to_the_role_of_women_in_The_Lord_of_the_Rings.

Miéville, China. "Tolkien—Middle Earth Meets Middle England." *Socialist Review* no. 259 (January 2002). http://www.socialistreview.org.uk/socialist-review-archive/tolkien-middle-earth-meets-middle-england/.

Mohammadi, Farid. "Mythic Frodo and His Predestinate Call to Adventure." *International Journal of Applied Linguistics and English Literature* 2, no. 5 (September 2013): 117–126. http://www.journals.aiac.org.au/index.php/IJALEL/article/view/960.

Molyneux, John. "Tolkien's World—A Marxist Analysis." Personal blog. http://johnmolyneux.blogspot.it/2011/09/tolkiens-world-marxist-analysis.html.

Moorcock, Michael. "Epic Pooh." In *J.R.R. Tolkien*, Bloom's Modern Critical Views, edited by Harold Bloom. New York: Infobase, 2008.

Morgan, Richard. "The Real Fantastic Stuff." suvudu.com, February 18, 2009. http://suvudu.com/2009/02/the-real-fantastic-stuff-an-essay-by-richard-k-morgan.html.

Muir, Edwin. "A Boy's World." *Observer*, November 27, 1955.

———. "Strange Epic." *Observer*, August 22, 1954.

Pearce, Joseph. "Hobbits and Heroines." *The Imaginative Conservative*, January 6, 2016. https://theimaginativeconservative.org/2016/01/hobbits-and-heroines.html.

———. *Tolkien, Man and Myth: A Literary Life.* San Francisco: Ignatius Press, 2001.

Politi, Marco. "Ratzinger Contro Harry Potter: 'una Saga Che Corrompe I Giovani'" [Ratzinger against Harry Potter: 'A saga that corrupts young people']. *Repubblica*, July 14, 2005. https://www.repubblica.it/2005/g/sezioni/spettacoli_e_cultura/harrypotter/harrypotter/harrypotter.html.

Purtill, Richard L. *J.R.R. Tolkien: Myth, Morality, and Religion.* New York: Harper & Row, 1984.

Randolph, Burt. "The Singular Incompetence of the Valar." *Tolkien Journal* 3, no. 3 (1968): 11–13. https://dc.swosu. edu/tolkien_journal/vol3/iss3/2/.

Reynolds, Patricia, and Glen H. Good-knight. *Proceedings of the J.R.R. Tolkien Centenary Conference.* Mythopoeic Press and The Tolkien Society, 1995.

Richardson, Maurice. "New Novels: Review of *The Two Towers.*" *The New Statesman,* December 18, 1954.

Santoni, Vanni. "Il Signore Degli Anelli Ha Una Nuova Voce" [*The Lord of the Rings* has a new voice]. *Corriere della Sera,* December 22, 2019.

Schwarz, Guido. *Jungfrauen Im Nacht-themd: Blonde Krieger aus dem Westen* [Virgins in nightgowns: blonde warriors from the West]. Würzburg: Königshausen & Neumann, 2003.

Scull, Christina. "Open Minds, Closed Minds." In *Proceedings of the J.R.R. Tolkien Centenary Conference,* edited by Patricia Reynolds and Glen H. Goodknight. Mythopoeic Press and The Tolkien Society, 1995.

Shippey, Tom. *J.R.R. Tolkien: Author of the Century.* New York: HarperCollins, 2000.

_____ *The Road to Middle-earth.* New York: HarperCollins, 1993.

Smol, Anna. "'Oh... Oh... Frodo!': Readings of Male Intimacy in *The Lord of the Rings.*" *Modern Fiction Studies* 50, no. 4 (Winter 2004): 949–979. https:// www.jstor.org/stable/26286386.

Stimpson, Catharine. "J.R.R. Tolkien." In *Columbia Essays on Modern Writers No. 41.* New York: Columbia University Press, 1969.

Timmons, Daniel. "Hobbit Sex and Sensuality in *The Lord of the Rings.*" *Mythlore: A Journal of J.R.R. Tolkien, C.S. Lewis, Charles Williams, and Mythopoeic Literature* 23, no. 3 (Summer 2001): 70–79. https://dc.swosu. edu/cgi/viewcontent.cgi?article=1319 &context=mythlore.

Vallini, Gaetano. "La Magia Non è Più Un Gioco Sorprendente" [Magic is no more a surprising game]. *L'Osservatore Romano,* July 13–14, 2009. https:// www.vatican.va/news_services/or/or_ quo/cultura/159q05b1.html.

Vink, Renée. "'Jewish' Dwarves: Tolkien and Anti-Semitic Stereotyping." *Tolkien Studies* 10 (2013): 123–145. https://www.academia.edu/4638819/_ Jewish_Dwarves_Tolkien_and_Anti_ Semitic_Stereotyping.

Williams, Raymond. *The Country and the City.* London: Chatto & Windus, 1973.

Wilson, Edmund. "Oo, Those Awful Orcs!" *The Nation,* April 14, 1956.

Wolf, Mark J.P. *Building Imaginary Worlds: The Theory and History of Subcreation.* New York: Routledge, 2012.

Yalçın, Oğuzhan. "Racism Has No Place in the Middle-earth and in *The Lord of the Rings.*" Thesis, Karabük University, 2015. https://archive.org/details/Raci smHasNoPlaceInTheLordOfTheRings AndMiddleEarthOuzhanYalln.

Yatt, John. "Wraiths and Race." *The Guardian,* December 2, 2002. https:// www.theguardian.com/books/2002/ dec/02/jrrtolkien.lordoftherings.

Zipes, Jack. *Breaking the Magic Spell.* Lexington: University Press of Kentucky, 2002.

Index